LITERARY FRANCE

LITERARY FRANCE

THE MAKING OF A CULTURE

PRISCILLA PARKHURST CLARK

University of California Press
Berkeley · Los Angeles · London

This book is published
through the generous contributions of
Braun-Brumfield, Inc.
to the
Campaign for the Humanities
of the Associates of the University of California Press
without whose financial support
it may not have been possible.

University of California Press
Berkeley and Los Angeles, California

University of California Press, Ltd.
London, England

Library of Congress Cataloging-in-Publication Data

Clark, Priscilla Parkhurst
  Literary France.
  Includes index.
  1. French literature—History and criticism.
2. Literature and society—France. 3. France—
Intellectual life. I. Title.
PQ142.C5 1987   840'.9   86-7132

Printed in the United States of America

1 2 3 4 5 6 7 8 9

For Neale and Richard Parkhurst
and
Jacqueline Duchêne

Books are only one of the forms in which the vast work of intellectual culture occurs and spreads.

Ernest Renan

The "writer" in France is something other than someone who writes and publishes.

Paul Valéry

Modern myths are even less understood than ancient myths, even though we are devoured by myths. Myths press upon us everywhere, they serve for everything, they explain everything.

Honoré de Balzac

Contents

Illustrations

Preface

Of making many books, there is no end.
Ecclesiastes 12:12

More than most works, a study that analyzes the impact of culture on writers and on books owes acknowledgment of at least the known sources of help, influence, and inspiration.

I am extremely grateful to the institutions that accorded me time and aid for research and writing: the University of Illinois at Chicago, which generously provided research and computer assistance, travel grants, and two sabbatical leaves; the George A. and Eliza Gardner Howard Foundation for a fellowship; the National Endowment for the Humanities for a fellowship awarded by the Newberry Library; the American Philosophical Society for a travel-research grant. At the Ministère de la Culture, at the Académie française, at the French Embassy in Washington, and at the National Endowment for the Arts various officials also gave generously of their time, expertise, and resources.

At my own university, Deborah Allen's very able handling of administrative affairs made it possible for me to chair the department and still undertake final revisions. Edward Samuelson's bibliographical research, editing, and exemplary proofreading and Charlene Tarter's retyping of most of the manuscript on the university computer made revision almost a luxury.

Of the many friends, colleagues, students, and readers who have patiently listened to questions, given comments and criticisms, suggestions and information, a few require particular mention. Jacquette Reboul steered me in and around Paris literary circles and helped me see French literary life from a participant's point of view. Jan Goldstein has been a special sounding board for things French. But I and this book owe most to Robert A. Ferguson, who managed the delicate art of instilling confidence even as he offered criticism. The enterprise and the author required both.

May 1986

Acknowledgments

M. Georges Dumézil, Professeur au Collège de France et Membre de l'Académie française, and M. Claude Gallimard, for permission to reproduce the invitation to the bestowal of the academician's sword.

Foundation Ascom for the reproduction of "Etes-vous Balzac?" publicity in *Le Monde*, July 1983.

Agence France-Presse for the photograph of François Mauriac and Jean-Paul Sartre.

Roger-Viollet for the photograph of the cover of *Le Cri de Paris*, 23 January 1898, print by Félix Valloton.

Agence de Publicité: TBWA for the photograph of ". . . et le Noir," advertisement for Johnnie Walker.

Eminence S.A. for the photograph of the advertisement "Prix littéraires, Soyez à la page."

The French Embassy Press and Information Division, for photographs of the Panthéon, Claude Lévi-Strauss, Marguerite Yourcenar, and François Mitterrand.

The Musée Victor Hugo, the Photothèque des Musées de la Ville de Paris, for the following photographs: the caricature of the candidates to the Académie française, the caricature of Victor Hugo and Paris, the engraving of Hugo's arrival at the Gare du Nord, and Hugo's funeral procession.

The Bibliothèque Nationale for the photograph of the crowning of the bust of Voltaire at the Comédie-Française.

The Bettmann Archive for the reproduction of Paul Cézanne's portrait of Paul Alexis reading to Emile Zola (held by the Museo de Saõ Paulo).

Magnum Photos for the reproduction of Guy Le Querrec's photograph of Jean-Paul Sartre's funeral at the Cimetière Montparnasse.

Prologue: Culture and Country

To Great Men the Grateful Country
Inscription on the Panthéon

I

On 21 May 1981, with great pomp and circumstance, television cameras rolling, the newly inaugurated president of the French republic ascended the steps of the Panthéon in Paris. He carried two red roses, which he solemnly placed on the tombs of two of the individuals buried in this gigantic crypt and monument to French glory: Jean Jaurès, the Socialist leader assassinated in 1914, and Jean Moulin, the Resistance leader tortured and killed by the Gestapo in 1943. With this gesture François Mitterrand opened his term of office, invoking great figures from the past as titular heroes of his presidency. The Panthéon stood as the visible symbol of the union between tradition and country, Mitterrand's gesture as the reaffirmation of the tie between past and present, the spectacle itself as a reminder to every French citizen of the grandeur of the nation.

As a symbol of the continuity between past and present, the Panthéon is even more to the purpose than Mitterrand may have supposed. But it is a more ambiguous monument than Mitterrand's ceremony of roses immediately suggests. For the building encompasses not one but many pasts. It has served many purposes and many regimes, monarchies and empires as well as republics. No symbol of unity has had a more divided history.[1]

The complexities involved are at least partially responsible for turning a mere monument into a veritable icon of France. The Panthéon was originally built as a church dedicated to

1

The Panthéon in Paris is at once the symbol of a culture and its battleground. The cross on the dome, the motto above the portico ("To Great Men the Grateful Country"), and even the bodies sanctified within its walls have been removed and replaced from one political regime to the next. Yet at each stage of its tumultuous history, the Panthéon has been a monument of things peculiarly French. (Photograph courtesy of the French Embassy Press and Information Division)

the patron of the city of Paris, Sainte Geneviève, the result of a vow made in 1744 by Louis XV in gratitude for his recovery from a grave illness. Not until 1764 did the king place the first stone, and the edifice itself was barely completed twenty-seven years later when the Assemblée nationale decreed its metamorphosis into a pantheon of and for the great men who honor France by word and deed. The inscription placed on the building renovated to republican purpose—"To Great Men the Grateful Country"—bore witness to the will of the new republic to govern the very landscape. Mirabeau was the first patriot interred in the Panthéon, in April 1791, followed by Voltaire in July, in great (and costly) ceremony, and by Jean-Jacques Rousseau in October 1794. But rendering public space consonant with public ideology was a risky enterprise at a time when regimes shifted with bewildering frequency. Mirabeau was soon replaced by Marat, who was himself removed as the Revolution rewrote its history and sorted out its heroes.

Regimes in the nineteenth century continued to fix on the Panthéon to assert particular ideals and ideologies. Napoleon returned the building to an ecclesiastical function. Louis XVIII placed a cross on the dome and a new inscription in Latin proclaiming Sainte Geneviève the protectress of the church, his grandfather Louis XV as founder, and himself as restorer. Rededication in 1822 meant relegating Voltaire and Rousseau to an unconsecrated corner of the reconsecrated church. After the 1830 revolution Louis-Philippe reinstated the Panthéon, put Voltaire and Rousseau back where they had been, installed a new frieze, reinscribed the original motto, and substituted a flag for the cross on the dome. Scarcely twenty years later Louis-Napoleon Bonaparte, then president of the Second Republic, effaced the inscription and once again placed a cross on the dome, though he kept the July Monarchy frieze in which his uncle Napoleon I figured so prominently. This church remained unchanged throughout the Second Empire and the Commune of 1871 and well into the Third Republic. But with the death of Victor Hugo in

1885 the republican government reconverted the structure into a pantheon to receive the figure who symbolized the Republic for so many. The original inscription reappeared, to coexist with the cross on the dome in a final reconciliation of contraries. The Panthéon as it stands today bears all these reminders of its pasts, from the ancien régime to the present, the myriad cultural complexities reduced and contained within the apparent simplicity of a single monument. Somehow its very history, despite the divisiveness it records at almost every moment, redefines itself as a precious identification of country.

It is no accident that the many contradictions of these tumultuous years of French history were settled in and around the figure of a writer. In a country where politics divides so bitterly, literature can offer a vital source of union. The prominence of those whom I call public writers is a function of their ability to articulate a sense of country that both comprehends and transcends politics. Romain Rolland later explained the extraordinary outpouring of emotion at Hugo's grandiose funeral: "For us the name of the old Hugo was wedded to that of the Republic." A fellow student said more simply, "Victor Hugo is our religion."[2] Thus does the simultaneous association with and distance from the political process transform public writers in France into representatives of the country. This sort of public writer is a characteristically and indeed uniquely French figure. Every country, every literature, has politically committed writers, but only France has a tradition of writers who transmute those commitments into an encompassing identification with country. Only France has a literary culture that elects the writer as spokesman and invests literature with such powers.

A symbol of country, the Panthéon carries a special burden. The men buried there—military men, statesmen, scientists, and writers—recall in their diversity the original Greek conception of the pantheon as a temple for all the gods. The French heroes incarnate the public figure in the broadest and most various sense of the term, the individual whose life and work exemplify the best that France has achieved. Writers occupy a privileged position among those buried in the Panthéon, and they do so because they articulate the definition of country that is personified by the others. The writers in the Panthéon—Voltaire, Rousseau, Victor Hugo, Emile Zola—fused the public world of country with the private word of belief.

By virtue of this identification with country French literature has the crucial task of defining and sustaining that country. Writing from occupied Paris in 1941, Jean Giraudoux, playwright and diplomat, turned for solace to his literature.

> Our literature is not the Champs-Elysées [down which the conquering German army had marched in triumph]; it is the intangible, incorruptible, active domain of our true value and of the adventure of France in this world. . . . [This is] our true history, [the history] of our spirit and our language, the history of which everything survives.[3]

Giraudoux's statement is impressive not just because of its aspirations in a difficult time but because of the concrete meaning carried by its vague language. Literature here is as large as it is vague—"the intangible, incorruptible, active domain of our true value." Only a firm sense of context can also make it "our true history." What stands behind the conception of literature as an "active domain"? To understand Giraudoux's statement, to understand the milieu in which the statement itself can make sense, to see the Panthéon for what it has become, we must look to the culture that has shaped the literary enterprise in France. Although histories of French literature abound along with innumerable studies of individual writers, movements, and particular literary institutions, no study has concentrated on the largest source of shared meaning when French men and women talk about literature. No study has tried to define and analyze the specific sense of culture that gives direction to the whole configuration of writers, readers, and literary institutions. This book makes that attempt. *Literary France* seeks to analyze French literary

The Square of Writers Who Fought and Died for France near the Bois de Boulogne was dedicated in 1929. Like the Panthéon, though on a smaller scale, it articulates the bond between writer and country central to French literary culture. (Photograph by Priscilla Clark)

culture from its beginnings in the seventeenth century to the present, from Voltaire to Sartre.

II

The methodological difficulties of such an undertaking are considerable. Defining a culture and determining the ties between literature and its culture present major problems. That the connection is a necessary one, however, can scarcely be doubted. When the Vicomte de Bonald declared at the beginning of the nineteenth century that "literature is the expression of society as words are the expression of man," the claim was already a commonplace.[4] Since Vico at the beginning of the eighteenth century and most especially Voltaire, intellectual circles had more or less assumed the interdependence of the arts and the societies that create and practice those arts. Like most aphorisms, de Bonald's deceives in its simplicity. Controversy arises as soon as one looks beyond the well-turned phrase to inquire precisely what is "expressed," in which "society," in what kinds of "literature," and, for that matter, what "expression" itself means. Nor does a consensus exist concerning the proper mode of inquiry. How indeed should one approach the social relations of literature? What medium translates social forces into the symbolic discourse of literature? Just how is any analysis supposed to move from literary forms to social structure (and back again)?[5]

These very questions make a number of theoretic assumptions about the nature of literature and about the connections literature sustains in the worlds beyond the book. I take as axiomatic that literature implies a profoundly social endeavor and that it depends on the efforts and the expectations of a great many individuals and institutions. Some of these interconnections are obvious—for example, books need publishers, publishers need books. Other dependencies are more subtle. Education, less visibly connected to the literary enterprise than writers or publishers, nonetheless influences the way this enterprise occurs in society. Schools set up what is in effect a literary tribunal that chooses and judges literature, elevating some works and some authors while disdaining others. Beyond perpetuating a canon of works, education instills a sense of the literary, an attitude toward the writer, and a definition of literature—what it is and what it should be. That is, education participates fully in any literary culture.

For literature to exist in any form whatsoever then, whether book or text or institution or concept, many elements must interact, some best described as aesthetic and intellectual, others predominantly economic, cultural, or political. *Literary France* undertakes to identify and then explore both the texts and the contexts where these elements realize, indeed create, the possibilities of literature in one particular setting—France.

The coalition of forces responsible for the production of literature becomes increasingly apparent as modern societies accord ever more autonomy to the literary enterprise. With increasing specialization and the division of labor in contemporary society, a constellation has emerged of mutually sustaining institutions, ideologies, symbols, and codes that together define a distinct subculture in the larger society. This subculture I call literary culture, and I see it as a vital link between literature and society, a mediator between the two poles that translates the literary into social terms and the social into a literary mode.

The explorations of French literary culture in the chapters that follow will illustrate its meaning better than any pronouncement *ex cathedra*. Nevertheless, a definition will help set, and thereby clarify, the terms of inquiry. The concept of culture itself is so elusive, so maddeningly loose in its multiple and even contradictory usages, that many commentators sidestep definition altogether and rely on the context to determine the concept.

Modern discussions of culture, certainly in the Anglo-Saxon world, usually descend in one line or another from the definition advanced by the British anthropologist E. B. Tylor in 1871: "Culture or Civilization, taken in its wide ethnographic sense, is that complex whole which includes knowledge, belief, art, morals, law, custom, and any other capabil-

ities and habits acquired by man as a member of society."[6] By
these lights culture comprehends virtually anything and
everything that makes the individual a social being. Capa-
cious to the point of vacuity, this definition offers little in the
way of methodological precision. On the other hand, it has
the great merit of focusing on the intangibles, on modes of
existence, rather than on such easily circumscribed signs of
culture as institutions or artifacts.

In our own century Claude Lévi-Strauss has offered a more
useful working definition. He pursues the implications of Tylor's claim as well as those inscribed in the eighty years or so
of ethnographic practice since Tylor, his own work in particular:

> We call culture the ethnographic whole which, from the point
> of view of the study, presents significant differences from
> other such entities. . . . We see that the notion of culture can
> correspond to an objective reality even as it is a function of the
> kind of research undertaken. . . . The term of culture is used
> to group an ensemble of significant differences whose bound-
> aries, experience tells us, approximately coincide.[7]

Because culture is construed in terms of difference, its distinctive characteristics emerge strikingly from comparisons.
French literary culture stands out against literary cultures
elsewhere and also against other subcultures in French society. But the *maker* of the comparisons—"the point of view of
the study"—inevitably intrudes on the seeming objectivity.
Identifying the concept and the coordinates of culture gives
the ethnologist a share in the existence of that culture. French
literary culture is partly a function of this book—"the kind of
research undertaken"—and it is well to admit as much from
the outset.

Contemporary sociological research tends to shift the focus
from the whole of small, usually non-Western societies and
their "primitive" cultures to parts, or subcultures, of techno-
logically advanced and organizationally complex Western societies. The sociologist has, then, the advantage of working
closer to home than the anthropologist. But proximity exacts
costs as well. The more complex a society and the longer its

history, the more meanings inhere in the term *culture*.[8] Inevitably, the ethnographic definition of culture clashes with the older and still current definition of culture as an ideal, as the sum of the intellectual and aesthetic accomplishments of a society or even an individual. In no domain is the confusion greater than in that of literary culture. The tensions that subsist in any culture between the ideal and the norm, and hence between the insider and the outsider are exacerbated for literary culture by the value invested in literature. It is difficult to stand apart from those values and to analyze literary culture without in some measure participating in it. Moreover, the resistance to analytic incursions into the realm of the aesthetic can be fierce indeed on the part of those who perceive—quite correctly—that such analyses take literature from the ethereal to the very terrestrial.

The construction of literary culture faces a further obstacle. Literary culture is grounded, not in a circumscribed, easily contained social group, but rather in a social practice that affects many individuals who otherwise may have little in common. Literature involves much more than writers, and even they do not form the well-defined group that would facilitate the task of locating literary culture. Like the intellectuals whom they frequent and with whom they are often identified, writers elude the familiar social categories. Long association with the liberal professions cannot transform writing into a profession in any truly sociological sense. Nor can writers qua writers be readily assimilated into any other social status: they are not capitalists or workers in the classical definitions; they are not rentiers or peasants, nor bureaucrats or bourgeois, and their many institutional affiliations only complicate the situation. There remains a heterogeneous assemblage of individuals isolated by their work and torn by dissent almost as much as they are bound by a common, ambiguous position in society—a position about which many voice considerable ambivalence.

Neither individuals nor institutions operate in a vacuum. As literary culture circumscribes individual creativity and interpretation, so too it constrains institutions. It is useful to distinguish literary culture—the values, norms, and behavior that suffuse literary life—from the literary institutions that circulate literature in society—publishing houses, journals, schools, and the like. To the extent that literary activities in different settings rest on a common economic base, they share literary institutions. Capitalism, after all, makes similar demands in France and the United States, in Japan and Australia, just as patronage once imposed its logic indifferently on English and German as on French cultural life. Yet the many countries that share certain literary institutions do not share a literary culture. For culture keeps to the particular. By linking economic and social institutions to cultural and literary traditions, literary culture moves these institutions to act in particular ways.

Thus French literary culture is embedded in institutions, in individual behavior, in literary works, all of which may be read as signs to and forms of the culture, which they serve to preserve and to perpetuate. In the words of M. M. Bakhtin,

> Cultural and literary traditions . . . are preserved and continue to live not in the individual subjective memory of a single individual . . . but rather in the objective forms that culture itself assumes (including the forms of language and spoken speech), and in this sense they are inter-subjective and inter-individual (and consequently social); from there they enter literary works, sometimes almost completely bypassing the subjective individual memory of their creators.[9]

How one chooses to address the whole problem of tradition—the "objective forms" beyond "individual subjective memory"—reveals a great deal about one's definitions of culture, both implicit and explicit. As the biological referent of the word implies, culture sets the very conditions of life.[10] So too literary culture poses the conditions of literary creativity, the constraints within which the writer must work, the opportunities inscribed in the legacy with which every writer must contend. As T. S. Eliot noted almost a half century ago, tradition provides the indispensable context of creativity. Every writer must measure and be measured against others, in the past as in the present. To appreciate is to compare. Yet if every creation bears the imprint of tradition, some times and some writers—Eliot singled out the French—pay more attention to traditions than others.[11]

For Eliot literary tradition meant primarily a succession of works that stand in some vital relation to one another—as in the tradition of English or French literature, of European literature, of the novel, of realism. But he of all people would have agreed that literary tradition is not reducible to aesthetics. Texts and aesthetic principles invariably touch on values and perceptions, ideologies and ideas. Thus, for example, the celebrated dictum "What is not clear it not French" states an aesthetic principle with implications that are social, ideological, and even political. The clarity so often ascribed to the French language and prescribed for French literature constitutes a basic element in French literary culture and determines much about the ways literature in France is conceived and written, interpreted and read.

III

To summarize the foregoing and to essay a definition: French literary culture is the complex configuration of ideals and practices, comportment and conviction, custom and discourse that characterizes the literary enterprise in France. This "ethnographic whole," to take Lévi-Strauss's formulation, sets that enterprise apart from other literary cultures and apart also from other subcultures in French society. The fabric of this culture is woven of many strands. Some originate in the social, economic, and political structures of French society. Others come from literary, intellectual, and aesthetic traditions both within and beyond France. Other literary cultures and other cultures in France may share one and another of these elements with French literary culture. The Panthéon, for example, played a specifically political role in Mitterrand's inauguration, and the public writers who so well represent the union of culture and country also belong to specific aesthetic and intellectual contexts. But no other culture offers the distinctive combination of these elements that characterizes French literary culture; no other culture has its patterns. It is, to return to Lévi-Strauss, an "ensemble of significant differences."

Literary France considers this ensemble from different but complementary perspectives, synchronic and diachronic, institutional and ideological, sociological and historical. Chapter 1 opens with the most basic question of all: how do we know that this literary culture is "French"? What does it mean to say that French literature or French writers are "French"? Does this literary culture exist independently of the literary works that we are trying to understand in the first place? Only cross-cultural comparisons offer the possibility of answering these questions, and the first chapter compares a variety of cultural indicators, with particular focus on France and the United States. While these two countries differ greatly in size, population, and age, for example, they also share a great deal as advanced industrial societies and representative democracies. It is precisely these resemblances that throw the distinctiveness into high relief.

Chapters 2 and 3 trace French literary culture to the institutions and ideologies of the ancien régime that assimilated literature to an essentially aristocratic culture. After the Revolution effectively destroyed this milieu, the nineteenth century greatly expanded the market for literature. The values of this newly dominant market clashed with the literary values bequeathed by the ancien régime, and this confrontation produced new institutions as well as ideologies to support them. A specifically literary culture evolved out of the antagonisms that pitted the aristocratic traditions inherited from the ancien régime against the bourgeois ethos supported by the market.

Chapter 4 turns to the new breed of nineteenth-century writers who had to cope with an alien, seemingly omnipotent market. Whether they used the market or tried to circumvent it, these writers set many of the features of French literary culture as we know it today. On a different tack, chapter 5 sketches a portrait of this literary culture, or what the nineteenth century would have called its "physiology," drawn from the definitions proffered over several centuries by foreign as well as French commentators of what exactly makes the literature and the writers of France recognizably French. In the mosaic of these characterizations we read the patterns of French literary culture and the literary sensibility it sustains.

Chapters 6 and 7 move from synchrony to diachrony to present French literary culture not as a phenomenon fixed in time and place but rather as a dynamic that individual writers respond to and, in their responses, redefine. Each in his time and for his time, Voltaire, Victor Hugo, and Jean-Paul Sartre stand as the incarnations of French literary culture, their work its fullest expression. Finally, the Epilogue speculates on the future of this literary culture and its remarkable capacity to make use of and renew the tradition that spans three centuries from the ancien régime to the late twentieth century.

Taking our cues from the ethnologist, we must seek out the relevant signs and symbols, scrutinizing institutions as well as ideologies, the values sustained as well as the strategies employed, the modes of expression encouraged as well as the writers glorified in the process.[12] For beyond the place of writers and literature in this society, at issue is the nature of literature in France and hence, as de Bonald reminds us, the nature of French society.

1

Locating Literary Culture

But really what they do do is to respect art and letters, if
you are a writer you have privileges, . . . and it is pleasant
having those privileges.

Gertrude Stein, *Paris France*

Nowhere else except in France do writers have the exorbi-
tant privileges they enjoy in Paris in public life.

François Nourissier,
Les Chiens à fouetter

I

All cultures resist definition. Where analysis would general-
ize, culture resolutely espouses the particular. Literary culture especially frustrates. It possesses no geographical unity,
no natural boundaries, and the artifacts it produces—
books—are perhaps the least of what literary culture is all
about. Certainly this holds for France where, as Paul Valéry
observed some time ago, the writer is something other than
a man who writes books that are published.[1] Nevertheless,
the conviction, indeed the belief that this is so, that something makes literature in France distinctly French, does not
immediately help in determining what that something
might be.

A logical approach takes us to and through comparison.
Thus Lévi-Strauss's definition in terms of difference requires
comparisons.[2] We need not be ethnographers to make comparisons. We all make them all of the time, and never more
so than when we deal with cultures that are not our own.
Most often these comparisons remain implicit and are for-
mulated vaguely; a systematic analysis of culture, presum-

ably, need only make them explicit and rigorous. But what can or should be compared? For an American, the United States presents the logical, even "natural" term for comparisons with France. Yet many of the most obvious bases of comparison do little to distinguish one literary culture from the other.

Almost any reader of France and America is likely to register surprise, if not disbelief, at the remarkable similarities of France and the United States in standard indicators of literary activity—books published, book sales, reading habits, subventions available to writers, and prestige accorded writers in general surveys. Wherever a distinctive literary culture lies, it is manifestly not here.[3] On the contrary, the similarity of these measures seems to credit the claim that contemporary society reserves little or no space for national cultures. At one end of the spectrum, critics of varying persuasions argue that mass culture, however determined, has obliterated such differences. Mass communications, so the argument runs, have transformed the world into a global village.[4] At the opposite end of the spectrum is the argument, made for France most recently and most emphatically by Theodore Zeldin, that the French are becoming less and less alike and that social fragmentation and tolerance have progressed so far that it is misleading, if not impossible, to speak of a truly French culture at all.[5]

Measures of books produced, sold, and read and of writers supported testify that on some issues, differences between France and the United States are much less significant than they were a hundred years ago when France published many more books than the United States. Today, now that the United States has more or less caught up, parity in book production, readership, and the like proves only the prevailing logic of the literary market in modern society, which is itself subject to the imperatives of an industrial economy. To locate literary culture, we must look elsewhere, beyond *what* a society does with and for literature to *how* it does what it does. The hows of literary life bring the uniqueness of literary and cultural traditions into play. We must, in short, construct other indicators to capture the special qualities of that culture and the principles around which it coheres.

Fortunately for the would-be ethnographer, signs point to a distinct literary culture in France. What makes French literary culture distinct is not the amount of moneys available to writers but the source and the functions of those moneys. It is not the gross production and sales of books that set France apart but the modes of marketing those books, not a generalized social judgment of writers but the prestige writers gain by association with upper-class milieux and notably with the government. Cultural differences show up in the particularities of symbolic activity, not in aggregate assessments of productivity. This is so because any culture keeps to the particular, engaging the incident, the otherwise unremarkable event, the anecdote, the turn of phrase by which it narrates the world. All these signs are the signs of and to a culture; they are the signs by which outsiders recognize that culture, the signs also by which participants identify and identify with that same culture. When read with care, the least detail can provide a key to cultural meaning. Like the archaeologist who studies fragments of physical artifacts, shards, tablets, and inscriptions on stone, the analyst of culture must look at fragments, bits and parts that can perhaps be pieced together to form a whole. At stake is an imaginative grasp of the nuances and patterns that encourage a sense of belonging to *this* culture and no other.

We find the signs to French literary culture in emblems of literature, of writers, of the literary enterprise. We read these emblems as so many manifestations of ideals and ideas conveyed to society at large. French bank notes give pride of place to literary figures. And although vast claims cannot be made for public recognition, it seems wonderfully apt— and ironic—that prostitutes should pay off the police with "des Pascal"—street slang for the five-hundred-franc note that bears Blaise Pascal's mournful countenance. Paris street names integrate writers into the urban text. Again the resonance is uncertain, but surely other Americans have reacted like Edmund Wilson, who thought it "quite wonderful" to

The text as artifact in a commercial world. Here the full-page advertisement from *L'Express* dissociates the indissociable by removing the first term from Stendhal's classic, *The Red and the Black*. The Johnnie Walker Red Label—the only color variation on a black, white, and grey page—then rescues the literary order. "WITHOUT THE RED," runs the caption, "NOTHING WORKS." (Photograph courtesy of Agence de Publicité: TBWA)

find a Paris street named for one of his favorite writers, and have reflected as he did on the situation at home, where efforts to rename Washington Square for Henry James, who was born there, came to naught. How different from France, where the young Jean-Paul Sartre could be confident that literary success meant "his" streets in Paris and the provinces as well.[6]

Literary prizes also suggest the subtle (and sometimes not-so-subtle) ways in which French literary culture works within economic constraints even as it alters their logic. Although all of the vast number of literary prizes awarded in France do not have a great impact on sales, the most notable ones have a spectacular impact. The Prix Goncourt, awarded since 1902 to the "best work in prose" published during the previous year, regularly sells 200,000 to 400,000 copies—a direct market influence not replicated in its absolute predictability by any American prize, not even the Pulitzer. The five or six other "marketable" French prizes sell fewer books, but even the 20,000 or so copies of a "difficult" Médicis (established expressly for experimental fiction) push sales well above the average. The great round of publicity that attends the announcements of these prizes, invariably followed by a mixed but strident chorus of acclamation and denunciation, has consecrated the award ceremonies as an essential ritual of the Paris literary season and, for the writer, a veritable rite of passage.

The news media pounce with delight on these ceremonial occasions and often give extensive coverage to literary affairs generally. Even television—surely the quintessential mass medium—gives greater prominence in France than elsewhere to cultural and literary programs. Television works within established patterns and preferences, not against them. Still largely a state monopoly, it reinforces the empire of Paris and magnifies the effects of French literary culture.[7]

II

The meaning of any culture lies in the specific configuration of social, economic, and political circumstances on which

Victor Hugo's name rebounds from street to plaza to storefront and café, while other stores on the writer's street take the names of his heroes and heroines. The street sign explicitly renders the association with country: "Writer, Poet, and Politician." (Photographs by Priscilla Clark)

PRIX LITTÉRAIRES, SOYEZ A LA PAGE.

Il ne suffit pas de connaître ses classiques pour aborder la course aux prix littéraires. Il faut aussi renouveler le genre. Avec le caleçon Style City d'Eminence, vous vous définissez en quelques lignes, certes comme classique dans la tradition du style français, mais avec une invention, un brio, une fraîcheur qui sauront séduire un public d'aujourd'hui. Et vous aborderez les prix littéraires dans le plus grand confort, sûr d'avoir l'étoffe d'un grand écrivain. En améliorant votre académie vous vous donnez même des chances d'y être reçu.

GINGKO

"LITERARY PRIZE WINNERS, BE UP TO DATE. It is not enough to know your classics to enter the race for literary prizes. You have to know how to renew the genre. With these shorts you can define yourself in a few lines, as a classic in the tradition of French style, but also with an inventiveness, a brio, a freshness that will seduce today's public. And you will take on the literary prizes in the greatest of comfort, sure of having the material of a great writer. By improving your academy, you give yourself a chance of being received by the academy."

The underwear advertisement, appearing in *L'Express* just prior to the attribution of major literary prizes, insists on the connection. "Académie" is both the technical term for the lower torso and the identification of an awarding institution (Académie Goncourt, Académie française, Académie des Jeux Floraux de Toulouse, inter alia). (Photograph courtesy of Eminence S.A.)

it depends. Governmental centralization has characterized French society since the early seventeenth century. The concentration of literary life in Paris is itself part of a the more general concentration of social, economic, and cultural resources, most of which were originally tied in some fashion to the government. As chapter 2 will show in greater detail, Louis XIV exercised a quasi-monopoly over patronage of the arts through direct subsidies to individuals and through institutions like the Académie des inscriptions, the Académie des sciences, and, the most revered, the Académie française, whose foundation in 1635 makes it the oldest (almost continuous) cultural institution in France. Charged with writing a dictionary and a grammar, the Académie has continued to regiment the use of the French language. Although there are other academies in France, there is only one French Academy. If its importance should not be exaggerated, neither should it be minimized. The Académie exemplifies a characteristic mingling of writers and the upper classes in and around a central cultural institution. Academicians have been and indeed still are recruited from all the traditional sectors of the upper classes—the aristocracy, the clergy, the military—to which have been added the new aristocracies of academics, savants, and politicians.

In the nineteenth century the educational system took up where patronage left off, inculcating the values of literature and perpetuating the norms and the expectations of French literary culture. The long-term consequences of the lycée program, which the Ministry of Education determined in exceptional detail, can scarcely be exaggerated. Even for students specializing in mathematics, philosophical and literary studies predominated. French was taught through translation from Latin (the *version*), and Latin, along with the general culture it bespoke, united the upper classes at the same time that it distinguished them from everyone else. The curriculum stressed the development of a "correct" style and effective oral and written expression, almost invariably with reference to literary models. Students might be asked to imagine Sophocles writing to Racine to console him for the lukewarm

reception of *Athalie* or Mme de Sévigné recounting the premiere of Racine's *Esther* to her good friend Mme de Lafayette.[8]
Insofar as these institutions central to French society propagated literary values and norms, they created a public for
literature that extended beyond readers to include the much
larger population touched by these institutions directly or
indirectly.

The strength and the persistence of these upper-class connections go far to account for the prestige so often attributed
to the writer in France. Already in the eighteenth century the
English were complaining that "men of learning enjoy not
the happiness of a free and easy intercourse with the great,
unless there is a prospect of turning their abilities to political
use." By contrast, "the uncommon regard paid in France to
persons eminent in literature, is no less extraordinary than
commendable."[9] By the nineteenth century this preeminence
had become virtually an article of faith. Writing in the 1830s,
the novelist Edward Bulwer-Lytton affirmed peremptorily
that a writer in France is like a writer nowhere else: not in
America, where there is not the "superstition for the arts"
that prevails in France; not in Germany, where one needs a
von before one's name to get anywhere; and not in England,
where men are immersed in politics and women are preoc-
cupied with fashion. Bulwer-Lytton made the customary
identification of literature with learning but argued that notwithstanding the greater spread of education, England possessed neither France's "ardent passion" for literature nor its
"vast respect" for men of letters. In England, this aristocrat
lamented, a man known as a writer was assumed to be poor
and not a gentleman, whereas in France the state made writers peers and gave them important responsibilities.[10]

The twentieth century concurred. Ford Madox Ford, for
one, thought that writers in France were almost a "national
value." The German literary historian E. R. Curtius contended that France was the only country that made a "religion" of literature.[11] But it was the Americans who marveled
most. The Southern critic Allen Tate asserted categorically
that there is "no other country where the writer is so much

honored as in France, no other people in western culture who understand so well as the French the value of literature to the state."[12] Of the many American writers and artists who went to Paris in the early twentieth century, Gertrude Stein was perhaps the most inveterate expatriate and the most indelibly American. The consideration with which she was treated in France impressed her greatly:

> But really what they do do is to respect art and letters, if you are a writer you have privileges, . . . and it is pleasant having those privileges. I always remember coming in from the country to my garage where I usually kept my car and the garage was full more than full, it was the moment of the automobile salon, but said I what can I do, well said the man in charge I'll see and then he came back and said in a low voice, there is a corner and in this corner I put the car of Monsieur the academician and next to it I will put yours the others can stay outside and it is quite true even in a garage an academician and a woman of letters takes precedence even of millionaires or politicians, they do, it is quite incredible but they do, the police treat artists and writers respectfully too.[13]

Stein's garageman was not likely to have read the works of Monsieur the Academician and even less likely to have read hers, but he was well aware of their rank as figures in the world of letters. The deference honored the status rather than the individual—a striking and, for writers, gratifying effect of the upper-class relations of literature.

French politics also bears a literary stamp, imprinted both by the writers who have taken on serious political duties and by the politicians who have figured prominently in literary life. Long connected to the government, accustomed to the company of political figures and familiar with their concerns, French writers frequently and naturally entertain political ambitions of their own. An impressive line of writers has been directly involved in politics. Chateaubriand was foreign minister during the Restoration as well as ambassador to England and to the Holy See. Benjamin Constant was a deputy to the Assemblée nationale during the Restoration, Alphonse de Lamartine and Alfred de Vigny during the July Monarchy. Lamartine played a vital role in the revolution of 1848. Victor

Hugo sat in the Chambre des Pairs during the 1840s and was elected deputy twice, during the Second Republic and at the very beginning of the Third Republic; he was senator thereafter. Maurice Barrès sat in the Assemblée nationale for many years; Paul Claudel, Jean Giraudoux, and Saint-John Perse were all ranking diplomats in the foreign service; André Malraux served as the first minister of culture under the Fifth Republic. And so on.

Of equal moment for French literary culture are the literary aspirations of politicians. By its transmission of the practical into the higher discourse of art, literature legitimates politics in subtle and complex ways. The act of writing still secures important "symbolic capital," much as it did for the aristocrats of the ancien régime. The republication of Napoleon's literary works recalls the young strategist's dreams of literary as well as military glory. Napoleon III hoped (in vain) that his biography of Caesar would gain him election to the Académie française, and Valéry Giscard d'Estaing confessed that he too would once have preferred literature to politics had he been certain of equaling Flaubert and Maupassant. François Mitterrand has written some twelve books. Indeed, the Fifth Republic may already have set a record in absolute numbers for the production of political memoirs, programs, essays, and sundry reflections.[14]

This nexus and the reciprocal fascination of writers and politicians are intensely French. As one veteran political journalist commented in a review of the book Giscard d'Estaing published while president, one can hardly imagine Gerald Ford as a novelist, Helmut Schmidt as a historian, or Leonid Brezhnev as a philosopher.[15] The comparison with the American political scene is especially sharp, and here the inevitable politicians' memoirs confirm the hypothesis. The French rightfully boast of a long line of such memoirs, beginning with the Cardinal de Retz in the seventeenth century and illustrated most remarkably in the twentieth century by Charles de Gaulle, who wished to be known, as indeed he was, for his style. His memoirs belong to an esteemed literary tradition as Richard Nixon's or Henry Kissinger's or Jimmy

Carter's do not. American campaign autobiographies are often ghosted: the French tend to write their own. And although Spiro Agnew wrote a novel upon quitting politics, no one ever imputed literary ambitions to him. One cannot conceive of an American politician, in or out of office, being praised, as de Gaulle once was, for the "natural and sumptuous" style of his press conferences or being taken to task for the "irresolution" of his commas.[16] Carter's or Reagan's commas attract little attention, and Nixon's language has been scrutinized for everything *but* style. Style is not even a minor consideration of political life in America, where grammar remains at best a casual concern. (Think, for a moment, of the quite extraordinary exchange during the congressional Watergate hearings: "Who was 'we'?" to which the response came automatically, "'We' was us.")

The practice of politics comes naturally in a literary culture that produces so many of what I call public writers, that is, writers who conflate their social and literary commitments and who resolve to place them before the public. This lineage of Voltaire, of Victor Hugo, of Jean-Paul Sartre, to take the exemplary figures discussed in the final chapters of this work, lies at the heart of French literary culture. Public writers may also be tempted by practical politics—Voltaire dreamed of fulfilling diplomatic missions for Frederick the Great, and Hugo actually entered political life, though with a resounding lack of success. Yet the public writer never forswears the primary allegiance to the word and to literature as the medium of engagement. The authority of such figures is moral, not practical, and their power is symbolic, residing in their ability to focus attention and to galvanize opinion. In 1960 the originators of a declaration supporting French soldiers who refused to serve in Algeria went naturally to Sartre, whose signature set the moral authority of the public writer against the legal authority of the government and the power of the state.[17]

The prominence of the public writer can be ascribed to his dual status as insider and outsider, the ambiguous position that writers have occupied since the ancien régime, when they participated in aristocratic society without being an integral part of it. The prestige of the public writer in France can be traced not only to the centuries-old ties to political figures but also to the even older association of the poet with the prophet, the outsider who sits in judgment on the exercise of power by those same figures. Is influence power? One must caution against confusing the symbolic power of moral authority with political power in a strict sense. To Sartre's request for permission to hold the war crimes tribunal in France, President de Gaulle deferentially addressed his reply, "Cher Maître," even as he declined the petition.

III

How distinctive are these French connections? Once again, the particular context makes the difference. Neither Germany nor England exhibits the single most conspicuous feature of French society, namely, the centralization of government and the consequent concentration of cultural resources. The German cultural world has never had an undisputed cultural capital. The large urban centers—Berlin, Dresden, Vienna—preempted the many lesser states, but when that lesser state was Weimar and its most illustrious inhabitant Goethe, the periphery could easily, if momentarily, become a center.

Since the thirteenth century the University of Paris has enhanced the stature of Paris, drawing to the city French citizen and foreigner alike. Even today, after powerful moves to break the dominion of Paris in the university system, thirteen of the seventy-two universities in France are to be found in the capital. Universities in Germany have always been spread over the whole country, and in England the two medieval universities, residential as the Parisian faculties were not, were located outside London—not all that far, to be sure, yet far enough to make the university a world apart. Founded in 1836, and hence overshadowed by venerable Oxbridge, the University of London has never played the role that devolved on the University of Paris.

Court life similarly diverged to set France apart. Aristocratic society in England, the closest parallel to France, never knew the relentless centralization that has so marked France; consequently London has never dominated cultural life in England as Paris has dominated it in France. The English court, like the French, drew people of all kinds and callings to the capital, but the English monarchs viewed the advent of urbanization differently from their French counterparts. In the early seventeenth century, when Louis XIII and Richelieu were striving to concentrate political, social, and cultural life, the Stuarts were protesting against the congregation at court of individuals who ought instead to have been off keeping peace and order on their estates. In 1615 James I enjoined all the gentry and those of the nobility without special business in London to return home: "Therefore as every fish liues in his owne place, some in the fresh, some in the salt, some in the mud; so let everyone liue in his owne place, some at Court, some in the Citie, some in the Country."[18] The French court, by way of contrast, instilled an invincible prejudice against provincial mud. Queen Elizabeth took her court to the countryside on her many famous progresses; Louis XIV realized similar social and political control through the contrary strategy of impelling the nobility to Versailles. We see here the emergence of radically different attitudes toward the notion of a capital.[19]

Cultural control in England has been simply more diffuse. No major institution has ever regimented English letters. No English academy has matched the Académie française. In 1664 the Royal Society, founded in 1662, set up a committee to improve the English language, but it remained a dead letter even though an English academy was proposed several times during the course of the eighteenth century. No dictionary undertook to rule on English grammar. Indeed, the very notion of such cultural control ran counter to English custom. Samuel Johnson, in the preface to his own *Dictionary* (1755), voiced what must have been the prevailing sentiment on the subject: "If an academy should be established . . . I . . . hope the spirit of English liberty will hinder or destroy [it]."[20]

The spirit of English liberty was a spirit of laissez-faire, at least as English monarchs interpreted it. Patronage of letters never became the tool in England that it was in France. Notorious for her parsimony, Elizabeth I gave little material return for the many poems written in praise of her virtue, beauty, and sagacity. Writers did better—though not all that well—with noble families like the Sidneys whose patronage, once again, took writers to the country, away from the court and the capital.[21] Elizabeth's Stuart successors were somewhat more lavish, but neither the civil war nor the Protectorate offered artists much in the way of support. The extent of Charles II's debt both at the Restoration in 1660 and after was so great that if he perhaps had the inclination to spend great sums on the arts, he lacked the means to do so. By the early eighteenth century whatever patronage existed was fast becoming overtly politicized, one more weapon in the arsenal of party politicians. Not until 1945 did Great Britain reestablish government subvention of literature.[22]

The expansion of the market in eighteenth-century England countered and hastened the decline of patronage, and this commercialization had the effect of making writers far more dependent on booksellers than on patrons. By midcentury patronage was increasingly a thing of the past. Samuel Foote's play of 1757, *The Patron*, details the tribulations of Dick Dactyl caused by his would-be patron, Sir Thomas Lofty, and his publisher, Puff; Puff definitely dominates the scene. Dactyl can do without Sir Thomas, but he cannot do without Puff. The newly independent author energetically refused the inequalities inseparable from patronage. Samuel Johnson's famous riposte to Lord Chesterfield's belated offer of assistance said it all: "Is not a Patron, my Lord, one who looks with unconcern on a man struggling for life in the water, and, when he has reached ground, encumbers him with help? The notice which you have been pleased to take of my labors, had it been early, had been kind; but it has been delayed until I am indifferent, and cannot enjoy it, till I am solitary, and cannot impart it; till I am known, and do not want it."[23]

Such a tone would have jarred the proudest and most arrogant of Johnson's contemporaries in France. Although

Rousseau rejected the offer of a royal pension, some years later he accepted with alacrity the support that allowed him to go his own way. French writers were dissatisfied certainly—dependence must always gall. Yet they curbed their tongues, at least in public, partly because no acceptable alternatives existed to patronage, partly because of a greater attention to and respect for hierarchy. It is worth recalling that in England this hierarchy had no legal status comparable to that of the three estates by which Frenchmen of the ancien régime were classified into the clergy, the nobility, and everybody else. The frontiers between these estates could be crossed, and they were, but they existed. If the three estates were a legal fiction, that fiction commanded assent until 1789.[24]

As one would expect, American literary culture is the product of other traditions. American federalism, by according autonomy to state and local governments, supported strong regional identities. Localism, in turn, sustained and was sustained by a recurrent populism in American society. Local authority and local pride fostered suspicions of national elites and national authority. From the beginning the United States repudiated aristocratic models of society and of literature. Despite isolated examples of governmental patronage, Americans had no established patronage of letters or the arts.[25] Jacksonian democracy effectively quashed John Quincy Adams's dream of a national academy of arts and sciences, and when Senator Charles Sumner made a similar proposal some forty years later, the very idea of such an academy was an anomaly.

Those who marked American literary and artistic culture were not the aristocrats and their successors but the "new," "modern" self-made men and their wives whose fortunes came from business and commerce and went to foundations, museums, libraries, and universities scattered about the country, endowments that reflected local pride and accentuated the dispersion of American cultural life. Of these various cultural institutions, colleges and universities have come to be most closely associated with writers. They are now the largest single source of literary prizes and, more important, have provided a haven for writers ever since Henry Wadsworth Longfellow was appointed to Bowdoin, then to Harvard. Most of these writers have been employed, as Longfellow was, to teach literature courses (Longfellow began by teaching French), but beginning with Robert Frost's residency at Amherst College, the poet/writer-in-residence became an increasingly common figure on American campuses. Especially in the past decade or two, the proliferation of "creative writing" courses, programs, and even degrees means that many writers are able to teach as well as practice their craft. Not so in France. French education has no equivalent to "creative writing." Indeed, the French language cannot even translate a term so utterly alien to French notions of writing and style.

In the United States, at least since the middle of the nineteenth century, the worlds of politics and letters have gone their separate ways. Only sporadically has political life tempted the literary minded. Ralph Waldo Emerson exhorted the writer to lofty concerns and away from the political hustings. Henry Adams's distaste for the whole business of politics, so evident in his novel *Democracy* (1880), may be extreme because so patently aristocratic, but few American writers have bothered to disagree with him, and even fewer have entered politics themselves. Lawyers, not writers, are the more typical politicians in America, and not since the first half of the nineteenth century have lawyers had much to do with literature or literary life.[26]

Of course, American political figures have taken up the pen. Among the presidents, one can point to the Thomas Jefferson of *Notes on the State of Virginia* (1787) as an important writer and an authentic American philosophe. John Quincy Adams wrote poetry and was well known for a work on the nature of oratory. Ulysses S. Grant's memoirs were published by Mark Twain, Grover Cleveland published *Fishing and Hunting Sketches* (1906), Theodore Roosevelt was celebrated as a serious historian and biographer and hailed for his stirring narratives of the West. Woodrow Wilson was known for his various works on political theory, and John F. Kennedy won the Pulitzer Prize for *Profiles in Courage* (1956). Generations of school children have memorized Abraham Lincoln's "Gettysburg Address" as a model of humanitarian patriotism and as a model also of style. Yet America places the emphasis elsewhere. None of these men belonged in any sense to a literary milieu as did Lamartine, Vigny, and others cited above. Thus John Quincy Adams's poems were originally published anonymously and were collected under his name only after his death. His poetry was, as the publisher noted, for his "leisure moments," and even then duty beckoned the poet, not delight:

> Behold the lettered sage devote
> The labors of his mind,
> His country's welfare to promote,
> And benefit mankind.[27]

Geography confirmed the separation of literature and politics. The intensity promoted by the concentration of people and resources in Paris was simply not possible in the sprawling United States, especially in times when travel was slow and difficult. Equally significant was the lack of an indigenous American literary history to which writers and political figures alike could relate. Not only could French writers find social, intellectual, and at times financial support in the upper-class milieux where literature and politics mixed with ease, but they also had the incalculable added advantage of working in a prestigious literary tradition and with a language that laid claim to European supremacy. Americans did not have such a literature to call their own, and many early Americans viewed European customs with great suspicion. Revolutionary and postrevolutionary France had both a literature and a language around which the new nation could be formed; the French language was a powerful instrument in creating a French nation. Americans had to build their nation without such aid. They had to build a country and a literature, and the country came first. Literature was for "leisure moments," an indulgence unless infused with a strong sense of duty and moral purpose, and even then not of the greatest consequence. Although Jefferson loved literature, he directed his energies elsewhere. Fifty years after the Revolution Daniel Webster analyzed the situation: "But the times were times for action, rather than contemplation. The country was to be defended, and to be saved, before it could be enjoyed. Philosophic leisure and literary pursuits . . . were all necessarily postponed to the urgent calls of the public service."[28]

Early on John Adams set the priorities for serious Americans. Writing to his wife from Paris in 1780, Adams owned that it would be nice to take another walk about Versailles and review its pleasures in detail. But he had no time. "It is not indeed the fine Arts, which our Country requires. . . . I must study Politicks and War that my sons may have liberty to study Mathematicks and Philosophy. My sons ought to study Mathematicks and Philosophy, Geography, natural History, Naval Architecture, navigation, Commerce and Agriculture, in order to give their Children a right to study Painting, poetry, Musick, Architecture, Statuary, Tapestry, and Porcelaine."[29] No wonder John Quincy published his poems anonymously. Poetry had come at least one generation too soon! The fullness of time eventually would endow the United States with literary traditions of its own. Yet the prejudices in the early patterns linger on, fortified by literary institutions and by the literary culture that grew up around them.

A different literary ethic functions in France. Writers there have the prestige and the privileges they do because of their ties to political life, because of the moral authority of literature, because the writer is a public figure, and, above all, because French literature reaches decisively to the political past. Literature in France speaks of the ideals and aspirations of a country. No doubt every literature harks to the past, every writer looks to predecessors. In France the institutions that infuse literature with a sense of history restore this past to the present.

Precisely this continuity defines this characteristically

French mode of dealing with modern society and with the economic and social constraints imposed on literature by that society. Here are the differences that count, the differences that tell us something essential about literature and the importance of a given social setting. The locus of French literary culture, then, is in the dynamic conjunction of past and present. To appreciate the force of this continuity we must turn to the ancien régime; to the logic of patronage; to the configuration of king, court, and salon; and to the culture they bespeak.

2

The Logic of Patronage

> The relations that exist between the social and political
> state of a people and the genius of its authors are always
> very numerous; whoever knows the one is never com-
> pletely ignorant of the other.
>
> Alexis de Tocqueville,
> *De la démocratie en Amérique*

French literary culture is a modern phenomenon. The logic
of patronage in force during the ancien régime blocked a
strong sense of literary self or community by subordinating
literary activities to essentially aristocratic definitions of literature and culture. Not until the nineteenth century, when
the disappearance of patronage and the expansion of the
market destroyed the literary world of the ancien régime,
did intellectual and institutional support emerge for a properly literary culture. The transformation was not unique to
France. Nor was it confined to literature. Although the chro-
nology and staging of literary events varied from one country
to another, the scenario was similar for most of Europe: patronage declined and the market grew. Everywhere new publics for literature changed its very nature.

To determine what *was* unique to France, we must follow
de Tocqueville's suggestion and look at the social and political
state in which France found itself in the early nineteenth century.[1] Patronage continued as a support for literary activities
until almost the end of the eighteenth century. The transfer
from patronage to the market as the primary support for literary activities, the expansion and consequent redefinition of
the reading public, the rise of the novel as the representative
genre of modern society—French society did not feel the full

force of these developments until the early nineteenth century. French literary culture still bears the mark of the late date at which these profound changes took place.

Then, of course, there was the French Revolution. Whereas England experienced a gradual and peaceable transition from patronage to the market from the late seventeenth century through the eighteenth, in France the traditional literary world dissolved abruptly and in a climate of violence. Born of this political upheaval, the new literary world, like the new literature, carried a heightened sense of the political.

The concentration of these changes in time and place dramatized transformations that were dramatic in and of themselves. This heightened drama exacerbated the conflict between the French writer and the increasingly alien market. This alienation, in turn, intensified by the recent memory of the ancien régime, had much to do with the persistence of patronage and traditional literary institutions long after the disappearance of their economic and social bases. French literary culture emerged out of these confrontations of the old and the new.

I

He did too well by me for me to speak ill of him,
He did me too much ill for me to speak well of him.
Pierre Corneille,
"Sur le Cardinal de Richelieu"

The modern literary market is characterized by relatively rationalized economic relations and by relative autonomy. The institutions of the market both signal and sustain the multiple publics that the market must attract for literature to circulate in society and hence to survive. The ancien régime kept books in another world. True, beginning in the fifteenth century the printing press created important markets for books, literary works were bought and sold, and some writers made money from these transactions. Nevertheless, literary life during the ancien régime revolved not around the market and sales of books but around patronage and the support of writers. Unlike the market with its impersonal commercial relations, patronage built on the relations of individuals. Patronage provided much more than financial support; it sustained a way of life and was in turn sustained by values and beliefs opposed to those of the market. The clash was inevitable.

Whereas the instability of the market follows from the unpredictability of sales to the public, the instability of patronage derives from the unpredictability of individuals. And although patrons then were no more disinterested than publishers are now, their interests differed considerably. Glory, not profit, was the coin in which the aristocratic patron hoped to be paid. Art provided a ticket to immortality, at least according to artists in search of patrons. Virtue, beauty, prowess might be celebrated for all eternity: "So long as men can breathe, and eyes can see / So long lives this, and this gives life to thee." Though Shakespeare was presumably addressing a lover in this sonnet (number 18), the argument held for patrons as well and was used *ad nauseam*. Because it was intangible, verse had an advantage over other, more perishable, arts. In the nineteenth century Théophile Gautier (for reasons unrelated to patronage) based the superiority of poetry on just this premise: "The Gods themselves die / But sovereign verse / remains / stronger than brass."[2]

Some patrons had a greater stake in immortality than others. The traditional celebratory function of such literature afforded kings and princes a posthumous reign of sorts. And even as it traded in the hereafter, patronage dealt with the present. As a vehicle of cultural, social, and political control, it fulfilled definite functions in the here and now. The legendary Maecenas of antiquity (*mécène* and *mécénat* are the standard French terms for patron and patronage) dispensed largesse in the service of the emperor Augustus who sought to legitimate his rule. Virgil's *Aeneid* justified the empire and the emperor to contemporaries long before it spoke of history. Most other royal patrons presumably acted from considerations similar to those of Maecenas. A poem that celebrated military exploits, quite as much as a statue or painting of the monarch in military regalia, reinforced the traditional aristocratic association of physical prowess and political power and symbolically legitimated that power. The splendors of Versailles, though they were extravagant luxuries, conveyed significant values. Patronage and the display at court that gave it meaning kept everyone busy. Occupied and forced into debt by the incessant round of activities at Versailles, potentially disruptive malcontents lacked time, money, and the context to assert their independence or otherwise contest monarchical authority. Louis XIV deserves his reputation as the patron of the arts par excellence not because he was so prodigal or because his reign was so magnificent but because he made patronage an integral part of national policy.

In the realization of this policy, writers joined with architects and gardeners, painters and decorators, composers and performers of ballets and operas—all of those who embellished and celebrated the golden servitude of the aristocracy. Writers stood on a different footing, however, distinguished from other artists by both the nature and the context of their work. Writers competed for patronage at a disadvantage because literary works can be, and are usually intended to be, shared by many persons. The printing press altered the nature of books and transformed them into the first mass medium. Exclusive possession of a painting or a statue is possible; exclusive ownership of published writing is not. Specially bound copies and dedications palliated the disadvantage only slightly. (One enterprising seventeenth-century writer managed to insert a different dedication sheet in each of several copies of his work.)

Too public because of their general distribution, literary works were also, paradoxically, too private. If a patron could not possess a work of literature as he could own a painting, neither could he direct the consumption of literature as he could influence performances of a ballet or a drama or the spectacle of Versailles itself. By virtue of their more public consumption, the court premieres of dramatic works identified the play with the patron, asserted his control over the author and the actors, and indirectly affirmed his authority over the audience. Accordingly, drama provided ancien régime France with its most characteristic genre. Insofar as the literary work constituted a public good destined for private consumption, the writer was not in a position to reciprocate patronage as fully as an artist whose "product" the patron could control absolutely. Aristocrats who created nothing at all yet received royal pensions labored under an even greater obligation to give the king something for his money. One solution for writer and aristocrat alike was deference to the patron. Deference added the requisite particularism to the more public literary work. Writers like Racine and Boileau were accomplished courtiers. Others, like Voltaire, who found himself exiled after an indiscreet remark, or Rousseau, who judged himself inadequate to the exigencies of salon society, were not so skilled and not so well patronized.[3]

The patron strove to keep the patronage relationship asymmetrical, that is, with all the power on one side. To lend credence to its supposed spontaneity and disinterestedness, patronage was bestowed at irregular intervals. The list of Louis XIV's literary and scholarly pensioners was revised annually; those fallen from favor were unceremoniously dropped, like the aging Corneille in 1675, while rising stars received increases. Racine's initial 600 livres in 1663 grew to 2,000 by 1680. Total appropriations fluctuated as well, from an initial 77,500 livres in 1663 to a high of 110,000 livres in 1669 and a low of 49,000 livres in 1676, a year of heavy military engagement. Nor was payment punctual. Others no doubt concurred with Corneille's backhanded New Year's wish to the king: "May all your years have fifteen months / Like the ones your lackeys make for us!"[4]

Patronage assumed many forms, varying according to whim and circumstance. Outright gifts, pensions, and subsidies were only part of the picture, perhaps because they did not have enough strings attached. Works could be printed free of charge at the royal press, or they might be guaranteed a minimum sale. Alternatively, a writer might receive free room and board: La Fontaine had his place at Mme de La Sablière's and Corneille his with the duc de Guise in 1662, while Voltaire spent time being feted and fed at the court of Frederick the Great and Rousseau had the use of a cottage on the Montmorency estate. Then there were the offices (*charges*) that carried considerable revenue and even ennoblement. Racine accumulated nominal ecclesiastical posts (*bénéfices*) and was eventually named gentilhomme ordinaire de la chambre du roi. When Voltaire received this same post in 1746, it carried an annual income of sixteen hundred livres. Ever the speculator, Voltaire sold the post three years later for thirty thousand livres even as he retained the title.[5] The seemingly countless positions attached to royal and aristocratic households (private secretary, tutor, librarian, historiographer) were not necessarily sinecures. La Bruyère was tutor to the grandson of the prince de Condé, Bossuet tutor to Louis XIV's son, Fénelon to his grandson (for whose edification the prelate wrote *Les Aventures de Télémaque*), and none of the pupils was docile. (The royal tutor could, however, take some comfort in virtually guaranteed election to the Académie française.)

Patronage had clear disadvantages for both parties. Writers could rarely count on a steady income, and the logic of patronage meant that they could not depend on any one individual but had to be ever alert for new patrons, offices, sinecures, pensions; they had to calculate their dedications and endure the vicissitudes of personal fancy and political expedience. Corneille's epitaph for Richelieu (the single most important source of financial support for writers of the time) put the ambivalence succinctly: "He did too well by me for me to speak ill of him / He did me too much ill for me to speak well of him."[6]

Instability worked to the disadvantage of patrons as well. By multiplying potential sources of income, writers escaped the influence of any one individual. Inevitably, the patron with the greatest interest in social control, the Crown, sought ways to render more permanent the dependence fostered by patronage. The Académie française was established just for this purpose. Founded in 1635 under the protection and vigilant eye of Cardinal Richelieu, the Académie accorded official recognition to literary activities, which it thereby redefined as worthy of royal interest and surveillance. The success of such institutions as mechanisms of control encouraged imitation. The same desire to extend political dominion that prompted Richelieu to transform an informal gathering of writers into the Académie, a formal organization under the aegis of the state, subsequently incited Louis XIV to make Versailles the cultural center of France. By tying literary activities to official auspices, the kings of France made it clear that culture very much concerned the state.[7] Similar national academies founded in the latter half of the seventeenth century extended jurisdiction to architecture, the beaux arts, and science. A number of provincial, usually all-purpose academies resulted from local initiatives, although several moved quickly to solicit the privileges of royal protection and thereby to associate themselves with the center.[8]

The state also extended its prerogatives into the market. Publishing in the ancien régime was closely regulated. For a work to be published, a writer had to contract with a publisher, and that publisher had to belong to the book guild. Once a manuscript was in the hands of a publisher, the author had no further claim to it. He might receive a flat fee from the publisher, or he might receive only free copies of the printed work. Descartes, for example, received two hundred copies as sole and full payment for the *Discours de la méthode*. The publisher then applied for a *privilège du roi*, which guaranteed him a sales monopoly for one, two, ten, or even fifty years. The publisher alone negotiated censorship permits (*permissions*), set the price, and fought pirated editions; and he alone could renew the *privilège*. Small wonder that many writers did not even bother trying to make money on their works and preferred patronage or, like Voltaire, looked elsewhere: "I have seen so many men of letters poor and despised that I concluded a long time ago that I ought not increase their number."[9]

Technological restraints played their part in these restrictions. Editions were limited by the capacities of the wooden handpress, by the laborious hand setting of type, by the unwieldy thick paper, and by the equally unwieldy distribution circuits. Even so, one cannot help thinking that had there been a will, there would have been a way around the restrictions. The fever of discovery that animates Balzac's tale of David Séchard's frenetic search for a cheap paper in *Illusions perdues* reveals a temper of the times that is vastly different from the traditional spirit of the guilds and of authors and patrons.

Because the market offered economic support only, it could not compete with patronage, which offered extensive social support as well. Patronage could define literary life because no real alternative sources of support existed. Prior to the great expansion of the market in the nineteenth century, writers could not hope to realize substantial income from the sales of their books. When Voltaire groused that a good book commonly sold fifty copies, a runaway success five hundred, he exaggerated, but editions in the ancien régime rarely exceeded two thousand copies.[10] Even after a notable expansion of the reading public in the eighteenth century, opportunities remained circumscribed. Lesage, the playwright and novelist, and Abbé Prévost, the novelist, by and large did earn their living by writing, but they were paid mostly for journalism of the hack variety, and in any case both were poor most of the time and constantly in debt. Prévost resorted to forging checks and complained bitterly about the "alimentary literature" to which he was reduced. Rousseau noted with chagrin that he received more for the performance and publication of his opera than from all of his major literary and philosophical works together. In desperation he took to copying music to secure a small but steady income that placed him under no obligations to either patron or publisher. Diderot was not poor, but besides an allowance and an eventual inheritance from his father, he could depend on income from both the sales of the *Encyclopédie* and his own salary as editor. Even so, worry over his daughter's insubstantial dowry led him to sell his library to Catherine the Great—a form of patronage since the books went to Russia only after Diderot's death. These and other writers were somewhere between the extremes occupied by the millionaire Voltaire and the Grub Street hacks for whom literature shaded into police spying, pornography peddling, and similarly suspicious pursuits.[11]

The ideology of *honnêteté* raised another significant obstacle between the writer and the market. This ideal of cultivated amateurism supported the integration of literary and elite activities and inhibited the development of a professional ethos. To be fully noble, literature had to be untainted by either commercialism or specialization. "A man of letters, when he sits down to write," decreed one late seventeenth-century author, "ought to have only the public good in mind. The commerce he enters into with his pen . . . diminishes his quality to that of a merchant."[12] Aristocrats took particular care to avoid classification as writers since the specialization represented by any occupation violated the norms of *honnêteté*. Printing turned literature into an impersonal exchange and made one a "slave," as Boileau complained, to the caprices of any buyer.[13] Even more devastating, the impersonal logic of the market took no account of the individual. "Works alone must speak for" the writer—no special pleading allowed. To be sure, norms may or may not coincide with practice. Corneille was taken to task for his commercial avidity ("Corneille is excellent, but he sells his works").[14] Boileau, in his *Art poétique* (1674), exhorted writers to "work for glory" and castigated those of his fellow writers who would hire out "their Apollo" to a bookseller and make "a mercenary trade out of a divine art."[15] While complaints were numerous enough to make one suspect a good many violations, the sense that commercialism did constitute a violation attested to the strength of the code.

The social composition and the consequent predispositions of the upper-class milieu that the French called *le monde* further buttressed this aristocratic ideology of *honnêteté*. In the diffuse support it gave to literary life in the ancien régime, *le monde*, like patronage, provided far more than pecuniary subsidies. But whereas the logic of patronage favored the other arts, *le monde* favored literature. Alone among the arts, literature permitted, indeed encouraged, access to the salons frequented by *le monde*. Since literature had no association with manual labor, the creation of literary works was never considered incompatible with nobility. Writing did not provoke the loss of aristocratic prerogatives (*dérogation*); painting did, unless it could be proven uncontaminated by commercial dealings.[16]

An even more important factor integrating writers into *le monde* was the unspecialized, untechnical nature of literature. Writers needed no training beyond the general education of the time, and they used a medium that was essentially an instrument of the elite. Furthermore, both the "nobility" of writing itself and the numerous aristocratic writers conferred upon literature a power of enoblement. Aristocratic writers like le duc de La Rochefoucauld, la comtesse de La Fayette, and le baron de Montesquieu were born with an entrée into *le monde*. Their talents gave writers born lower on the social scale, like Corneille, Racine, Voltaire, and Rousseau, entry into these same circles. The elite associations that make writing in France prestigious even today can be traced to these salons of the ancien régime.

The symbol of these ties was the Académie française. As patronage mixed upper-class or royal patrons with writers of lower social status, the Académie française mixed literary with other elites. Men of letters were to be in the minority in the Académie, whose function, as the saying went, was to make "letters more noble, and nobles more lettered." "Every day at court," Boileau complained, "a well-born fool can render silly judgments with impunity."[17] Accusations of aristocratic boorishness crop up fairly often, prompted and exaggerated by disgruntled writers both envious and scornful of the class from which their patrons came.

The interaction of writers and the aristocracy in the Académie française, at court, and in the salons of which the Académie was an extension subordinated literary to social concerns. *Honnêteté* was in effect both an ethic and an aesthetic that grounded literary practices.[18] Legal and commercial practices confirmed these social constraints, associating writers with a distinct milieu and making literary activity a social affair subject to the imperatives of social discourse. This weighting of literature toward the social precluded the differentiation of roles and institutions capable of supporting a distinct or separate literary identity.[19]

Writers in general lacked a specifically literary consciousness because they were not a distinct occupational group, and they did not form a distinct occupational group because writing itself was not a distinct occupation. Writing was rather a practice fit for consumption in Paris salons or in the royal salon at Versailles. Not all literature was suited to salon presentation, but a number of genres favored in the seventeenth century were: much poetry was read aloud; plays were given private readings prior to public performance; maxims and portraits, composed more or less on the spur of the moment, were all the rage for several years. Courtiers and even the royal family might perform in works presented at court. Louis XIV himself danced in ballets and turned a sonnet or two. (Asked for his opinion of these literary efforts, Boileau replied with the skill of a consummate courtier, anxious to retain patronage yet aware that his favor depended on his critical judgment: "Sire, nothing is impossible for His Majesty. He wanted to write bad verse, and he has succeeded.")[20]

Of course, aristocratic culture did not always operate according to principles. The ideal of harmonious integration of literary and elite social activities was just that, an ideal that influenced but did not absolutely dictate behavior. Neither the overt control of censorship or patronage nor the community of values that fortified such control excluded conflict. Literary causes célèbres were well in evidence in the seventeenth century—in the Querelle du *Cid*, in the affairs of *L'Ecole des femmes* and *Tartuffe*, in the Querelle des Anciens et des Modernes. If the Académie had reservations about *Le Cid*, Corneille was vindicated by his rousing success with the discriminating public of *les mondains*. Even the censorious Boileau recognized their sovereignty: "In vain against the Cid a Minister intrigues / All Paris for Chimène has the eyes of

Rodrigue. / No matter if the Académie moves to censure / The Public in revolt stays to admire."[21] Molière could defy the pedants in *L'Ecole des femmes* and the ecclesiastical cabal in *Tartuffe* because he had the king and the *honnêtes gens* on his side: to his detractors he could riposte that "the great art is to please, and this comedy [*L'Ecole des femmes*] having pleased those for whom it was made, I consider that it need not worry about the rest."[22] Though they might disagree over the particular game being played at any one time, the players generally agreed on the rules of that game and on the conception of literature implied and imposed by those rules.

II

I do not feel up to taking on Voltaire.
la duchesse de Choiseul,
letter to Mme du Deffand

The death of Louis XIV in 1715 ended an age. His extraordinarily long reign (1643–1715) made the century very much his, as indeed Voltaire baptized it, so firmly were aesthetics, ideology, and policies identified with the king. Autocratic monarchs still reigned in the eighteenth century, the regent until 1723, Louis XV until 1774, Louis XVI nominally until 1791, but the collective epithet bestowed on the period defined it as the Enlightenment, the age of the philosophe, *l'Age des Lumières*. The eighteenth century that began in 1715 and ended in 1789 broke the association with the monarch and loosened those controls exercised by the Crown: the legal controls of absolute monarchy, the bureaucratic controls of a centralizing administration, and the aesthetic constraints of French classicism.

Yet though these many controls were relaxed in practice, eighteenth-century France never forswore either the idea or the ideal of control.[23] Despite the increasing numbers that climbed up the social ladder, French society retained its commitment to hierarchy. Indeed, the crossing of legal and social barriers served to confirm their existence. An entrée into upper-class milieux did not put writers on equal terms with

other salon habitués, for like patronage, *le monde* presumed
the inequality of the parties involved. The ancien régime was
highly sensitive to all the nuances of social hierarchy and
insisted on the minutiae of rank. Voltaire was not likely to
forget the drubbing he received from the lackeys of the chevalier de Rohan nor his subsequent imprisonment. The rise in
prestige of the man of letters, or what the eighteenth century
called *considération*, was real but also slow, irregular, and far
from uniform. The duchesse de Choiseul, for one, had no
desire to consort with men of letters, not even Voltaire, except
in their books.[24]

The eighteenth century, in sum, brought the tensions of
ancien régime France closer to the surface of social life. In no
domain was the strain more apparent than in the literary enterprise. Talent pressed its claims against hierarchy, achievement protested the rewards bestowed on birth, the individual
rebelled against tradition. Increasingly prominent as the century progressed, these tensions found only partial and tem-
porary resolution in the abolition of the ancien régime and
the instauration of another.

Although the logic of patronage continued to dominate
much of literary life through the eighteenth century, the
sources of moneys diversified. Posts multiplied in royal and
princely households while the growing periodical press required directors, censors, and writers, all official appoint-
ments.[25] The state retained considerable interest in directing
the world of letters. The police kept track of comings and
goings and on occasion employed impecunious men of letters
to keep watch on their fellows.[26]

As a social control, the censorship system in the ancien
régime was both inefficient and ineffective, in part because
the function devolved on several authorities, which frequently worked at cross-purposes.[27] But however ineffectual,
censorship did exist and could make life uncomfortable for
writers who stepped over the line. Both Voltaire and Diderot
spent time in prison, the former in 1726 in the Bastille for a
satirical poem, the latter in the Château de Vincennes for his
impious *Lettre sur les aveugles* (1749). To escape the same fate

after *Emile* (1762) was burned by the Parlement of Paris, Rousseau fled into exile. *Les Confessions* recounts the myriad negotiations surrounding the publication of *Emile*, which had neither a *privilège* nor a *permission* but which Rousseau had been encouraged to publish by Malesherbes, the liberal directeur de la Librairie from 1751 to 1763. Rousseau's friends in high places endeavored to allay official fears, but to no avail. As Rousseau narrates the incident, he was in his carriage leaving the country when he passed the four officials coming to arrest him in their carriage. They tipped their hats![28]

These and similar incidents point to the precarious situation in which eighteenth-century French writers could find themselves. Political and religious authorities had the upper hand and did not fail to show it. At the same time, these collisions between writers and political powers reveal a shift in cultural authority. Censorship and persecution testified, if perversely, that the Republic of Letters had become a force to reckon with. Although individual writers might be bested, the collectivity gathered force.

This rise in esteem was a commonplace by mid-century. Publicly caned by the servants of a nobleman in 1726, Voltaire was received like a great lord a quarter century later; and a quarter century after that, in 1778, he made a spectacular triumphal return to Paris. The submissiveness of Molière to the judgment of *les honnêtes gens* gave way to Voltaire's acerbic comment that the greatest misfortune to befall a man of letters was to be judged by idiots or d'Alembert's more tempered but still insistent conviction that the literary judgment of great men is valid only to the extent that the critic is himself a man of letters.[29] The duchesse de Choiseul's refusal to encounter Voltaire betrayed distrust as well as disdain, an implicit acknowledgment of the cultural authority that the Republic of Letters had come to exercise.

In part this relocation of cultural authority expressed the gradual removal of cultural life from the court at Versailles to the salons in Paris. *Le monde* spread and diversified, thereby loosening connections between literary life and the court.

Then too the international prestige of the French language and French literature lent luster to the latter-day practitioners of each. But most of all, the Republic of Letters in the eighteenth century was identified with intellectual ferment. The political implications of the philosophes' works, like the commitment to reasoned discourse, pushed French literature to explore new realms. De Tocqueville attributed leadership of public opinion to the French philosophes who led and also misled their public by the very brilliance of their speculations.[30] Politics entered French literature with éclat, never really to leave. French literary culture, as it crystallized during the nineteenth century, preserved this political sensibility.

These were the contributions of the philosophes—a political sensibility, a social commitment, and a critical mode. They resisted the characteristic controls of the ancien régime, the controls of patronage in particular. They were conservative in the main, yet the Revolution is hardly conceivable without them—an ambiguous position vis-à-vis politics occupied by the writer ever since. The French tradition of *engagement* commences in the Enlightenment with these writers at once committed to social commentary and forced to compromise with society, its conventions and traditions.

The Revolution mounted a direct attack on the controls that both restricted and sustained literary life. The overthrow of the monarchy eliminated the patronage dispensed by royal households, and the confiscation of property belonging to émigré aristocrats destroyed the power of *le monde*, bringing traditional patronage of the arts in all its guises to an abrupt end. Once disbanded, *le monde* never again played the role it had once assumed in literary life. When the émigrés returned in good grace and even with the compensation offered by the Restoration government for their financial losses, they had neither the resources nor the inclination for largesse to writers.

Censorship was lifted, with the suppression of the corps of royal censors. (Indirect censorship, often in the form of special taxes and penalties, was reinstated in due time and enforced with greater or lesser vigor according to the fears of the particular regime in power.) The Assemblée nationale also—and with greater effect, both immediate and long-term—reformed the archaic commercial regulations that so severely checked competition among the printers, publishers, and sellers of books under the ancien régime. The Convention nationale abolished the book guild in 1790 and the monopoly of the state theater (the Comédie-Française) in 1791 and in 1793 passed the first French copyright law (England's dated from 1711). The rights of authors—*les droits d'auteur*—followed hard on the heels of the Rights of Man.[31] Henceforth, upon expiration of a contract with a publisher, the rights reverted to the author, who might then sign a new contract with whomever he saw fit.

The abolition of the book guild removed legal obstacles to competition and enabled publishers to take advantage of an increasing literacy. Whereas only a minority of the population was literate at the time of the French Revolution, a century later the literacy rate exceeded 95 percent.[32] And although literacy itself did not necessarily make even the simplest of literary works accessible, it nevertheless indicated a trend that eventually destroyed traditional literary institutions through the sheer numbers of new readers, writers, publishers, booksellers, and journalists.

The new readers clustered in cities, especially Paris. Versailles lost its *raison d'être*. Under the Revolution and Napoleon, the centralization of French society proceeded apace to make Paris the undisputed and overwhelming cultural center that it has remained ever since. Technological innovations both stimulated and responded to the demands of the new readers. Steam presses on metal rollers replaced the laborious hand-presses; cheap wood pulp replaced linen or cotton rag in paper manufacturing. The reading publics did not simply increase; they changed. More and different readers demanded and received different literatures. The popular literature(s) of the nineteenth century responded to the influx of readers whose rudimentary education had given them little familiarity with, and even less interest in, the rules of classicism. These readers remained untouched by the fierce debates that pitted romantic against classic, and their sheer numbers weighed heavily in the literary balance. To take account of new tastes, critics found themselves in the uncomfortable position of redefining literary norms of long standing. *Taste* acquired a plural form that created havoc among writers and critics unaccustomed to dealing with the nether regions of Parnassus and unsympathetic to what was produced down there.

To be sure, the ancien régime had a popular literature, but it differed in both substance and form from the works labeled "popular" by the nineteenth century. This older popular literature was not literary as *le monde* understood the term, for it operated under conditions and assumptions other than those inscribed in the logic of patronage. Hawked from village to village by peddlars (*colporteurs*), this *littérature de colportage* addressed a rural and largely illiterate population, a public with no connection to *le monde* and the writers seeking its patronage. The books themselves were crudely assembled and shoddily printed, without pagination, on ragged paper. The works themselves were short, usually between eight and fifty pages and drew not on the high culture of the Enlightenment but on oral tradition, popular farce, medieval epics, and Renaissance tales. The nonliterary works were often how-to books on gardening, manners, and religious conduct.[33]

In contrast, the popular literature of the nineteenth century participated in the same literary market as serious works and, like them, was a largely urban phenomenon. Popular and serious works shared publishers, booksellers, and readers. To the distress of many, it was often difficult to say what was popular and what was not.[34] Indeed, the confusion of nomenclature is instructive. *Popular* might refer to the mode of production (serial novels), to the characters' lower-class status, or to the audience presumably addressed (though every class read Eugène Sue or Victor Hugo). Of course, not everything associated with the ancien régime was high class (in every sense), and novels as a genre were popular insofar as they did not fit classical criteria. But eighteenth-century critics worked earnestly at assigning novels a place.[35] The nineteenth century questioned the fairly well-defined, and definitely subordinate, literary space occupied by the novel as such.

A sure indicator of the effect of these new publics is the steady rise in the number of new book titles. From the 600 to 800 new titles published annually during the eighteenth century, the number of titles registered in the *Bibliographie de la France* rose to over 7,600 in 1850 and reached a high of almost 15,000 in 1889, with an average of about 12,000 new titles annually between 1890 and 1900. If most of these titles were not literary works, a good many were. An average of 450 new novels and poetic and dramatic publications appeared between 1840 and 1870, 790 from 1876 to 1885, and slightly over 1,000 from 1886 to 1890—a handsome increase in new novels alone from the average of 54 published annually between 1751 and 1789. Journals participated in, profited from, and increased this growth, providing outlets for literary works as well as supplementary and even primary income for writers. The 1,200 copies printed by *La Gazette* in 1638 had grown only to 12,000 by 1762—not spectacular considering the century and a quarter that had elapsed. The combined (weekly) political press in Paris, which totaled some 56,000 copies in 1824, reached 200,000 copies in 1846. By 1899 *Le Petit Parisien* alone sold more than 775,000 copies daily, and circulation reached 1,500,000 by 1914. The inauguration of the serial novel in 1836, coupled with the introduction of advertising to cut the price, made *revues* or magazines a real force in literary life. The end of the century also saw a great many small, frequently ephemeral, journals: 601 new periodical publications appeared in 1857, the first year the *Bibliographie de la France* kept records of periodicals, another 269 the following year, and an average of 824 every year between 1890 and 1900![36]

Those writers able to strike a responsive chord in the new reading publics encountered unpredecented opportunities, whence the success of the prodigiously prolific Alexandre Dumas, Paul de Kock, Eugène Sue, Victor Hugo, Emile Zola. However different their conceptions and practices of literature, their works sold astoundingly well. For all that Balzac groused about the phenomenal success of Eugène Sue,[37] his own works did well on the market—just not well enough to subsidize Balzac's extravagant habits. Novels were most obviously aimed at a broad market, yet Lamartine's *Méditations poétiques* (1820) sold thirty thousand copies in the three years following publication, a figure any writer or publisher of poetry would envy today. Zola's first best-seller, *L'Assommoir* (1877), saved his publisher from bankruptcy. Even *Madame Bovary* (1857) sold well, although Flaubert did not benefit from the notoriety since he had sold his rights to the manuscript before the trial for obscenity and the publicity it produced.

A writer could earn a living, even a handsome one, from writing books and books alone. Few writers actually did so. The obverse of the shiny coin of success bore the dark tones of failure. For every modest success, there were many failures. In contrast to Eugène Sue, guaranteed an annual salary of 100,000 francs for fifteen years by the *Constitutionnel*, Champfleury estimated that over his entire career he had realized no more than 3,000 francs a year from his journalistic work as well as his short stories. The Société des gens de lettres paid for Gérard de Nerval's funeral. While Alexandre Dumas was paid 2.50 francs per line, total sales of Baudelaire's *Fleurs du mal* (1857) came to only 250 francs. Moreover, the book was successfully prosecuted for obscenity, and the publisher went bankrupt. If *Madame Bovary* sold well, Flaubert's next novels, *Salammbô* (1862) and *L'Education sentimentale* (1869), did very poorly, and Flaubert ended his life hounded by creditors.

The market thus restructured literature for good and for ill. After providing marginal support under the ancien régime, the market in the nineteenth century became the primary motor and the major source of support for literary activities. Individuals might or might not achieve success in the market, but the state of literature was now defined by it. What little patronage still existed could not alter this growing dependence on an essentially new set of rules—rules that

ÊTES-VOUS BALZAC?

Vous avez un diplôme de grande école ou de 2ᵉ cycle? Ou vous travaillez depuis plusieurs années dans les métiers de la communication? Vous voulez aller plus loin? Vous pensez qu'à l'âge de la télématique, le jeune Balzac ne resterait pas passivement assis sur les bancs d'une vieille université? Qu'il chercherait à connaître toute la nouvelle panoplie des outils de communication : radio, vidéo, télévision, presse, médias informatisés? Mais vous ne regrettez pas ce que vous avez appris dans vos premières études?

Vous pensez que la «communication», en soi, cela ne veut rien dire, que le problème est d'avoir quelque chose à communiquer?

Vous voulez être de ceux qui concevront et réaliseront ces fameux programmes que les modernes machines à communiquer attendent impatiemment? Vous voulez être les créateurs des grands médias de l'avenir?

ALORS VENEZ A LA FONDATION POUR LES ARTS ET LES SCIENCES DE LA COMMUNICATION, LA PREMIÈRE GRANDE ÉCOLE DE COMMUNICATION MULTIMÉDIA.

Vous y deviendrez un(e) généraliste de la communication, en un an d'études complémentaires intensives à Nantes. Si du moins vous avez déjà une tête bien faite et bien pleine. Avec des idées et des projets. S'il y a du Balzac en vous... Et si vous réussissez le concours, en septembre 1984. Trente élèves seulement (littéraires, scientifiques, artistes, IEP, managers).

Documentation, inscriptions : Fondation ASCOM, 3, allée des Tanneurs, 44000 NANTES. Tél. : 16 (40) 35-79-80.

FONDATION ASCOM : LA PREMIÈRE-NÉE D'UNE NOUVELLE RACE D'UNIVERSITÉS

The announcement of the Ascom Foundation from *Le Monde* in 1983 demonstrates how forcefully the tradition of literary France plays with a changing society.

"ARE YOU BALZAC? . . . You are thinking that in this age of telecommunications, the young Balzac wouldn't be just sitting around in an old university. He would set out to master the new means of communication. . . .

"You can become a generalist in communications studies . . . if you have any Balzac in you, . . . and if you pass the entrance exam. . . ."

Thus Balzac, who conquered the mass media of the 1830s and 1840s, becomes the Balzacian hero on the make and at home in the electronic world of contemporary education.

ratified literature as a commerce and writing as an occupation.

Nevertheless, the commercialization of literature remained imperfect. Books did not constitute ordinary merchandise, nor were writers run-of-the-mill workers. Indeed, one is struck by the ways in which the market failed to run true to its logic. Some publishers behaved like patrons. François Buloz, editor and publisher of the canonical *Revue des deux mondes*, made loans to George Sand and invited her to family dinners. Dr. Véron, editor of the *Revue de Paris* and then of *Le Constitutionnel*, in the early 1830s took what he termed a weekly "course in comparative literature," visiting "his" authors, offering encouragement, consulting on manuscripts. Véron subsequently endowed a prize of ten thousand francs for the Société des gens de lettres. Mme Charpentier, the wife of Flaubert's publisher, worked hard to arrange a state pension for the writer. Publishing was, after all—as Balzac discovered when he tried it—a chancy affair, not likely to interest someone devoid of literary sensibilities.

The vast economic base that the market offered literary activities created new social structures, new literary institutions, new roles, even new attitudes, all of which endowed literary activities with a theretofore unknown independence. These were the changes responsible for the emergence of a distinct literary culture in France. The market made its most obvious impact in the number and range of literary institutions that it supported. As had been true for patronage, writers could not depend on any one source of income. The superiority of the market lay in the greater variety of paraliterary occupations that it supported and that made even the commercially unsuccessful writers dependent on the literary market.

Not everyone greeted these transformations with choruses of joy. The market wrought transformations equally profound through the antagonisms it engendered. The increase in the number of poets, dramatists, and novelists was striking, but the number of people involved in the production and diffusion of literary works was triple that of the writers. Unhappy writers—and they were legion—focused their resentment on the critic and the publisher, all-too-visible reminders that the market defined literary activity. "There is no virtue," as one of Balzac's journalists says, "that doesn't have a vice. Literature engenders publishers." Publishers were men of business with hearts of stone, men of "the old school"; Balzac noted of the publisher to whom the naive Lucien de Rubempré tries to sell his poems that he was "a man from the time when publishers wanted to keep Voltaire and Montesquieu locked in an attic and dying of hunger." The sales of another publisher make him seem "like the minister of literature." As Lucien soon learns, journalists sell their souls and their pens to the highest bidder, while critics are simply "impotent writers." "Today, as everything becomes materialistic, criticism has become a sort of customs office."[38]

Inevitably, the conspicuous success of the few attracted many more writers than the market would support. "You do not know," another publisher assures the hapless Lucien, "the trouble produced by the success of Byron, Lamartine, Victor Hugo. . . . Their glory has brought us an invasion of barbarians. . . . In the past two years poets have bred like mayflies."[39] Balzac sided with his poet, but he also knew that a publisher cannot dispense charity. The publisher had simply adapted to the market, and so, eventually, must Lucien. As Lukács recognized in pointing to the commodification of literature, Balzac expressed the resentments and disappointments of a generation.[40] To that generation French literary culture owes the articulation of some of its most basic attitudes.

The impersonality of literary transactions in the market stood in marked contrast to the personalism of patronage. How could one know the thousands of readers one might have except by hearsay—and sales? Publishers naturally regarded sales as the logical measure of success, a rule as brutal as it was simple. Unlike patronage, with its characteristically loose sense of obligation, the market required a strict accounting of debits and credits. The obtuseness and severity with which writers taxed individual publishers derived logically from the market requirement of immediate tangible return on investment. A patron had the leisure to consider the long term, but a publisher could not afford either the immortal or the immaterial. The market dealt in numbers of books sold, not sentiments expressed.

Dissatisfaction with the market also stemmed from the close contact it required between writers and the world of commerce. Whereas the ancien régime had put writers in the company of the aristocracy, the market took them away from the court, out of salons, and put them in offices where they encountered a breed of men ignorant of *le monde* and its mores. The secular disdain for specialization and for commerce fueled the resentment that set writer against publisher in the nineteenth century. The violent intrusion of the market into literary domains intensified the scorn that had been heaped on the bourgeois during the ancien régime and gave writers new ammunition for an old and familiar target. But the bourgeois—now promoted to the capital status of a stereotype as Bourgeois—was no longer only despised; he was feared and condemned all the more strongly as the materialism of the market impinged ever more on literary life.[41]

The clash between the market and the values, attitudes, and behavior bequeathed by the ancien régime set the stage for the literary culture that took form during the nineteenth century. French literary culture expressed, and simultaneously provoked, a consciousness and a defense of aesthetic values, however variously these might be defined. Because this literary identity originated in opposition to the institutions supported by the market, literary culture by its very existence set itself against social structure. From the beginning French literary culture was an adversary subculture within the larger society. Its members, partly by choice, partly by circumstance, formed a minority on the margins of that society. Bourgeois by birth for the most part, writers became antibourgeois by conviction. This stance signaled a radical transformation in the relationship between "literature" and "society," between literary activities and the social and cultural contexts in which they operated. The elite culture of *le monde* did not oppose but rather extended traditional literary institutions; culture elaborated social structure. Nineteenth-century literary culture, quite to the contrary, existed in and through opposition to social structure as represented by the market. Literary culture signaled the disintegration of what had been a fairly coherent sociocultural unit. Henceforth this literary culture and the larger society went their separate ways, mutually dependent but mutually suspicious as well.

The ideals of the ancien régime were all the more tenacious, and the more remarkable, for the shock incurred in the dissolution of the ancien régime itself. The adversary subculture that formed around literature claimed the privileges of superiority and was at the same time infused with nostalgia for a time when business was not the order of the day; when men of letters lived in harmony, in the "sweetness of friendship"; when they "effectively governed their country, . . . patriots out of habit, philanthropists from sympathy." "The century that we saw end," as one writer summed up sentiments in the 1830s, "far from being ungrateful for men of letters, assured them a special existence that had its priviliges."[42] From this almost palpable sense of loss French literary culture drew prejudices, fashioned institutions, and proclaimed ideals.

3

Institutions and Ideals

One is invariably struck, when looking at French society, by the overwhelming presence of the past and the degree to which this society turns to the past to legitimate the present and justify the future. The "modern" nineteenth century in many respects was not very modern at all. In spite of the many "revolutions" from 1789 onwards—political, social, and economic—French society held fast to familiar views of the world and one's business in it. Observers of French society ever since have noted how much of the ancien régime survived into the new, a survival that sustained a characteristically French tension between past and present, between tradition and modernity.

The institutions and ideologies that gradually took form did not replace but took their place alongside existing institutions and ideologies. The newly expanded literary market of the early and mid-nineteenth century transformed literary life as much through the resistance it provoked as through the new support it provided. The market was challenged on three fronts economic, social, and ideological. It had to contend with the vestiges of patronage. It faced opposition from literary institutions ranging from the conservative Académie française and the equally conservative salons to the more militant literary groups, known as cénacles. Finally, the logic of the market had to counter highly charged emotional definitions of literary creativity in the traditional moral conception of art, in the hyper-aestheticism of art for art's sake, and in the objectivity proposed by the scientific method.

Yet at the same time that these institutions and ideologies sought to subvert the market, they competed against each other for a place in it. The resulting tensions are fundamental to any interpretation of French literary culture. Indeed, one of the lessons to be learned from the proliferation of institutions and ideologies in nineteenth-century France is the subtle way culture works to incorporate difference and to subsume conflict. Some institutions and some ideologies were more obviously traditional, others more aggressively modern; some looked to the past, others to the future. French literary culture builds on them all—on the whole constellation of institutions and ideologies working in concert and in conflict across the nineteenth century and beyond.

I

In French literary culture the constitutive tensions between continuity and change appeared most vividly in the institution most solidly entrenched in the aristocratic ethos and practices of the ancien régime, namely patronage. For patronage influenced French literary life long after it had ceased to support literary activities in any meaningful economic sense. In many ways patronage continued to furnish the norm, whence its symbolic importance in the absence of any economic justification.

To be sure, kings and emperors who reigned in France until 1870 could dip into privy purses, and some did. Victor Hugo received a pension during the Restoration; Leconte de Lisle benefited from the largesse of Napoleon III, as did Théophile Gautier, who was also a protégé of the princesse Mathilde, the emperor's cousin. But privy purses were private and limited. Patronage had largely passed from individuals to institutions, from heads of state to cabinet ministers. The emperor might himself accord a few small pensions—3,000 francs to Gautier, 3,400 francs to Leconte de Lisle—but he called on the legislature to vote the 25,000 francs needed to save Lamartine from destitution and appointed Sainte-Beuve and Mérimée to the Senate to secure them a comfortable 30,000 francs annual salary.[1] The Ministry of Public Education reserved a budget item to "encourage" scholars and writers. Guy de Maupassant, who worked there in the 1870s, claimed that the ministry annually awarded as many as six hundred pensions, some of them on the order of 5,000 to 6,000 francs.[2] But Maupassant must have been exaggerating for his own purpose, to persuade the reluctant Flaubert to accept a pension. Indeed, the actual budget allocation would not have gone that far.[3] Only a few men of letters could benefit and even they had to share the pie with scholars. Priorities were clearly elsewhere. It was appropriate to notions of imperial splendor that the 1862 budget reserved far greater sums for prizes to horses than for rewards to men of letters and that it allocated more money to purchase horses for the imperial stables than books for the Imperial Library.

Bureaucratization further diminished the effect of patronage by eliminating the patron, which made patronage relations even more asymmetrical than they had been under the ancien régime. Ministers changed often enough to preclude personal relations of any consequence, and in any event the bureaucrat acted not on his own but as the agent of a government. Consequently, the writer felt no personal obligation— no one felt moved to pen dithyrambs to the Ministry of Public Instruction. Once the foundation of the literary enterprise, patronage had dwindled into a matter of charity. No wonder Flaubert looked on the very idea of a pension with such distaste.

The prevalence of sinecures also illustrated both the bureaucratization of patronage and its growing association with the administration. By the nineteenth century the multiple posts that had once attached writers to aristocratic households tied them instead to the government. As in the ancien régime, libraries were thought to be appropriate havens for impecunious men of letters, but the personal libraries had likely become state dependencies. The Arsenal Library was originally the property of the comte d'Artois, who gave it to the state when he became Charles X in 1824, and the perquisites for the head librarian included a spacious apartment in addition to a salary. Similarly, the Ministry of the Interior (which, as one contemporary mused, had no library) found a librarian's spot for Alfred de Musset in 1837, and the Ministry of Public Instruction did likewise under the Second Empire. The Mazarine Library (at the Institut de France) at various times appointed Sainte-Beuve, Jules Sandeau, and Flaubert. When the fall of the empire ended Leconte de Lisle's pension from the emperor, the Senate library obligingly found him a post, which subsequently went to Anatole France. And so on.

These posts paid only modest sums but required little work. Anatole France eventually resigned from the Senate library in 1890 after the chief librarian voiced a loud and indignant complaint that Monsieur France had not cataloged a single title in eight years.[4] Given the connections with governmental circles and the contacts one might make, these posts carried considerable prestige, a prestige their clear elevation above the market could only increase. Marcel Proust's career as a librarian showed the system at its most bizarre. To convince his father that he had a regular occupation, Proust managed to get an appointment as honorary librarian at the Mazarine in June 1895. In July he applied for the first of a series of leaves of absence (dusty books aggravated his asthma and even the most nominal duties interfered with his vacations). The farce did not end until 1899, when after a general inspection Proust was ordered to work. He, of course, resigned.[5]

All posts, however, were not sinecures. Prosper Mérimée acquitted himself exceptionally well as inspector of historical monuments, and Stéphane Mallarmé took his work seriously enough as a lycée professor of English to write an English grammar. The expansion of civil service further amplified writers' connections to the government. In the twentieth century Paul Claudel, Jean Giraudoux, and Alexis Saint-Léger Léger (Saint-John Perse) entered diplomatic service, where they served with distinction; Romain Rolland taught first at the Ecole normale supérieure (history) and then at the Sorbonne (history of music), and Jean-Paul Sartre and Simone de Beauvoir, among others, taught in lycées.[6]

It is clear that bureaucratization did not eradicate so much as it modified patronage. Though expunged in principle from administrative subventions to writers, the personalism characteristic of traditional patronage surfaced in different guises. As governmental associations weakened writers' ties to the market, these intensely personal connections countered the impersonality of economic transactions.

The newly expanded market of the early and mid-nineteenth century wrought many changes in French literary life. Although contemporary and later critics lamented that literature during this period became a commodity, in fact it had always been one. But the implacable market seemed vastly more intrusive and more foreign to the literary enterprise than patronage had ever been—in part because patronage had so long supplied the norm, in part because the market worked to eliminate the personal relations intrinsic to patronage and to the writer's sense of mission.

Faced with the uncertainties of the market and only the barest remnants of patronage, writers looked elsewhere for support. They turned to groups that seemed to promise a refuge from the market and its alien conceptions of the literary enterprise. But these groups did not operate in a vacuum. They could not escape the larger society and indeed realized their goal of protection most effectively in their connections with that society, its traditional social and literary institutions and even the despised market. The prevailing rhetoric of separation notwithstanding, these groups were always more than "literary."

Salons maintained traditional elite ties for some literature and certain writers. Unlike their ancien régime predecessors, nineteenth-century salons often led back to the market through the publishers, critics, and journalists who also frequented them. Mme Charpentier, the wife of Flaubert's and Zola's publisher (and the subject of Renoir's painting in the Metropolitan Museum) even had a salon of her own.

To the degree that salons were an extension of *le monde*, they sustained the traditional elite associations of literature, most notably with the Académie française. The Académie depended on the government to the extent that it was subsidized by the state. Moreover, the head of state had to approve the election of every member (as he does even today). But the Académie was never simply the mouthpiece of the government, not even under the ancien régime. Its members created strong ties to the government but also to other elites in French society, to the Church (eventually including Protestants), to the aristocracy and the military, and to the "new aristocracies" of talent—writers, scholars, and scientists.[7]

The prestige of the Académie lay in its exceptional capacity to assimilate the modern without relinquishing tradition and to reedefine each one in terms of the other. In its general assault on the bastions of privilege, the revolutionary government made a clean sweep in 1792 by dissolving the Académie française and the other national academies as well. Barely three years later, another revolutionary government resurrected them as the collective Institut de France. Whatever the differences between the new Académie française and the old, the two bespoke continuity, not revolution. This symbolic continuity with the past cannot be underestimated, especially in a country where political regimes changed with such frequency and in a society that tagged the seventeenth century as le Grand Siècle and its writers as classics. Few writers could be indifferent to the lineage of Corneille, Racine, and La Fontaine. Paradoxically, the Revolution turned the Académie française into a national treasure much like Versailles, Notre Dame, and the Louvre. The traditions embodied in this most traditional of literary institutions help explain why the Académie mattered at all. Continuity with the past, even a repudiated past, remained peculiarly significant.

Similar arguments might be advanced for the Académie des sciences, founded in 1666 and therefore almost as venerable as the Académie française. More specialized, the Académie des sciences was *a* French academy; it was not, and still is not, *the* French academy. If science contributes to the glory of France, it is not identified, as were French literature and the French language, with "l'esprit français."[8] At the end of the eighteenth century the abbé Maury summed up prejudices that died hard: "The Académie française alone was esteemed in France and gave real status. No one thought much of the Académie des Sciences. . . . D'Alembert was ashamed of being a member. . . . At the Académie française we looked on the members of the Académie des Sciences as our valets."[9]

One could scarcely hope for a stronger expression of *honnêteté* and of the position that academicians guarded so zealously. It was this weight of tradition rather than governmental interference that made the Académie so much more *arrière-garde* than avant-garde. To maintain its exemplary prestige the Académie could not give prestige away, which is why elections typically acknowledged established values. Not until 1862 did it elect a novelist *as* a novelist. Other academicians had written novels, to be sure, but their claim to membership in the Académie française, like that of Victor Hugo, rested on work in the established genres of poetry and the drama. The election of Octave Feuillet finally recognized a genre that had been practiced in France for over two hundred years. Not surprisingly, the first official representative of the genre was a literary conservative. No naturalist was ever elected; their "littérature putride," as one critic put it, could not hope for the seal of moral approbation that the Académie implied. No one could discuss the sordid things naturalists wrote about, and in many respects the Académie resembled a salon. Then too the Académie did not bestow but required elevated social status. Counseling Balzac to straighten out his complicated finances, Charles Nodier explained that "the Académie . . . faints at the idea of a loan that can sent you to debtors' prison. It has neither sympathy nor pity for the genius who is poor or in straits. So . . . get a position . . . and you'll be elected."[10] Balzac never did get a position and never was elected.

The political conservatism of the Académie was only secondarily attributable to its governmental associations. Its conservatism reflected above all the conservatism of *le monde* and its conventions, its habits, its attitudes, its personalism. Edmond de Goncourt explicitly acknowledged the conservative influence of *le monde* in an observation to the princesse Mathilde, the cousin of Napoleon III whose salon was much frequented by literary men: "Oh Princesse, you don't know what a service you've rendered the government, how much hatred and anger your salon has disarmed, what a buffer you have been between the government and those who wield a pen. Flaubert and I—if you hadn't bought us off, so to speak, with your grace, your attentions, and your friendship, we both would have spent our time attacking the Emperor and the Empress!"[11] Had the Second Empire been as generous with Zola, Goncourt reasoned, he would never have taken up with democratic newspapers and would never have become politicized.

The filiation of these traditional literary institutions from the ancien régime was clear. However, the context in which they operated had altered radically. The Académie could remain faithful to its traditions but it could no longer assume, as it once had, that those traditions represented all of literature. The Académie and the salons had to recognize the existence of other literary institutions even as they vehemently opposed them. Salons had always competed among themselves. Henceforth they competed with a self-conscious, combative literary group, defined by a commitment to a specific aesthetic ideology. By their very existence these avant-garde literary groups defined the traditional and the classic as *arrière-garde*. None of them could claim the identification with country and with history that distinguished the Académie française. What they did claim was modernity.

The archetypical literary group was the cénacle. The term, which originally referred to the Last Supper (from *cena*, Latin for "evening meal"), was borrowed by the romantics to designate a small gathering of writers, artists, and intellectuals committed to the same ideal. The gatherings occurred in a social setting and often around a meal of some sort, but they differed from the salons in that the company seldom mixed socialites with artists. Whereas socially exclusive salons were intellectually open, receptive to almost any topic that would exhibit "l'esprit français" at its most brilliant, cénacles were typically closed to ideological outsiders, though ever hopeful of converts. As the word *cénacle* implies, the principle of recruitment was attachment to a belief. Théophile Gautier's account of the romantics' *petit cénacle* around Victor Hugo confirmed the aptness of the extended metaphor, and Coppée noted wryly that the Parnassians went to Leconte de Lisle's salon as "believers go to Mecca."[12] Balzac's poet, fresh from the provinces, found an "oasis" in the "desert" that was Paris, a meeting of sympathetic souls in the Cénacle de la rue des Quatre Vents. All the members were "superior beings" who bore "the stamp of a special genius" on their foreheads. Lucien had to wait to be deemed worthy of joining "this Cénacle of great minds." When he betrayed its ideals by succumbing to the temptations of journalism, Lucien was simply read out of the company.[13] Although the term went out of vogue by mid-century, the cénacle became a permanent feature of French literary culture.

The strengths of the cénacle also determined its weaknesses. Like traditional literary institutions, but for different reasons and with dissimilar effects, the cénacle ran the risk of isolation. Its solidarity cut it off from the broader literary world. Since the cénacle sought to publicize its particular definition of literature, intellectual exclusiveness constituted a definite hindrance—or it would have, were it not that cénacles typically mustered their forces for assaults on the outside literary world. The boisterous premiere of Hugo's drama *Hernani* (1830) offered a spectacular example of how a cénacle could mount an attack on the literary establishment.

Less dramatic but in the long run probably more effective was the extension of the informal cénacle to a more formal organization, the better to mobilize resources. Turning toward the market, literary groups founded or annexed literary reviews and publishing houses. In so doing they took on the distribution and production of literary works. The naturalists followed Zola to the publisher Charpentier. The symbolists were associated with the *Revue blanche;* Péguy had the *Cahiers de la quinzaine* publish his articles and reviews, and while the *Nouvelle Revue Française* did not speak for any one group, it certainly considered itself a prime spokesman for "modernist" literature. While this movement into the market especially characterized the end of the century, the tendency had appeared much earlier, in the Hugo brothers' journal, *Le Conservateur littéraire* (1819), in Gautier's editorship of *L'Artiste* (1856), and in countless other journals more ephemeral still.[14] Every literary tendency seemed to have its journal and every journal its literature, the cénacle writ large and, more important, written down, its conceptions of literature ready for dissemination.

Like many imitators that followed its lead, the Académie Goncourt formalized the cénacle much as the Académie française gave the *esprit de salon* an organizational base. The Académie Goncourt was officially established in 1902 by the will and with the legacy of Edmond de Goncourt. The idea, however, goes back to 1880, to a wish of both brothers. The ten members, originally named in Goncourt's will, were to receive a yearly stipend of six thousand francs, hold regular dinner meetings, and award an annual prize of five thousand francs to the best imaginative work in prose published during the previous year. This last directive, in practice, has meant a novel. The Académie Goncourt was directed above all against the market whose demands the two brothers deplored, for Edmond de Goncourt intended the stipends to free the ten academicians from the time-consuming and demeaning demands of journalism. The Académie Goncourt was also directed explicitly against the Académie française and its mixed recruitment. Goncourt made it clear that "to have the honor of belonging to this Society, it will be necessary to be a man of letters. Nothing but a man of letters, we will accept neither great lords nor politicians." Small wonder that newspapers in 1880 were already speaking of it as "an academy that would revenge and console" the unfortunates who never made it into the Académie française.[15]

Although the Académie Goncourt claimed to protect its members against the depredations of the market, it reached, even more than the cénacles, beyond the strictly literary: witness the annual prize, the help to needy men of letters, and the "encouragements" to young writers stipulated by the statutes (the latter not much attended to). And again like the cénacles, the Académie Goncourt had an impact on literary life precisely to the degree that it engaged the market. Within a few years of the first award it was known to affect sales. Today, the Prix Goncourt all but guarantees to the work chosen sales of 200,000 to 400,000 copies—an extraordinary feat considering that fewer than .5 percent of literary works in France sell over 100,000 copies and the average printing of novels runs from 3,000 to 5,000 copies. Five or six other prizes significantly influence book sales, although none as much as the Goncourt.[16]

II

Literary institutions did not operate in an intellectual vacuum. Similar forces were at work in the intellectual debates surrounding definitions of literature. The institutional conflicts that set tradition against modernity also fueled the intense competition between forms of literary creativity. To understand the lines of battle drawn around these literary institutions and to comprehend their role in defining French literary culture, one must confront the aesthetic ideologies that circumscribed the institutions.

Three ways of defining literature in the nineteenth century stand out: the traditionalism that judged literature against moral standards, the aestheticism that proclaimed the inviolability of literature, and the scientism that preached objectivity and defined literature in relation to its value as truth. These literary modes competed both with one another and against the reduction of literature to a commodity in much the same way that literary institutions competed among themselves and against the market. And as with literary institutions, no one view of literature was as important as the tensions that governed the relations among the different views.

Until the nineteenth century there was general agreement that literature was to be judged by criteria that might assume a specifically political, religious, or social guise but remained fundamentally moral. In Western thought this moral view of literature claimed the authority of Plato, who drastically limited the depredations of literary discourse by banishing poets from his republic. The more positive note discernible in Horace's dictum *utile et dulce* still adhered to the basic premise that art must be subordinated to moral imperatives.

Because what was moral depended on particular circumstances, moral criticism varied considerably. Outrage expressed by an individual was one thing; backed by the authority of Church or state it was quite another. Official censorship in France covered the spectrum from the convoluted system of the ancien régime to severity under the First and Second Empires to the rather more relaxed surveillance of most of the July Monarchy and the Third Republic. But such intervention did not even begin to account for the anticipatory self-censorship on the part of the writers, publishers, and editors.

Moral criticism did not have to be dogmatic. The least dogmatic of nineteenth-century critics, Sainte-Beuve, placed himself squarely in the moral tradition: "For me literature is not distinct or at least separable from the rest of the man. I can enjoy a work, but it is difficult for me to judge it independently of knowledge of the man himself. Literary study leads me naturally to moral study."[17] Victor Hugo's declaration was at once simpler and more categorical: "Truth contains morality; the great contains the beautiful."[18]

Traditional conceptions of literature could also take a more activist turn, and in nineteenth-century France they often did. Following on the path opened by eighteenth-century philosophes and adopting their use of literature as a weapon to spread the Enlightenment, nineteenth-century writers espoused causes that ranged over the entire political spectrum. Under the banner of social romanticism writers wrote works inspired by feminism, socialism, and a general humanitarianism. They lobbied for divorce, for penal reform, for the improvement of working class conditions, for the end of slavery. Much of what was written under the rubric of reform was exceedingly vague, evidence of a generous impulse rather than a specific program: Eugène Sue intended *Le Juif errant* as "a work of conciliation between the two classes placed at the two extremities of the social ladder."[19]

Commitment for these writers almost transcended partisan politics, for nineteenth-century writers, again like the philosophes, came to view themselves as general legislators for humanity. The declaration of principles in the avant-propos to the *Comédie humaine* spoke for an entire generation and for an engagement thereafter associated with writers nowhere more so than in France. Balzac enjoined the writer to "consider himself a teacher of men." A royalist, Balzac nevertheless agreed that this injunction applied regardless of political views: "Early on I took as a rule these great words, which are the law of the monarchist writer as well as the democratic writer."[20]

The often contradictory forms assumed should not obscure the basic unity of traditional definitions of literature. Whatever the divergence of goals, literature in all these conceptions of creativity was seen as a means to some higher end that was therefore judged by necessarily extra-literary standards. More revolutionary, the aesthetic theory of literature that came into prominence in the 1830s dissociated the good, the true, and the beautiful and claimed that literature could be defined in purely artistic terms. The philosophic justification for this aestheticism could be found in Kant's argument that one must consider as distinct and incommensurable the realms of the conscience (ethics), the imagination (aesthetics), and the intellect or reason (metaphysics or epistemology). Consciously or not, a good many nineteenth-century writers acted and wrote on this premise, arguing in effect that these same distinctions obtained for literature itself.

One thinks of art for art's sake, which defended the aesthetic as a law unto itself, but aestheticism, the commitment to an aesthetic standard, involved more than a given moment in literary history. It was less a movement than a sensibility, less a doctrine than a belief in the superiority of true art. "We believe in the autonomy of art; for us art is not the means but the end."[21] As such, aestheticism and aesthetic definitions of

literature became permanently inscribed on the literary landscape.

It was considerably more difficult to define what strictly
aesthetic criteria might be. For despite impassioned proclamations to the contrary, there was no single measure. As the
context ultimately defined traditional conceptions of literature, so too the milieu determined what form aestheticism
might take. Formalism was one answer. Leconte de Lisle enjoined the poet to "realize the Beautiful . . . by the complex,
skillful, and harmonious combination of lines, colors, and
sounds." However, even those firmly committed to aestheticism realized that a uniquely literary language, even if it were
conceivable, would by that fact alone lose its ability to communicate. So arcane and so technical were discussions
around *L'Artiste* during Gautier's tenure as editor that the
Goncourt brothers felt that they had "fallen in the midst of a
battle of grammarians of the Late Roman Empire."[22] Leconte
de Lisle perceived the ultimate sterility of formalism as well
as anyone else, which led him to add to the formal components of poetry "all the resources of passion, reflection,
knowledge, and fantasy."[23]

The impossibility of an objective, general aesthetic standard meant that like traditional moral definitions of literature, aestheticism varied with those who waved its banner.
Like the more politically activist literatures, aestheticism
flourished in opposition—opposition to the market, opposition to traditional literatures, and especially opposition to the
institutions that gave those literatures authority. Insofar as
aestheticism proposed anything, it advanced the independence of literature, freedom from repressive institutions,
freedom from constrictive definitions.

Such opposition engendered extremist positions and truc-
ulent opinions voiced in a peremptory tone: Gautier an-
nounced, condemning the market, "the only thing that is
really beautiful is something that cannot be used for anything; everything useful is ugly." And since aestheticism was
as much a matter of style as of substance, he added for good
measure: "The most useful spot in the house is the latrines."[24]

The extravagant dress and behavior of Gautier and his fellow bohemians in the 1830s reinforced this opposition to the materialism of the bourgeois society that supported both the market and the morality associated with traditional literary institutions.

Even the scientism and the objectivity so emphatically expressed late in the century by the proponents of realism and naturalism were variants of aestheticism. In his preface to his *Poèmes antiques* (1852), Leconte de Lisle enjoined art and science to unite their efforts.[25] "Science" soon became a watchword, brandished in the cause of a new aesthetic. Zola was the best-known advocate of the "scientific" approach: "Whoever is with science should be with us." Going one step further than Auguste Comte, who decreed sociology queen of the sciences, Zola placed the novel "at the end" of the same path to knowledge. The experimental novel, in its author's eye, was "a consequence of the scientific evolution of this century." It was "the literature of our scientific age."[26] Zola was not alone. A half century earlier Balzac had been every bit as influenced by the scientific ideal, although his notions of science differed greatly. Even Leconte de Lisle included the resources of science among the elements of poetry (he was undoubtedly also playing on the older meaning of "science" as knowledge).

Partisans of literary change thus found themselves at an impasse in their effort to define the new and the different entirely in their own new terms. The task proved impossible. Opposition required reference to the opponent, to the past that was being opposed. Writers found it all the more difficult to avoid tradition because even writers without political pretensions were inclined to think of their literature, if not of themselves, in missionary terms. The intellectual difficulty of divesting oneself entirely of traditional criteria was exacerbated by the prominence of the traditional literary institutions that perpetuated them. Hence even the writers most opposed to the imposition of morality on art had recourse to the familiar vocabulary of moral concepts. Partly as a tactic but partly too because of the real intellectual quandary, art was presented not as amoral, aesthetic, or scientific but as a higher morality. "There are several moralities. There is the positive, practical morality that everyone ought to obey. But there is the morality of the Arts. This one is entirely different."[27] This from Baudelaire's introduction to *Les Fleurs du mal* (1857), a work prosecuted, and condemned, for immorality. Leconte de Lisle offers another example. At the same time he insisted that "the Beautiful is not servant to the True," he fell back on tried-and-true terms. A work that does not realize the Beautiful, he declared, "is a bad deed, a cowardly act, a crime, something shamefully and irrevocably immoral."[28] And for all his clamoring about science, Zola made the same confusion, almost to the point of caricature. "One is very guilty when one writes poorly," Zola intoned; "in literature this is the only crime I see." And this self-proclaimed advocate of science ended his diatribe against censorship with an astonishing pronouncement: "A well-made sentence is a good deed"![29]

And what were the connections between these literary institutions and the definitions of literature? The correspondence was never so absolute nor so neatly drawn as one might wish. True, traditional literatures had natural affinities with solidly entrenched traditional institutions, and avant-garde aesthetics tended to be linked to more ephemeral groups. The Académie française did not elect anarchists or proponents of extreme aesthetic positions. But literature was not static and neither were its institutions. Aesthetics once considered extreme eventually entered the cultural patrimony, and the outrageous became ordinary. The most vociferous opponents of tradition knocked on the door of the Académie française and often passed through. The enemy, the Académie française, was also the focus of a good many aspirations. "Run it down—but try to get in," was how Flaubert summed up the ambivalence.[30]

Election to the Académie concerned more than the individual. It consecrated an aesthetic. Baudelaire, Balzac, Gautier, and Zola all presented their candidacies more than once. Assuredly they sought personal honor. They sought as well honor and legitimacy for the literatures in which they believed. Where they failed, others succeeded. With Lamartine, Vigny, Hugo, and Musset, romanticism conquered and in the process altered the Académie by broadening its conception of literature. At the same time acceptance by the Académie altered the avant-garde. The triumphant romanticism that Victor Hugo brought into the Académie française in 1841 was not the romanticism of the combative *petit cénacle* arming itself for the premiere of *Hernani*. In 1830 both romanticism and its authors were on the line.

Such ready co-optation of the avant-garde by traditional literary institutions showed just how much these aesthetics were bound by the very traditions they defined themselves against. By incorporating these new aesthetics, literary institutions demonstrated adaptability—an adaptability that transcended the minutiae of momentary conflicts and ideological definition. Neither the intellectual nor the institutional lines of force were absolute or rigidly drawn, for both acknowledged the tensions between past and present as a norm of French literary culture. Change never went smoothly but always came to be accepted because acceptance assumed a larger sense of the whole. Tradition controlled through the very opposition it engendered. It set the terms of intellectual debate. We see as much in the way individual writers struggled with and against these terms in working through their own specific theories of creativity.

4

Collective Strategies and Individual Rewards

> Day by day literary production becomes more enormous, more threatening. Books rise, overflow, spread out; it's an inundation. From overcrowded bookstores comes a torrent of yellow, blue, green, and red cascading from displays that make you dizzy. You have no idea of all the names torn from the depths of the unknown which this floodtide throws up for a moment on the crest of its waves, rolls about pell-mell, and then flings away onto a forgotten corner of the beach, where no one passes, not even beachcombers.
>
> Octave Mirbeau, *Les Ecrivains*

Octave Mirbeau, one of the second-generation naturalists, was one of the fortunate few who made a success of a literary career, but he was acutely aware of the oblivion that awaited the vast majority of aspiring writers.[1] Balzac's Lucien de Rubempré in the 1820s focused all his attention and energies on getting his work published, hence all his resentment of the hard-nosed publishers who refused even to consider his poetry; by the 1890s when Mirbeau was writing, however, it had become obvious that publication alone could not make a reputation or a career. The expansion of the market and the consequent multiplication of literary institutions and aesthetic ideologies together changed the rules for literary success. Collectively and individually, writers took stock of the new state of literary affairs, and after assessing both what they had and what they wanted, they elected various strategies to reconcile the two.

What they perceived as rampant commercialism and un-

78

mitigated competition—Mirbeau's torrent of books—drove writers to join forces and seek allies in the battle for success. In consequence, literary groups of all sorts proliferated, especially toward the end of the century as competition became more acute. Many of the groups were ephemeral, but others—including the three examined below, the romantics, the Parnassians, and the naturalists—emerged as important forces in French literary life. Still, as the evolution of these three groups makes clear, any collective endeavor was fraught with tension. Every group was fragile, sapped at its foundation by the myth of the great poet, the genius who had no peers. These tensions between the exemplary individual and the group have defined French literary culture ever since.

I

The collective nature of writers' strategies to cope with the market ties literature to ideology, that is, to the interpretations by which groups cope with the larger society.[2] Neither *theory*, a concept that emphasizes logic of argument, nor *philosophy*, a term that implies abstract speculation, conveys the special relationship of ideology to a social group. Nor, for the most part, do theory and philosophy transmit the highly charged symbolic discourse that distinguishes ideology. As translations of relationships between one recognizably distinct social group and the rest of society, ideologies are "objective" insofar as they take root in the history, the social composition, and the economic, political, and cultural position of an identifiable social group. At the same time ideologies are "subjective" to the extent that they express the experience of that group in society.

The ideology of aestheticism in nineteenth-century France took its meaning from the context in which or against which it was elaborated. Yet though aestheticism pushed in many directions, all varieties assumed the superiority and the marginality of the artist in the modern world and the independence of art. Defined thus, aestheticism claimed to speak to and for the artist in modern society, with special pleading and a special place for the writer. Balzac's presentation in the *Comédie humaine* might appear especially aggressive, but he was neither unusual nor atypical in vaunting the writer whose "law . . . makes him equal and perhaps superior to the statesman."[3]

Although aestheticism did not concern only writers, and even though writers were not the sole beneficiaries or advocates of aesthetic promotion, writers nonetheless benefited from conspicuous privileges. Beyond the vatic associations that devolved on the poet, writers enjoyed the further advantage over artists who worked in more specialized media of making their art from the common intellectual and social discourse. Writers spoke for aestheticism because literature could articulate the ideology that bid to legislate the very idea and practice of art.

Circumstances and temperament accounted for the many variations on this theme. The direct attack mounted in critical writing made explicit the discontent that was implicit in a more strictly literary mode. The bourgeois, for example, came to stand for all that the artist detested in modern society. The exaltation of the writer found its mirror image in the denigration of the bourgeois, with the result that both figures transcended sociological categories to attain almost mythic proportions. For the artist, the bourgeois was the Other. If few artists actually lived *la vie de bohème*, the extravagant presentation of self characteristic of those who did live a bohemian existence publicized a dissent from society that extended well beyond the eccentricities of the few. At the same time, artists' extravagances—Gérard de Nerval taking a leashed lobster on a walk in the Palais Royal—bid for the attention of the same bourgeois, the only possible public.[4]

Given the ground they shared, writers naturally discovered grist for their literary mill in the work of artists, painters, and musicians, whose good offices they sought to enlist in their literary battles. Gautier began his career in a painter's studio, which he found very much attuned to literary battles—"we read a lot then in studios"—and he hesitated for some time before opting for literature.[5] Courbet's painting that included Baudelaire in attendance with all the painters recalls that the term *realism* was born in Courbet's studio. Zola, for his part, annexed the impressionists, most notably Manet, and until he took umbrage at Zola's portrait of the artist in *L'Oeuvre*, Cézanne was a close friend.[6] In part such ties were a logical extension of particular aesthetics, and in part they derived from the natural overlap of artistic milieux. Nineteenth-century Paris, we should not forget, was a center for all of the arts.

The stress upon the common plight of writers and artists should not obscure the fact that the writer came in many exemplars. Beyond the ideology of aestheticism lay many particular aesthetic ideologies, the literary movements, currents, and practices that contributed so heavily to the constitutive tension of French literary culture—the strong strains and often overt and strident conflict between groups and the fundamental, all-encompassing tension that set the individual against the group and against the entire social order. On the one hand, the ideal of the writer inherited from romanticism insisted on the unicity of the creative work. On the other, the growing disproportion in forces between the individual and the market prompted writers to make common cause in the struggle to impose themselves and their literary ideals. Accordingly, as the market expanded during the century and dominated literary life, collective strategies became increasingly salient. The loosely grouped romantics in the 1820s and 1830s were succeeded by the far more closely knit Parnassian poets in the 1860s and 1870s and by the tightly integrated naturalists in the 1870s and 1880s.

The marked identities of these groups and their internal coherence set them apart for both their contemporaries and later generations. The three also represented the principal modes of literary creativity in contention throughout the century. In the 1820s and 1830s the romantics were a fairly disparate group whose members marked every genre. They cohered around basically traditional conceptions of literature, which they renewed by redefining the place of literature and of the writer in modern society. The modern image of the writer as marginal yet also superior comes to us from the romantics and their ceaseless campaigns of self-promotion. Some years later, in mid-century, the Parnassians—all poets—rallied to the banner of Leconte de Lisle's austere aestheticism, ambitiously calling their collective publication *Le Parnasse contemporain*. Finally, in the 1870s and 1880s the naturalists vocally espoused the scientism preached by Zola, aiming to portray the "real" world and to make the novel a "slice of life." The varying success of these literary groups, the strong images they projected on society and on literature, and their social and literary status attested to the increasing significance of collective strategies in French literary culture as well as to the conflicts engendered by those strategies.[7]

These collective strategies can be seen as so many moves to stake out territory for a particular group and for its conception of literature. The first step toward self-definition was to claim intellectual and aesthetic territory. The clamorous public statements that publicized aesthetic beliefs in effect endowed the group with an identity and a *raison d'être*. The more jarring the aesthetic to traditional sensibilities, the more necessary this aggressive journalistic criticism became—in Zola's metaphor, a hammer to be pounded in a bit further with every article.[8] The marked positions and the strident claims rallied supporters and provided a focal point for dissenters. Victor Hugo's resounding *Préface de Cromwell* in 1827, Leconte de Lisle's preface to *Poèmes antiques* in 1852, and Zola's *Le Roman expérimental* of 1880 established aesthetic coherence and ideological identity for members of the three groups and for outsiders. By such means groups took possession of literary space and made that space their own.

The institutional presence that fortified literary identity also linked individual practice to a broader social context. One can easily exaggerate the importance of writers' groups. But they were not simply artifacts of the overly tidy minds of latter-day literary historians trying to make sense out of a jumble of writers and literatures. Contemporaries faced the same disorder, and it was usually they who dubbed the

groups. But if those concerned did not devise their own labels, once the epithet was bestowed, they were likely to make
of it what Edmond de Goncourt called a flag word. Zola admitted that he didn't "care a fig for this word 'Naturalism.'"
Yet he kept on repeating it "because things need to be bap-
tised for the public to think they are new."[9]

If one can be skeptical about Goncourt's veracity as a recorder of conversations, his point was well taken. Just about
everybody waved one symbolic flag or another as part of the
campaign to take over literary institutions. The word itself,
the "ism," was only the exterior sign of an inner commitment.
But whereas the word might be silly, as Zola acknowledged,
and was often fortuitous, the ideal was anything but silly;
without an intellectual and literary foundation, organizational strategies were void of meaning. Balzac's short-lived
Société du cheval rouge caricatured the frenetic organizational strategies. As Gautier later recounted the rather hare-
brained scheme, the enterprise was purely instrumental, a
mutual aid society whose members would loyally (and se-
cretly) work to advance one another's careers. "We were supposed to take over the newspapers, invade the theaters, sit
in the Académie's chairs, make brochettes of all our decora-
tions, and end up, modestly, peers, cabinet ministers, and
millionaires."[10] But because these would-be literary condot-
tieri shared little more than a general sympathy and enthusiasm, nothing ever came of the project except Gautier's tall
tale. Balzac himself provided the explanation for the failure
in the *Comédie humaine.* The cénacle that gathered around
Daniel d'Arthez in the rue des Quatre Vents owed its effec-
tiveness to an aesthetic and intellectual commitment utterly
lacking in the Société du cheval rouge.

Obviously, convictions varied in intensity from one group
to another. The closer the ties, personal as well as literary, the
more cohesive the group and the stronger its identity. No one
led the romantics. They were so diverse and represented so
many currents that no single figure could focus aspirations
and give direction to all. If Chateaubriand served as the revered ancestor, or as Gautier put it, *le Sachem,* of French ro-

manticism, he held himself aloof from the battles waged by the more fractious younger generation. Hugo's striking success and strident calls to literary action, on the other hand, galvanized the slightly younger generation of would-be romantics. Gautier's marvelous account of his first meeting with Hugo right after the success of his romantic drama *Hernani* conveyed the special fascination Hugo exercised even as a young man (he was not yet thirty). So overwhelmed that he could not muster the courage to ring the great man's door bell, Gautier huddled on the stairs until Hugo sallied forth and almost stumbled over him. Notwithstanding his great admiration, Gautier did not become a disciple, though he fought valiantly in Hugo's troops to defend *Hernani*. In any case Hugo lacked the temperament to forge a really cohesive group. Leconte de Lisle and Zola later did form such groups, their example, energy, and reputation (not to mention the contacts) furthering the careers of the younger writers. Leconte de Lisle was twenty to twenty-four years older than the other Parnassians and Zola was eight to ten years older than his naturalist disciples; each worked hard both with and for their friends and followers. Leconte de Lisle took the Parnassians to his publisher, Lemerre, and Zola ensured that Charpentier published the naturalists. The disciples might return the favor when the opportunity arose. Of the Parnassians, Sully-Prudhomme was the first elected to the Académie française (1881). He obviously worked to good effect, since Coppée joined the forty Immortals in 1884, Leconte de Lisle in 1886, and Heredia in 1894.

Regular contact was important to strengthen group solidarity. Informal gatherings in cafés, at dinners, or in a salon associated the group with both a place and a ritual. In most cases the company was mixed. Salons mixed writers and upper-class society generally, much as they had during the ancien régime. But even writers among themselves might be a various lot, a gathering of friends and sympathizers rather than master and disciples. George Sand opened her country home to her friends, even those, like Balzac, with whose literary practice she emphatically disagreed. The dinners at

Magny's Restaurant that brought together Flaubert, the Goncourts, Sainte-Beuve, Taine, Turgenev, and even George Sand were typical of these "professional dinners." Other writers chose to be "at home" on specified days, Flaubert on Sundays, Mallarmé on Thursdays, Edmond de Goncourt on Sunday mornings at his suburban home (the gathering served as the model for his Académie Goncourt). And most writers moved in several circles.

But on some occasions groups closed ranks, and the more exclusive the meetings—the more limited to disciples and allies—the stronger the identity of the group. Leconte de Lisle's salon identified the Parnassians; Zola's country home at Médan concentrated attention on the naturalists. In general, prolonged contact with an acknowledged master afforded the most precious of literary apprenticeships, a means of testing ideas and receiving criticism. Heredia declared that Leconte de Lisle taught all the Parnassians how to write poetry. Cézanne captured the essence of the relationship, the deference, the role of the master, and the vital importance of his approbation in the portrait of Paul Alexis reading a manuscript to Zola, who is draped in an oriental robe and looking properly inscrutable and meditative.

A public manifestation of some sort frequently affirmed and publicized these affiliations. The premiere of *Hernani*, tomato projectiles and all, consolidated the conquest of romanticism and colored an image that has endured for 150 years. Less tumultuous, the poetic anthologies of *Le Parnasse contemporain* (1866, 1868, 1876) and the short stories in the *Soirées de Médan* (1880) similarly declared principles and served notice of intent. Leconte de Lisle's literary position was well known before the first issue of *Le Parnasse contemporain,* and Zola's indefatigable journalistic work had already made him the standard bearer of naturalism by the time the *Soirées de Médan* were published. The collection could not fail to identify the other contributors as naturalists and accentuated the divisions between literary groups and their aesthetics. Journalism too—Zola's hammer—sharpened distinctions and drew the lines of battle.

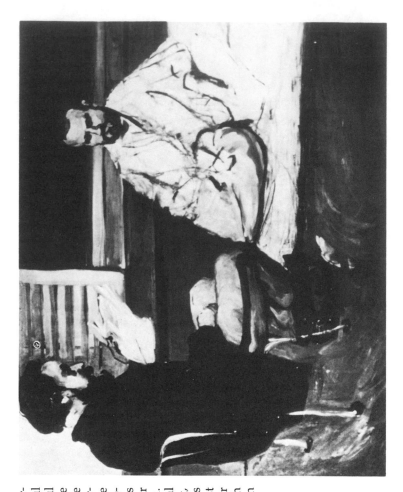

The dynamics of the literary group surface in Paul Cézanne's portrait of Paul Alexis reading to Emile Zola, which captures the essence of the master-disciple relationship. The disciple, seen only in profile, remains buried in his manuscript, submitted for the master's approbation. Zola's vaguely oriental garb, his lighter coloring, his frontal position, and his inscrutable mien all suggest the distance between leader and follower. (Photograph courtesy of the Bettmann Archive)

The intense literary competition that accompanied the establishment of these groups also posed a constant threat to their existence. Splintering was the inevitable consequence of rivalries within the groups. Proust's devastating portrayal of Mme Verdurin's salon was only just a caricature of the instability that jeopardized every such assemblage. Mme Verdurin's great fear of "defections" and her recourse to "assassination" of the unfaithful translated the fragility of all such semisocial, semiartistic relationships. These groups, even the most cohesive, lasted only a few years. The stress was great. Subordination to a master became progressively more difficult to accept. After a time the strong personality irritated more than it enthralled, and the disciples chafed at the collective identity that had attracted them in the first place. Leconte de Lisle's salon lasted until his death in 1896, but by the 1870s both Coppée and Sully-Prudhomme had inaugurated salons of their own. Only Heredia, the most faithful of the Parnassians (to whom Leconte de Lisle bequeathed his academician's uniform), waited for the death of the master before setting out on his own. A more strident declaration of independence was the "Manifeste des cinq" (1887), published in *Le Figaro,* in which five among the second generation of naturalists dissociated themselves from the path Zola had taken in his latest novel, *La Terre.* The disciples struck out decisively on their own, rejecting the status of apprentice for that of journeyman, ever hopeful of promotion to master.

II

The similarity of the collective strategies adopted by so many different writers contrasted with the varieties of fortune achieved. Necessary to literary success of every sort, collective maneuvers could not in themselves guarantee success, which was measured in relation to the individual rather than the group. Success depended both on the cultural context and on the resources at one's command. Whatever the strategies employed, neither aesthetics nor individuals were equal in the cultural assets or "cultural capital" on which they could draw.[11] In the nineteenth century as before, extraliterary factors weighed heavily in the balance.

The climate of intense competition that prevailed in nineteenth-century literary France made collective maneuvers essential, especially for those groups with fewer literary and cultural resources at their disposal. The more innovative, the more shocking and avant-garde the approach to literature, the more likely its proponents were to seek elsewhere the allies they could not find in literary milieux. Furthermore, writers with fewer resources were likely to be more combative than others. The naturalists had to fight; the more favored Parnassians did not. The former needed all the extraliterary support they could muster. More tangible forms of assistance also helped bolster aesthetic conviction. As Zola was quick to point out, Flaubert's family fortune, though by no means vast, meant that he could afford to disdain the market. Zola could not.[12]

Most obvious among the intangible extraliterary factors was social background. As the century progressed, the expanding market attracted proportionately more writers from lower social class backgrounds. The definite aristocratic connections among the romantics were almost absent among the naturalists and attentuated for the Parnassians. Of the eleven romantics, seven had some tie to the aristocracy—no dukes and no marquis, but a goodly number of lesser nobility. Lamartine, Vigny, and Musset were themselves of ancien régime nobility; Hugo's father was named count by Napoleon; Mérimée's grandmother was an aristocrat; and Dumas and George Sand were both descended, though illegitimately, from the ancien régime aristocracy. And although George Sand's spouse was one of the lesser personages in her existence, he was a baron. One might even take note of two aristocratic preromantics, Mme la baronne de Staël-Holstein and M. le vicomte de Chateaubriand, the latter still a significant figure in romantic literary and political circles.

The Parnassians counted three aristocratic members, the naturalists two—the two Goncourt brothers. Octave Mirbeau, himself a second-generation naturalist, correctly as-

sessed the situation at the end of the century when he observed how unusual it was to find an aristocratic writer who
was anything more than a dilettante.[13] Social recruitment of
writers moved down the social ladder: there were no petty
bourgeois among the romantics—Gautier later asserted that
he and his fellow bohemians were "all from good families"—
but there were two petty bourgeois among the naturalists and
Parnassians.[14] This shift attenuated but did not altogether ef-
face the upper-class character of French literary life.[15] Notwithstanding the decline of the aristocratic element and the
increase of the lower-class component, most of the romantics,
the Parnassians, and the naturalists came from the middle to
upper classes, which meant that stratification existed *within*
groups as well as between them. The eminently bourgeois
Balzac stood out among the aristocratic romantics. The end
of the century reversed the situation and made the aristocratic Goncourts the misfits.

Secondary occupations provided other associations. Naturally enough, given the opportunities each offered, writers
gravitated to the market or the government. Practically none
of these writers was without a link to one or the other: there
were no professionals, no doctors, no lawyers (though a few
writers either had law degrees or had studied law), and no
clergy. Of the twenty-nine writers in my sample, only three
had direct pensions (Victor Hugo during the Restoration, Leconte de Lisle and Gautier during the Second Empire), but
by the Third Republic the burgeoning bureaucracy of the
French state created a number of posts that enabled many
writers to profit by the extreme centralization of French administration and remain close to Parisian literary circles. That
same government might just as easily send its civil servants
to the far corners of France. Mallarmé counted himself lucky
to be named to a lycée in Paris, but Octave Mirbeau, as a
subprefect, was posted about France to one and another pre-
fecture. The market rivaled the goverment for writers' services. Journalism claimed more and more time and energy
over the century as writers struggled to keep up with the
proliferation of journals and newspapers. The romantics

counted two more or less full-time critics (Gautier and Nerval), the Parnassians three (Coppée, Mendès, and Glatigny),
and among the naturalists just about everyone except the
Goncourt brothers was actively engaged in journalism.

Education was another asset. The increasing incidence of
formal education during the century turned educational at-
tainment into a significant means of differentiation. Education came to form a new aristocracy, a situation that the twentieth century would accentuate. The romantics followed the
more traditional pattern (consonant with the aristocratic tradition of reliance on private tutors) of little formal education.
Only Balzac had a higher degree (law), although Mérimée
attended law school for a time. By the end of the century the
general level of education had risen noticeably. The *baccalauréat* degree and even attendance at a lycée or collège singled
out almost all the Parnassians and naturalists from the romantics as well as from the vast majority of their contemporaries. The *baccalauréat* degree alone signaled the elite status
of almost all these writers.

In addition, aesthetic resources worked in concert with the
principles of social, occupational, and educational stratification. The hierarchy of genres inherited from the ancien régime placed poetry and drama at the summit of literary creativity, and for much of the nineteenth century the poet
incarnated the literary impulse at its most intense. The poet
was the archetypal creator just as poetry was the essence of
literature. The hieratic voice of the writer-prophet was properly the reserve of poetry. Prose, and particularly the novel,
was more worldly because of its language. The novel, prosaic
by definition, had always been suspect because of its obvious
involvement in the quotidian world of the common reader
and tended to be dismissed in consequence. It ranked low on
the literary ladder, a bourgeois rather than a noble genre. The
seventeenth and eighteenth centuries considered novels
something of an indulgence, for writers as well as readers,
not to be judged by the same standards as drama and poetry.
The difference in prestige affected works and careers. Among
the romantics, the poets and dramatists enjoyed greater suc-

cess than the novelists. That many novelists also wrote plays (Flaubert, Goncourt, Zola, Daudet and Turgenev even held a dinner for *les auteurs sifflés*, "Authors who had been booed off the stage") had almost as much to do with the prestige of the drama as with the possible financial return. By the mid-nineteenth century commercialism further disgraced the novel as serialization and journalism tied the genre to a potentially mass market and defined it as still more ostentatiously plebeian.

However, like the bourgeoisie with which it was associated, the novel gained in stature. As the bourgeoisie came to dominate the social scene, so too the novel made stronger claims to the literary scene. The position of the novel itself paralleled the increasingly refined sense of gradation in the bourgeoisie. The genre reached in both directions, downward with the popular novel and upward as the novel gained its *lettres de noblesse* and proved itself fully as serious, fully as demanding as the traditionally noble genres. Still, it was accepted with reluctance. It is worth noting that the first novelist elected as such to the Académie française, Octave Feuillet in 1862, stood at the antipodes of realism, outside the lineage of Balzac and Flaubert. Feuillet was well aware of the taint on the novel. In his inaugural speech at the Académie française he acknowledged that until this final consecration the novel had been "forgiven rather than admitted" on equal footing with the other literary genres. Despite "some great examples," the Académie was not really sure that the novel could stand on its own as "a legitimate form of our national literature." Accordingly, Feuillet's most celebrated novel, *Histoire d'un jeune homme pauvre* (1857), was designed to reassure: aristocratic antecedents vanquish poverty and the hero inherits a fortune that enables him to wed his equally aristocratic ladylove and live happily ever after in her family château. Having fulfilled the "duties" of the novel, Feuillet could claim recognition of its "rights."[16]

And what of the success to which cultural resources predisposed these aesthetics? By the end of the century, two literary circuits evolved where there had been essentially one: one elite, defined as such by its circumscribed audience, and the other popular. The two overlapped but remained withal distinct.[17] The difficulty of trying to move from the mass to the elite circuit, from commercial to traditional success, testified to the significance of these distinctions for individuals and for the collectivity. To understand French literary culture is to see how the different elements in each circuit implied and reinforced each other and all but precluded a switch from one circuit to the other. Although tradition was continually redefined, it was almost invariably defined against the market and against the popular audience that market represented.

Their considerable social, economic, and cultural resources enabled and predisposed the Parnassians to seek their fortunes outside the market. They had introductions to elite milieux. The naturalists on the whole did not, and their careers were restricted in consequence. The aesthetic label attached to their leader further constrained choices. To the degree that a single individual can be said to incarnate an aesthetic for the public at large, Leconte de Lisle defined the Parnassians, Zola the naturalists. Moreover, the strong associations attached to the masters obscured the diversity of the new recruits. Coppée's petty bourgeois origins and relative lack of education ultimately mattered less for his literary reputation than his close connections with the aristocratic Leconte de Lisle. Refusal of these associations could lead others to keep their distance, like the aristocratic Edmond de Goncourt, who found Zola too much a parvenu for his taste.[18]

The romantics, the Parnassians, and the naturalists clearly illustrated the increasing opposition between commercial and traditional success. The romantics, on the whole, particularly the first generation of poets, Lamartine and Vigny, managed to combine a respectable market success with approbation by elite milieux. Lamartine's poetry sold well, and he entered the Académie française. The next generation of romantics in the 1830s, Hugo, Dumas, Balzac, and even George Sand, were men of letters as their elders were not. Literature became their livelihood as well as their life, and the market loomed larger in consequence. Of this group, only Hugo made it to the Académie, and then only after several tries.

If the romantics in the 1830s and the 1840s evidenced some disparity between success in the market and in traditional literary institutions, after mid-century those distinctions hardened. With a few exceptions, runaway commercial success did not fulfill the prescriptions of traditional literary institutions. Once the serial novel had tapped popular audiences, poetry was pushed to the margins of the literary market, retaining its prestige but presenting a decided commercial risk. Or rather, poetry remained prestigious insofar as it was uncommercial. The Parnassians, then, achieved suc-

To pass through the portals on the far right, candidates must first pay court to the "Old Lady," as the Académie française is popularly known, here depicted as an old and ugly concierge. Dumas père on the far left offers a knapsack of writings and Victor Hugo two armloads of his books; a plump, dandified Balzac presents his cane. Only Hugo, somewhat in advance of the others here, would ever gain admission. (Photograph courtesy of the Musées de la Ville de Paris, SPADEM © 1986)

cess with an elite public, the naturalists commercial good fortune. Four of the eight Parnassians entered the Académie
française, and one won the first Nobel Prize for literature
(Sully-Prudhomme). The naturalists presented another image altogether. Zola's works sold well enough to make him
almost a millionaire, Maupassant's works were invariably
best-sellers, and the others also enjoyed considerable financial return on their writing. But no naturalist ever set foot in
the Académie française.

These connections were not the work of chance. Writers,
like intellectuals generally, viewed the market with considerable ambivalence, eager to reach a public yet anxious not to
be thought unworthy of true art. Traditional institutions like
the salon and the Académie française allowed writers to define their work in terms other than commercial. As jealous as
he was of Eugène Sue's extraordinary popularity and consequent fortune, Balzac refused to define himself as a popular
writer. He played the literary market for all it was worth, but
he also sought the legitimation of aristocratic salons and the
Académie française. Zola did not frequent salons, but he too
sought the Académie's seal of approval. The obstacles each
encountered illustrated the difficulty in reconciling the two
modes of success.

In the effort to reconcile two kinds of success, a writer
could lose advantages and spend, even squander, cultural
capital. The Goncourts offer a case in point. Their espousal
of realism and their later alliance with the naturalists negated
the positive impact of their upper-class origins and effectively
disbarred them from more traditional success. Similarly, Gautier's long career in journalism negated the "nobility" his poetry conferred on him. He failed three times in the Académie
française sweepstakes. And given his bohemian life and general disreputability, Baudelaire's failure to be elected to the
Académie française belonged to the order of things as much
as the academic triumphs of the Parnassians, no more poetic
but infinitely more respectable. Zola's stance during the Dreyfus affair put the final seal of disapproval on the naturalists
as far as the Académie française was concerned, and it also

cut severely into sales of his works. His "democratic" orientation was in turn related to his lack of alternatives. Edmond de Goncourt, for one, thought that Zola had no firm political opinions and only started writing for "democratic" journals after he had been refused elsewhere.

The expansion of the market over the nineteenth century along with the proliferation of literary institutions and ideologies fostered keen competition among writers. The collective mode in which many writers chose to enter this battle for rewards intensified the characteristic patterns and distinctive tensions of French literary culture. United, writers could hope for a better chance of success. But the collective strategies evolved by these literary groups heightened the tensions inscribed in French literary culture. Certainly, the evidence suggests the significance of intense interaction among French writers in both the implied sociability and the contentiousness that was part of this esprit de corps. A still greater tension in French literary culture, however, subsumed all others, placing the individual against the group, not only in the immediate term and with respect to personal relations, but in the long term as well.

The fates of the romantics, the Parnassians, and the naturalists confirmed the disjuncture between individual and group. For if in their own time these writers made their way as groups, in ours they have survived as individuals. One remembers—or forgets—Balzac, Stendhal, and Hugo as individual writers, as strong personalities, irrespective of their connections to one another or to other romantics. Zola and Maupassant clearly dominate the Naturalists; Leconte de Lisle dominates the Parnassians. Epigones, the not-so-new lesson seems to be, slide into oblivion with the greatest of ease.[19] The fragility of these literary groups suggests that no one sensed more than the disciples themselves the confinement of a group and the pejorative connotations of collective enterprise. Invariably, writers refused group identity and swore by their independence. It is striking how many of the writers interviewed in the famous poll of literary figures conducted by the journalist Jules Huret in 1891 denounced literary labels, especially when applied to themselves.[20] Similarly, all the advocates of the *nouveau roman* in the 1960s complained about the injustice of that label.

Are these aggressively "terroristic" groups, as one critic recently suggested, a French specialty, applying themselves to impose a conception of literature and then disbanding, leaving only the strong personality, the great writer?[21] Certainly, the strain between the individual as exemplar and those who are exemplified is integral to French literary culture. Insofar as one depends on the other, it would be foolhardy indeed to pronounce for one or the other. French literary culture is both, needs both, and, even more, builds on the tension between the two.

5

L'Esprit de Géométrie et l'Esprit de Corps

The French have no really national work because they have a wholly national literature.

Louis de Bonald, *Pensées diverses*

"Anyone who really wants to understand French institutions," Edith Wharton admonished her American readers, "must bear in mind that French culture is the most homogeneous and uninterrupted culture the world has known."[1] Such a bald assertion must give pause. Yet the identity of French literature over several centuries and the coherence of French literary culture are remarkable. If the chronicles of French literature boast of no Dante, no Cervantes, no Shakespeare, no Goethe, no "universal" genius who both subsumes and stands apart from the entire tradition, the French *can* point with justifiable pride to a long and exceptionally continuous record of impressive literary achievement.[2] As a consequence, the literary tradition rather than any individual writer embodies the "incomparable personality" of France. In a similar fashion, the literature as a whole rather than any single part expresses this society.[3] Coming to grips with this "whole" of French literary tradition requires us to turn from events and institutions, from sequence and consequence, to the values and norms that integrate these many elements and give them a *raison d'être*. At issue are the modes of expression that mark this culture as distinctly, and distinctively, French.

I

French literary culture is French because of the peculiar and complex ways in which a sense of language and its possibilities structures not only means of expression but also modes of thought. Invariably, those who remark on the place of language in French society note the intricate intertwining— some would say confusion—of language as vehicle and language as value. More than a means of expression, even more than the medium of literary creation, the French language is itself a distinct cultural value. The much-vaunted clarity of the French language, to take the characteristic most likely to be mentioned in any discussion of French, is usually posited as both a linguistic feature and a cultural norm. The celebrated dictum "What is not clear is not French" is at once an analytical assessment and an article of faith, cited *ad nauseam* by the French and by foreigners alike to proclaim the intrinsic superiority of the French language. As one might expect, the phrase belongs to a Frenchman—Antoine Rivarol in his essay, *De l'universalité de la langue française* (1784). No raving chauvinist, Rivarol wrote his essay for a contest sponsored by the Berlin Academy, the terms of which assumed the universality and, by extension, the superiority of French.

Rivarol grounded his discussion on a vast number of what were, even in the eighteenth century, clichés about French. Along with many others, he ascribed the superiority of French to its fidelity to nature, which in linguistic terms means the direct order, verb following subject, object following verb. The clarity of French is "natural" because it follows the logic of thought in contrast to those languages that undermine logic, and hence thought, by an inverted word order, excessive use of metaphor, and similar aberrations: "What is not clear is still English, Italian, Greek, or Latin." Clarity is simultaneously a characteristic of this particular language that ensures its superiority, a norm for the usage of this language, and an ideal toward which *all* languages and literatures ought to strive.[4]

Freedom from the encumbering constructions that obscure the movement of thought fortifies the order imposed by the syntax of French. One seventeenth-century observer had to admit that French mores were not as pure as they might be,

but he felt that the "chastity" of the French language re-
dressed the balance.[5] Early on, this refinement, whatever the
moral overtones, acquired a specifically linguistic definition.
In the seventeenth century French was "purified" by critics
who reproved the Renaissance for its unrestrained borrowing
from the classical languages. Accusing Ronsard's muse of
speaking Greek and Latin more than French, Boileau ap-
plauded the orderly Malherbe for putting an end to such ex-
travagance: "Finally Malherbe came, and the first in France /
Put verse into a proper cadence: / Taught the power of a word
in the right place / And reduced the Muse to the Rule of duty."
So successful was this effort, so powerful its effects, that a
century and a half later de Bonald could tranquilly assert that
French was the "most perfect of all modern languages, and
perhaps of all languages" because it followed the "natural
order of beings and their relationships."[6]

Clarity in language and in literature followed from the primacy accorded reason and the intellect. Classical France subordinated lyricism to eloquence, sentiment to reason. Boileau
enjoined the writer to "love Reason," from which writing
should take all its luster and value. Inspiration helped, no
doubt, but literature and art were conceived as the products
of hard work. The would-be author should "hasten slowly"
and not lose heart even if he had to start over again twenty
times. "Polish ceaselessly, and polish again" was Boileau's
refrain; "add sometimes, but erase often."[7]

The cultivation of clarity and the exaltation of reason define the basic intellectuality of French literary culture. The
French language, French writers, and French literature appear "intellectual" in ways that other languages, other literatures, and other writers do not. Even other intellectuals do
not seem to measure up to those from the land of Descartes,
where, the argument runs, the spirit of Cartesian logic suffuses the entire culture to this day. Descartes's actual influence is considerably more problematic, for the influence of
the classical rhetoric taught in the collèges of the ancien régime and subsequently in the lycées was equal to, if not

greater than, that of any putative Cartesianism in fostering what Pascal—not Descartes—called the *esprit de géométrie*. Classical rhetoric, moreover, was an influence with direct connections to literature and literary culture.

This *esprit de géométrie*, the sense of order, system, and logic, found clear reinforcement in the literary rules taken from the classical authors of antiquity and reinterpreted for contemporary consumption. The rules themselves—the unities of time, place, and action, the *bienséances*—mattered less than the conviction that rules of some sort ought to guide literary practice. The intellect exists to order experience; to cite the poet Chapelain, a semiofficial spokesman for seventeenth-century views, "pleasure is the product of order and verisimilitude." Fundamentally disorderly, spontaneous effusions must be avoided at all costs. Chapelain's contemporary Guez de Balzac carried this prejudice to the point of preferring failure in a fully conscious effort to thoughtless good writing. A century later the naturalist Buffon yoked literary expression and rational thought just as forcefully when he defined style as "the order and movement of thought, to be judged by its properly intellectual beauties."[8]

The intellectualized view of literature sustained by the *esprit de géométrie* places a premium on what the French aptly call the *esprit critique* and, consequently, on the practice of criticism. French literary culture can freely mix criticism with literature because the same spirit presides over each enterprise. In Guez de Balzac's view, "meditation, study, work are the Apollos who inspire poets and make critics." Two centuries later Baudelaire was more emphatic still that a poet had to be a critic, and Sainte-Beuve, a professional critic, singled out France for its true critical faculty. The association between French "genius" and criticism amounted to an elective affinity; for many the critical spirit *was* the French spirit.[9] That this spirit was definitely French was beyond dispute, obvious to anyone who took the trouble to think about it and to look elsewhere, especially across the Channel. Writing to the English novelist Horace Walpole, Mme du Deffand summarized the canons of taste prevailing in the salons of the ancien régime that she knew so well: "You English submit to no rule or method; you let genius grow without making it take a particular form. You would have all the wit you do even if no one had any wit before you. We aren't like that at all. We have books; some are the art of thinking, others the art of speaking, writing, comparing, judging, etc. We are the children of art— a perfectly natural human being over here would have to be shown off at a fair. It would be quite a phenomenon!"[10]

Rule, method, form, art, books—all these terms mark a French conception of beauty. Together, they set art with civilization against nature, with clarity against confusion, with reason against sentiment, with books against experience. Art stands as order imposed, form triumphant. It embodies the *esprit de géométrie* and the *esprit critique*, the two "intellectual passions," in Paul Valéry's expression, that together sustain the cult of form so marked in France.[11]

A sense of form and the intellectuality with which it is associated are in turn supported by the cultural authority inscribed in literary institutions. The Académie française represents only the most prominent instance of the institutional underpinnings of this intellectual order. Has not the ambition of the Académie been to embody the *esprit critique* so often equated with the *esprit français?* As Ernest Renan put it, the function of the Académie is to act as guardian of useful prejudices, to resist rather than to create, and to resist in the name of a certain intellectual conception of literature and of culture. "The French genius," as Renan saw it, "is certainly the most complete, the most balanced, and the most able to create a form of general, intellectual culture."[12] The continued concentration of literary institutions in Paris and their multiplication over the nineteenth century strengthened the intellectual, critical cast of French literary culture so evident in the literary assumptions and practice of the ancien régime.

The *esprit de géométrie* and the *esprit critique* were of great consequence for French literature. When W. C. Brownell, later an important editor at Scribner's, proclaimed the Paris of the 1880s the very "apotheosis of the intellect," he was not thinking of literature alone, nor was Edith Wharton some years later when she explained to her American magazine readers that the "singular superiority" of the French lay in their "intellectual courage."[13] Nevertheless, both visitors saw that literature drew importantly on an assertive intellectuality and that it was greatly affected by the *esprit critique* and by the intellectual authority of the many French literary institutions.

Pondering the differences between France and England from across the Channel, Matthew Arnold too singled out the Académie française as the intellectual conscience of France, the source of a discipline absent or far less prominent elsewhere, particularly in England. The lack of such intellectual authority encouraged English eccentricities and willfulness, although Arnold admitted that it simultaneously favored the expression of poetic energies. Where Arnold commended the English for energy and honesty, he found the French notable for a quick and flexible intelligence, which is why he found it so natural to oppose English genius and French intelligence. The *génie français* was something else again, definitely not the poetic genius of the English but a critical spirit that produces an essentially critical literature. Writing at about the same time as Arnold and after a prolonged sojourn in France, the Portuguese writer Eça de Queirós echoed his contemporaries: "France is a country of the intelligence; we are a country of the imagination. The literature of France is essentially a critical literature."[14]

A critical literature, a literature that prizes the clarity of reason, is very likely prosaic in the strictest construction of the term. In any account prose dominates French literary history. Baudelaire lamented France's innate horror of poetry. Flaubert concurred: poetry was so detested in France that it had to be disguised. And the English poet A. E. Housman once startled André Gide by wondering (in flawless French) why France had produced no poets. Housman allowed Villon and Baudelaire but pronounced the four-century stretch between the two a vast wasteland of arid rhetoricians. (Gide responded some fifty years later with a misconceived anthology of "poetic" selections from six centuries of French poems.) The twentieth-century literary scholar Gustave Lanson recognized that the French were lyric almost by accident. And even though Valéry dissented from the common prejudice, arguing that the French language strives to eliminate harsh sounds and strident accents, he agreed that France's greatest literary creation was its incomparable abstract prose.[15]

These writers, and a good many others who could be brought to testify, were perpetuating another stereotype. The prose "genius" ascribed to French literature is a specifically literary consequence of the clarity assumed to reside in the very structure of the French language, whose "circumspect genius" works to arrest the poet's imagination. Rivarol's characterization of the language itself forced him to acquiesce in the inferiority of French poetry, but he did so only to vaunt all the more the superiority of French prose. Since prose, both in the original and in translation, crosses frontiers more easily than poetry, the undisputed brilliance of French prose literature greatly encouraged the pretensions of French language and literature to universality. "A dangerous work written in French," the arch conservative de Bonald boasted in fear and trembling, "is a declaration of war on all of Europe." Minerva's reasoned discourse rather than Apollo's lyre gave French literature a resonance that transformed the lack of a gift for poetry into a magisterial talent for prose. So complete was the substitution that by the time of the romantics the prestige traditionally associated with poetry and the vatic definition of the poet included the whole of literature, particularly the prose genres and notably the novel.[16]

The critical turn of French literary culture and the consequent dominion of prose favor an intellectual, critical perspective on literature. They also favor a literary conception of intellectual work that extends literary concerns to writing per se. The sophisticated public of the ancien régime did not compartmentalize its reading. The *honnêtes gens* read Descartes along with Molière, Buffon as avidly as Beaumarchais; and the Enlightenment in France and abroad flourished on the premise that the educated public could understand anything—anything, that is, that was properly presented. The key term is "properly," which in practice reinforced the philosophe's bias against specialized, nonliterary discourse— whence a French predilection for literary forms that reproduced salon conversation in a formalization of informality. Fontenelle chose to present his *Entretiens sur la pluralité des mondes* (1686) as a conversation between the scholar-narrator and a slightly frivolous and engaging *mondaine*. Montesquieu put his theory of population in the somewhat risqué *Lettres persanes* (1721); Voltaire weighed the relative merits of Descartes and Newton in the *Lettres philosophiques* (1734). Diderot's *Le Rêve de d'Alembert* (1769) recounts another conversation, between Mlle de Lespinasse, her lover the mathematician d'Alembert, and his doctor; an earlier section adds Diderot himself. In such instances the distinction between writer and scientist or savant cannot really obtain.

The most eloquent justification for the immixture of science and literature was made by the great naturalist Buffon, whose own scientific work, especially the monumental *Epoques de la Nature* (1778), was immediately recognized and continues to be praised for its literary merits. In presenting the edition of his predecessor's works in 1827, the zoologist Cuvier claimed that whatever criticisms might be directed to Buffon's scientific matter, the style was beyond reproach, and he placed Buffon among the great writers of French literature. Elected to the Académie des sciences in 1733 at the age of twenty-six, Buffon entered the Académie française in 1753. His "Discours de réception," generally known as "Sur le style," expresses perfectly the fascination of the French with their language and the belief that the manipulation of language by which literature is defined likewise determines the quality of intellectual work. "Posterity will retain well-written works and these alone. Knowledge, singular facts, even new discoveries cannot guarantee immortality." The precedence of form over subject is not simply a habit of long standing but a deep conviction that the intellectual qualities to be found in writing are as valuable as, perhaps even more valuable than, the content of the work.[17]

The relatively untechnical state of scientific and scholarly knowledge in the eighteenth century allowed learning and literature to be integrated in ways that became impossible by the late nineteenth century. Nevertheless, even today French literary culture assimilates specialized disciplines into a general intellectual exchange. Sometimes the assimilative works belong in the honorable French tradition of *haute vulgarisation* (with the emphasis on the quality of the popularization) that runs from Voltaire on Newtonian physics and Balzac on the phrenology of Franz Josef Gall to Zola's appropriation of Claude Bernard's physiology. Or specialists may do their own popularizing. Claude Bernard's treatise *Introduction à la médecine expérimentale* (1865) itself addressed a nonspecialist public. More recently Jacques Monod, recipient of the Nobel Prize in physiology and medicine, raised the concerns of his highly technical research to a different, more general, order in *Le Hasard et la nécessité: Essai sur la philosophie naturelle de la biologie moderne* (1970). "Science writers" are not confined to France. But in ways that other literary cultures do not, French literary culture connects the narrow world of science or scholarship to the broader world beyond.

Assimilation works in both directions. Specialized languages eventually redefine the general intellectual discourse. French literary culture today borrows from "outside" disciplines as it always has. What is new in the late twentieth century is not the fact of borrowing but rather what is borrowed and consequently turned to literary purpose. Criticism long ago adjusted to disciplines like philology, history, and history of the arts and more recently has accommodated sociology and psychology—disciplines as amenable to speculation and multiple approaches as criticism and literature itself. More recently, however, French criticisms have turned to other disciplines, to the more technical linguistics of Ferdinand de Saussure, the semiotics of C. S. Peirce, the poetics of the Russian formalists and the School of Prague, the anthropology of Claude Lévi-Strauss, the history of Michel Foucault, the psychoanalysis of Jacques Lacan, and the philosophy of Jacques Derrida, to mention only the most obvious figures. While these intellectual frameworks have particularly affected literary criticism, the close French ties between literary and critical work render literature itself exceptionally permeable to such influences. The many and varied domains integrated into French literary culture stress language all the more as the source, sometimes the only source, of commonalities.

The French conception of language has always reached beyond the "literary" in a narrow sense. Style—what the French invariably refer to as good writing—transcends the subject and may transform it as well. As early as 1728 the Swiss traveler Muralt had cause to remark on the "extreme veneration" in which the French held their language: "Quite aside from what is said, in France style is an important affair." He enunciated all the criticisms ever made from then until now about the French penchant for divorcing style and substance. "In other places thoughts give birth to phrases; here just the opposite is likely to occur; phrases often give birth to thoughts."[18] What seemed to Buffon a positive appreciation of the primacy of style appears different in the somewhat jaundiced view of a foreigner for whom French, though a native language, lacked the conspicuous prestige it had among the French.

Although style is a significant component in all French writing, it is central to works defined as "literary," and those who consider themselves writers of literature exhibit the linguistic consciousness of French literary culture in its extreme form. The most striking example of all, Flaubert, agonized over every phrase and raised that consciousness to a cult. For Flaubert style—the use, perhaps even the creation, of an ideal language—defined great literature. This ideal language was not extravagant or excessive, nor was it stuffed with metaphors and mannerisms. It was French, with its inherent clarity and logic. In the nineteenth as in the seventeenth century the writer was not called upon to innovate or invent so much as he was enjoined to revere a language that existed above and beyond the use individuals made of it. "Even in your greatest excesses," Boileau warned, "your writing must hold language sacred."[19] A privileged guardian, the writer remained a guardian nonetheless, who, like the Académie française, resisted in the name of tradition.

Insofar as French literary culture defines the French language as an absolute, the cultural medium predominates over individual usage. What linguists following Saussure see as an analytical distinction between language (*langue*) and the discourse (*parole*) in which it is realized acquires in French literary culture a resonance that is aesthetic and even moral. One could not ask for a clearer presentation of this unequal relationship between *langue* and *parole* than the following directive from Flaubert's disciple Guy de Maupassant: "The French language is a pure stream, which has never been and can never be troubled by affected writers. Into this clear current every century has thrown its fashions, its mannerisms. But from these useless attempts and ineffective efforts nothing survives. By nature this language is clear, logical and taut. It cannot be weakened, obscured, or corrupted."[20] However different his own language from that of his ancien régime predecessors, Maupassant's ideal was nevertheless theirs. One can easily imagine Maupassant decreeing like Boileau that "without style" even the best author is no more than a mere scribbler.[21] As supposedly "careless" and as "modern" a writer as Balzac concurred. Taken to task for his "poor" style—it was a commonplace by 1840—Balzac was in fact as imbued as any of his critics with the mystique of French. Reproached for making up a silly name in German for one of his characters, Balzac based his defense on his fidelity to French. He did not know German and, what is more, would not even think of learning German until he knew French perfectly. His compatriots would do well to follow suit: "If we all knew only French," Balzac intoned, "we would all know it better."[22]

The twentieth century brought precisely the redefinitions Maupassant had envisaged, but it also reordered priorities, something Maupassant had never imagined. An important incentive in this process of redefinition was surely the massive infusion of popular literature, notably those genres en-

dowed with the prestige of imports from across the Channel
and, more frequently still, from across the Atlantic. Because
they were not French, detective novels and eventually science
fiction did not need to adhere to the same canons of good
writing. True, Emile Gaboriau's Inspector Lecoq was detect-
ing crimes before Sherlock Holmes (who summarily dismissed Lecoq), and Jules Verne virtually created science fiction. Yet their very popularity made these writers suspect.
Detective novels and other avowedly popular works affronted
a strong sense of literary hierarchy. At the same time, this
popular literature confirmed the aesthetic hierarchy because
popular literature could be relegated to a category apart,
separate and unequal. Similarly, outright parody, which apparently transgresses every propriety, aims to subvert. But
parody also sustains. Proust's *Pastiches et mélanges* (1919) offers a telling example of the homage contained in parody: a
single incident recounted "by" Saint-Simon, Balzac, Flaubert,
the Goncourts, and others both exorcises the past and pays
it obeisance.

More disquieting for traditional sensibilities, foreign influences could not be so readily dismissed. American literature
in particular undermined the notion of aesthetic propriety by
its spirited mixing of styles and forms. So enthusiastic was
the reception given those works that the 1930s and 1940s were
dubbed the age of the American novel. The brutally direct
language of a Hemingway or the disconnected style of a Dos
Passos skewed the traditional perspective on style and language. As much as anything else, idiosyncratic, iconoclastic
language accounts for the hostility to Céline in the 1930s, to
Sartre and Camus in the 1940s, and to Jean Genet, Boris Vian,
Samuel Beckett and Eugène Ionesco in the 1950s—writers
joined only by their common dissent from the ideal of "good"
writing and "good" literature. The flat, matter-of-fact mode
of Camus's *L'Etranger* (1942), the vituperative exuberance of
Céline's *Voyage au bout de la nuit* (1932), and the linguistic inventiveness of Vian and Ionesco were equally destructive to
the studied elegance cultivated by three centuries of classical
rhetoric, equally devastating to the logic and symmetry im-

plied by that conception of language. These styles rejected the clarity and the order deemed inherent in the very structure of the French language and upset a good deal more than superficial linguistic order.

Given the many strictures on language and literature, it is not surprising that foreigners of one sort or another have played so significant a role in forcing these new literatures and redefinitions of the literary: Beckett the Irishman; Ionesco the Rumanian; Nathalie Sarraute the Russian (who credited her legal training for her ability to circumvent the constraints of *le beau style*); Alain Robbe-Grillet, foreign by his training as an engineer; Céline, a doctor who practiced far from *les beaux quartiers;* Camus, a *pied-noir* Algerian who did not even set foot in France until well into his twenties; Genet, whose language draws on the slang of prisons and homosexual milieux. Although everyone else did not navigate in the pure waters of Maupassant's crystalline French, the ideal retained sufficient force to turn these new approaches to a deliberate contest of styles and epistemologies. Much of French literary history can be read as a continually renewed attempt to undermine traditional notions of style, a contest between the *langue* of French literary culture and the *parole* of writers determined to contest that *langue*. Social discourse evolves to accept new modes of expression, but mostly under assault.

Contest quite as much as acceptance means that style remains, perhaps more than ever, "an important affair" in France. Like every other language, French changes with the times. Yet despite undeniable "loosening" of literary constraints, despite—and also because of—parody, the familiar and the traditional persist. For many, the French language remains a phenomenon apart, an object of wonder and even veneration. The Argentinian Borges spoke for many others when he attributed the richness of French literature to the richness of the French language. The wealth of the language itself has enabled and encouraged an identification that reaches to a spiritual homeland beyond mere country. "Madly in love with the French language," Albert Cohen, the contem-

porary Jewish novelist who wrote in French, cited French—
not France—as one of his countries, and across a generation
Bernard-Henri Lévy, one of the so-called New Philosophers,
had recourse to the same metaphor of language as country:
"My relation to language replaces geography. The French language is my dearest patient and my only possible country.
Asylum and hearth, . . . armor and arm, one of the places in
this world where I take my stand."[23]

II

> More than any modern literature, [French literature] has
> been in the most intimate correspondence with the social
> life and development of the nation producing it.
> Matthew Arnold, "Sainte-Beuve"

Language is never neutral. It cannot be divorced from an epistemology or from the particular social, political, and cultural
context in which that epistemology makes sense. The intellectual refinement of French literary culture, the associated
penchant for criticism, and the cult of form were inscribed in
a language and, by extension, a literature that were, and are,
vehicles of an exclusive social setting. An elite milieu defined
the language that embodied the *esprit critique* and so perfectly
expressed the *esprit de géométrie*, the language that was the
object of "extreme veneration." Linguistic, geographic, and
social boundaries coincided so that the French language sepa-
rated the knowledgeable, privileged few and also signaled
solidarity among the elect.[24] For French was the language not
of all France but of the Ile de France, the language not of the
provinces but of Paris and Versailles, the language not of the
peasant but of the courtier. French was the language of authority, the instrument of the administration and of the Académie française, the medium of the aristocracy and its culture,
the expression of *honnêteté* and its literature. In brief, French,
the language of the center, relegated all other languages
to the periphery occupied by dialects or patois. In many respects it still does.

Linguistic control manifested the overriding social and cultural control exercised by king and court. The two joined forces in the Académie française, which was officially charged with purifying the French language and making it a vehicle for all the arts and sciences. Although couched in general terms, a particular purity was envisaged—the refined usage identified with the polite society of *les honnêtes gens* and defined *against* the specialized jargon of law and theology (and eventually the exact sciences as well). Long before it became an international language, French laid claims to universality by excluding the particular, the local, and the idiosyncratic and by according importance to logic, order, and clarity. The French Revolution shattered these social and linguistic codes that had sustained the consensus of the ancien régime. When constituencies theretofore willfully ignored were admitted to the polity, the new regime was forced to recognize concerns that required a new means of expression. The Revolution required a language more varied and more open than the ideal instrument fashioned by Buffon and Rivarol. New realities forced recognition of the particular even as postrevolutionary political life imposed an essentially new discourse, which had to take account of styles and vocabulary and syntax far removed from the professed ideals of *le monde* and the monarchy.

These same architects of postrevolutionary France faced a more monumental problem: how to create a nation from the many peoples that inhabited the country. Even a simulacrum of democracy required nominal participation of the governed. The absence of a common language made this goal all the more difficult to realize. A study undertaken by the Convention in 1794 estimated that twelve million inhabitants of French territory, that is, somewhat over half the total population, could speak no French at all. Only three million spoke the language more or less correctly. The linguistic politics of the Revolution were designed to foster a consciousness of nationality through a national language and thereby to extend to the populace at large the social control that had been confined to an elite: "In order to extirpate all prejudices, de-

velop all truths, all talents, and all virtues, to meld all citizens
into a nation; to simplify and facilitate political life, there has
to be a single language. . . . Linguistic unity is an integral
part of the Revolution." So went the abbé Grégoire's official
report for the Committee of Public Instruction to the Assemblée nationale.[25]

The solution was to impose French upon France, to create
a national language out of what had been a class language.
French remained a dialect still, but it was now backed by the
authority and power of the government. The situation posed
problems. Because French had been a class language tied to
the monarchy, it was suspect. The alternative? There was
none. French had been the language of the educated revolutionaries, and it became the language of the Revolution.
Some of the more odious class distinctions were purged, and
for a time "citizen" and "citizeness" replaced *Monsieur* and
Madame, forms of address once reserved for the upper
classes. (The resulting ambivalence must have been like that
in the newly independent African nations in the 1960s: the
European language had been the medium of subjugation, but
it was also the only language not associated with a particular
tribe as well as the only means of communication with the
outside world.)

Such a drastic change in the social background of French
speakers necessarily affected the very conception of the
French language. No longer solely the medium of an elite
sociability, French was, more than ever before, the language
of the state. Like the new intellectual disciplines that multiplied over the nineteenth century, the new users of French
opened up the language to new worlds. The "purified" vocabulary vaunted by Boileau and the "nobility" of style advocated by Buffon ceded, though very gradually and in the
face of much resistance, before the invasion of realities that
had been the province of the languages and dialects spoken
in the countryside by the uneducated and illiterate. These
new usages displaced highly intellectualized discourse that
had been the ideal of the ancien régime. French was no longer

the exclusive preserve of an elite, though more than a century would pass before French became the native tongue of all the French.[26]

Contrary to the abbé Grégoire's hopes to abolish hierarchy in language and in society, the new and "popular" associations did not subvert the elite status of the language. Instead the pressure of popular concerns—in particular, the push for primary education beginning in the mid-nineteenth century—raised the linguistic consciousness of elites even as it spread French into popular milieux. French for the lower classes was conceived in strictly utilitarian terms. Primary education would suffice. Anything beyond the rudiments devolved on the highly selective lycée, whose decidedly non-utilitarian goals defined language against the everyday usage of ordinary people. A prominent Catholic educator based his conception of learning on just this linguistic distinction: "The objective is true language, . . . and this requires breaking and grafting primitive, natural, and vulgar language and giving it through art, . . . through true culture, and through a higher education a sort of new form, more noble and more elevated." Buffon and Rivarol and Mme du Deffand find echoes here. Art and education alone produce "true language" because only they are able to translate nature into higher and more noble realms.[27]

The noninstrumental usage of language acquired in the lycée fortified the elite associations of French and exacerbated the great distinction between modes of French. Thus language continued to serve as a means of social control and as a sign of distinction, much as it had during the ancien régime. This is the significance of the famous *dictée* Mérimée gave to Napoleon III and his circle, which was so full of tricky spellings and recondite terms that even Mérimée had to keep checking the original. The *dictée* is extraordinarily difficult, full of specialized vocabulary and homonyms ("cuisseaux de veau" and "cuissot de chevreuil"). The Spanish-born empress Eugénie made sixty-two mistakes and the emperor forty-five, but two writers (both eventually elected to the Académie française), Dumas fils and Octave Feuillet, made twenty-four and nineteen respectively, and Prince Metternich, the winner, only three.[28]

That dictation of a difficult passage in French was considered diverting offers further testimony to the pervasive sensibility to language. More significant still, the place this episode has earned in the annals of French literary history and the role the *dictée* has played in the teaching of French testify to the primacy of the written word in French literary culture. And the *dictée* lives on, most spectacularly in the Championnats Nationaux d'Orthographe. This monumental spelling championship, first organized in 1985 by Bernard Pivot of "Apostrophes" television fame and sponsored by the Crédit Agricole bank, attracted over fifty thousand competitors ranging in age from under ten to over eighty as well as the participation of prominent literary and political figures, who helped in administering the *dictée* throughout France. There could be no better illustration of the superiority accorded *langue* over *parole*, the fixed text over the ephemeral spoken word. The *dictée* betrays the concern, even obsession, with fixing thought, with containing the vagaries of oral discourse. Unlike the American spelling bee, which is based on isolated words, the French *dictée* calls on all one's linguistic resources—syntax and grammar no less than orthography. Moreover, one competes not against the others taking dictation but against the French language itself. It is possible to have no winner—Prince Metternich, after all, made three mistakes on Mérimée's *dictée*. Thus does French literary culture push to the extreme the domination of writing, this "modern mythical practice," that commentators have seen as characteristic of modern Western culture. A general trait of Western culture, this attitude toward language becomes also a trait specific to French literary culture.[29]

The French university in a sense formalized this linguistic consciousness; it translated to a higher level the concern for language evident in elite secondary education, and it connected the study of French literature and the study of the French language. Of the original eight chairs established by the Faculté des lettres of Napoleon's newly organized Université de Paris in May 1809, pride of place went to the History of French Literature and Poetry, and the sixth chair was for French Eloquence. By 1862 the sixteen faculties of letters in all of France had seventeen chairs of French literature (Paris had two); in 1881 sixteen of one hundred chairs (Strasbourg having become a German university after 1870) were concerned with French literature or language.[30]

For the English, by contrast, linguistic concerns were of less moment. Not until the end of the nineteenth century did Oxford and Cambridge give official academic recognition to the study of English language and literature. Even though the University of Edinburgh set up the Regius Professorship of Rhetoric and Belles Lettres in 1762 (Adam Smith lectured there on English literature as early as 1748), only in 1839 did the University of London introduce English and English literature into the examination system. But London did not enjoy the prestige bestowed on Oxbridge, and Oxbridge harbored strong prejudices against a subject that was reputed easy, attractive, directly useful, and connected with younger universities. Anyway English was not something to be learned, it was something everyone ought to know. So Oxford did not vote a degree (Final Honours School) in English Language and Literature until 1893 and waited until 1901 to establish a professorship in English literature alone. Cambridge was more reluctant still. The academic study of English started tentatively in 1896 with a lectureship, a professorship coming only in 1911 with an outside endowment; the full degree course was delayed until after the war.[31]

The English, one is tempted to say, were altogether dilatory about a matter that in France was the focus of intense national pride. No Englishman would (and no American could) claim that his linguistic conscience was nothing less than the national conscience. Yet it seems entirely fitting that a Frenchman should make such a statement in all seriousness.[32] What renders the assertion possible, if somewhat extreme, is the highly normative conception of French that so sharply demarcates levels of linguistic usage, far more so than in England or the United States. Where England has the queen's English, it also has BBC English, Oxford English, and any number of regional accents. Indeed, that is the point. Even elites in England show a linguistic diversity usually missing in France, where Parisian French *is* French. In some sense *every* speaker of English has an accent, whereas for French it would be truer to say that everyone *else* has an accent, that is, everyone who does not speak standard Parisian. French, the universal language of order and reason, serves as a bastion against the disorder, the emotion, the "foreignness" of other, necessarily particularistic, languages.

The elite associations of French and French literature survived beyond the ancien régime in a different social and intellectual setting. Linguistic consciousness turned into self-consciousness as the literary and social codes that had bound the traditional elite culture were broken and their language demoted, to be lost amid the welter of new literary languages. Class barriers fell with the linguistic ones, or so it was felt, which is why the ventures of Zola and others into lower-class language disturbed conservative critics convinced of the intimate relation between disorder in linguistic and social domains. The one surely portended the other—though assigning priority posed a problem for most.

Naturalism would not have raised such a fracas if the naturalists had not sought to redefine the very ideal of literature, to create a model against which all literatures were to be measured. Like realism and romanticism before it, naturalism laid claim to the top of the heap. Avowedly "popular" writers like Paul de Kock, Ponson du Terrail, or Jules Verne pressed no such claims to reorder the aesthetic hierarchy. Had Zola and the others renounced any thought of extending their example and their practice to a redefinition of literature and literary culture, they would have aroused far less opposition. But Zola aimed to rewrite French literary history to gain for himself and for naturalism more generally a hearing among those who constituted the social and intellectual elite. This was the public that really counted in the distribution of glory and honor, and this was the public that prized *l'esprit français*.

Zola's critical aggressiveness, like that of Balzac before him, bespoke the disparity between his socioliterary position and the standards of French literary culture. One needed the assurance, the tenacity, and the pugnacity of a Zola to persevere. Even when the lower classes supply the subject, the setting, and the characters, the bourgeoisie provides the writers and most of the public. If not altogether a contradiction in terms, proletarian literature remains marginal because it does not belong in French literary culture. True proletarian writers do not—for that matter cannot—fit any of the models it provides.

This exclusion has two effects, the first and most obvious being the neglect of literary works written of, by, and for a working-class audience. The Communist party newspaper *L'Humanité* chose to reprint André Gide's *Caves du Vatican* in 1933 instead of the works of "authentic" proletarian writers. As the definition of the French language excluded regional dialects or patois, so the French literary tradition excluded certain literatures as inappropriate. Mrs. Trollope might have been talking about the twentieth century when she observed that conservative writers (she named Chateaubriand and Lamartine) were held in higher esteem than the "revolutionaries."[33]

This literary divorce also pushes "outsiders" to write like "insiders." The historian Jules Michelet—himself from a lower-class background—knew whereof he spoke when he bemoaned the impoverishment of French literature resulting from strictures that trained out spontaneity, inhibited linguistic inventiveness, and blocked out harsh realities. Instead of writing from experience, working-class writers aped the language of abstract generalities and clichés that made up proper, acceptable French: "The lower classes, when they write, make the mistake of not writing from their hearts, where their force lies, but of borrowing generalizations and abstractions from the upper classes. These writers have the great advantage, which they do not appreciate at all, of not knowing this conventional language, of not being obsessed and pursued, as we are, by ready-made sentences, by phrases that come of their own accord when we write and settle on the page."

The working-class writers of whom Michelet spoke may stand for almost any "foreign" writer—African, Québecois, Breton, woman—confined by the straitjacket of this analytic conception of literature and the language appropriate to it, a conception that, as Michelet made clear, defined linguistic competence in social terms. The codified, highly intellectualized relations to the French language imbedded in French literary culture constrain the very notion of originality. "This is what working-class writers envy us for," Michelet continued, "what they borrow from us as much as they can. They dress up to write; they put on gloves and lose the superiority that workers have from their strong hands and arms."[34] Was he, one wonders, regretting his own loss as well?

French provided a passport to the wider world, to a civilization that laid claim to universality. "For us," Léopold Sédar Senghor declared in the name of his fellow francophones in Africa and the world, "Francophonie is culture, . . . a mode of thought and action, . . . a spiritual community . . . beyond the French language; it is French civilization." The Tunisian Jew Albert Memmi recounts his emotion at mastering this language that meant mastery of the universe.[35] Others recall instead the feeling of inadaptation, the oppression entailed by acculturation, the interdiction of native languages, and the scorn for indigenous cultural traditions.[36]

Writers, in particular, chafe under these constraints. How many shifts in literary sensibility have hinged on what amounted to a new language, or what was perceived as a new language? Victor Hugo proclaimed his ambition of revolutionizing literature by revolutionizing language, putting a revolutionary's red cap on the old dictionary, and Théophile Gautier's mock-heroic narrative of the battle of *Hernani* in 1830 likens Hugo's audacious run-on line to a ruffian thumbing his nose at classicism.[37] However much romantics may have disagreed about the exact shade of red for the dusty dictionary, most shared Hugo's advocacy of literary liberty.

But the battle of *Hernani*, tumultuous and triumphant as it

was, did not establish a new regime for all time. Each generation has its own version of the old dictionary to battle.
Céline found the French language in 1930 in as much need
of rejuvenation as Hugo had found it one hundred years earlier. Linguistic purification had worked too well. The aristocratic language imposed by seventeenth-century grammarians had snuffed out the boisterous popular, hence
authentically French, language of Rabelais. Three centuries
of linguistic "improvement" had produced what Céline condemned as "lycée" French, a "decanted, filtered, static"
French, the French of Montaigne, Racine, and the Prix Goncourt, a French "disgusting in its elegance, . . . the very epitaph of the French race."[38] A half century after Céline, the
division persists between what the avant-garde novelist and
critic Philippe Sollers sees as the "true, legitimate, official"
French and the other language of France. Two languages, two
cultures in almost complete contradiction—an old story, Sollers admits, yet up-to-date, so much so that a dictionary of
"unconventional French" published in 1980 was presented as
something of a rebellion against "legitimate" French. Nor is
it surprising that French feminists should denounce conventional French as "phallocratic," one more symbolic discourse
in the service of oppression.[39]

    The more French literary culture discriminates against out-
siders, the more it unites insiders. The resulting sense of
cohesion is often traced to the sociability deemed characteristic of elite French society. Early in the eighteenth century
Muralt noted that to the French "a life spent in company is a
good, orderly life. Man, they say, is made to live in society."
The French, he added, are "born courtiers." Jean-Jacques
Rousseau agreed with his compatriot's assessment and was
incensed that Molière should present this view in such a favorable light. That Molière made fun of the hero of *Le Misanthrope* was, for the outsider that Rousseau knew himself to
be, the unmistakable sign of a society perverted because it
prized conformity and condemned the individual who dared
to refuse society's specious definitions of self. The sociability
of French culture left no place for Alceste—or for Rousseau,

whose retreat from society was accompanied by great misgivings and attempts at justification. Jean-Jacques in tormented solitude had none of the serenity of a Thoreau, to call upon an example far removed in time and place but perhaps not in spirit. The French, Muralt observed, are tempted to reserve the term *owl*, or philosopher, for anyone with the least inclination to be alone.[40] By mid-century the intense sociability associated with the French philosophes had already given the lie to the equation of philosopher and solitude, making Rousseau even more of a misfit.

And so it continued into the nineteenth century. The redoubtable Mrs. Trollope did not fail to comment on the sociable temper of the French, and Taine even went so far as to assert that the French think best in a group: "Nowhere do we think better than when surrounded by other people; . . . our ideas come in flashes, prompted by the shock of someone else's ideas." Once again both the natural comparison and a striking contrast are to be found in England, where "*honnêteté* does not arise from sociability but from personal reflection." For that matter, *l'honnêteté* in the French sense is so preeminently a social trait that it did not really exist across the Channel—the term itself lacks an English equivalent.[41]

As it endowed literary activities with their own institutions, so the nineteenth century gave writers a milieu and a sociability they might claim as their own. The dissolution of salon society was countered by the emergence of a distinct literary milieu and a decided literary sociability. The English author Bulwer-Lytton was struck by the almost fierce esprit de corps of French *littérateurs:* "No men in France hang more together than literary men; no men defend their order with more tenacity." The reorganization of the literary world created a consciousness of literature defined against the rest of society—whence the esprit de corps noted by Bulwer-Lytton and the "clannishness" a more recent observer has imputed to a "messianic solidarity" that stands out against Anglo-Saxon collegiality.[42]

By all accounts literary life in France has long been a group affair, an echo of the salon milieu of the ancien régime. More than romantic movements elsewhere in Europe, French romanticism was defined, often contradictorily, by the circles, the cénacles, and the salons that propagated the faith and transformed a literary movement into a public affair. In these groups conversation might turn to debate, commentary into criticism. In the words of one contemporary, an "electrification of talent" resulted from interaction at close quarters with other writers, artists, and intellectuals. The *Journal* of Edmond de Goncourt offers an incomparable, minute record of the literary life of the last third of the nineteenth century—forty years of meetings, dinners, salon receptions, and gatherings of every sort.[43]

The vehicle of this sociability is the word, not the private words of the printed page but the public words of conversation. Conversation in France goes beyond communication and beyond mere talk (*bavardage*), Taine was quick to point out, to a veritable analysis.[44] Mme de Staël devoted a whole chapter of *De l'Allemagne* (1810) to "l'esprit de la conversation," so great was her own longing (she was in exile) for the pleasures of Parisian conversation. In Paris words "are not simply the means of communication they are elsewhere but an instrument to enjoy which revives one's spirits." Music plays a similar role in Germany where the language inhibits, even precludes, conversation, at least what Mme de Staël meant by conversation. Because German makes the listener wait for the verb until the end of the sentence, interruption is all but impossible—and for Mme de Staël interruption was a great pleasure—what French conversation was all about. No reader can miss her impatience with the invariably polite Germans nor her yearning for the sharp brilliance of French salon repartee.

As Mme de Staël recognized, interruptions are vital to the spirit of French conversation because contention is as characteristic of it as sociability. French conversation speaks to a milieu that prized brilliance of performance over profundity of thought. People are important in French conversation, ideas in German. It was just this personalism and stress on individual presentation, on *paraître* over *être*, that led Rousseau to refuse the pension offered him by Louis XV. Too much like Alceste of *Le Misanthrope* with whom he identified so strongly, Jean-Jacques withdrew from what he knew would be an unequal contest—not of will but of wit. If we are to believe Mme de Staël's portrait of the Germans, Rousseau might have fared better there, at least on this account. The Germans, Mme de Staël asserted, are lazy raconteurs and diffident conversationalists because their listeners are infinitely patient. The French speaker is a different creature altogether, a "usurper who knows himself surrounded by jealous rivals" and knows too that brilliant performance alone will allow him to keep the floor.

Mme de Staël was not speaking specifically about literary conversations, though she noted that in contrast to England where polite society talked about politics, Parisian society talked about literature. Indeed in France, she thought, one hardly read a book except to be able to talk about it, whereas in Germany a book took the place of company. Others who looked particularly at literature and literary life in France confirmed Mme de Staël's portrait of an aggressive sociability exacerbated by the multitude of rival groups, cénacles, and salons: the esprit de corps of literary men in France complemented and countered an *esprit de combat*. If, as Bulwer-Lytton claimed, no men hang together like French writers, he was quick to add that "no men in England pull one another so much to pieces."[45]

Time, and the increasing divisiveness of French literary life, increased this spirit of contentiousness. De Bonald was convinced that if the literary world had been as divided in the seventeenth century as it was thereafter, half the great writers would have scorned the other half and France would never have had a truly national literature. Later in the nineteenth century Taine characterized Parisian literary life as a "daily duel." In some cases real duels took place when literary honor was felt to be impugned. When Anatole France proclaimed himself "odiously outraged" by a newspaper interview given by Leconte de Lisle, the poet refused to apologize and immediately challenged France to a dual. France declined the honor (Leconte de Lisle was seventy-three).[46] Like most duels the whole affair was slightly ridiculous and for that very reason revelatory of the fragile sensibilities in French literary culture.

As the century drew on and competition became more dramatic, criticism became more polemical than ever. It was altogether appropriate for Zola to entitle a collection of his essays *Mes haines* (My hates) and to reject any notion of patronage (for himself or for anyone else) with the argument that "force is everything in the battle of letters."[47] The curious mixture of sociability and contention characteristic of ancien régime salons acquired new intensity in nineteenth-century Paris, which doubled its population in the first half of the century and benefited from the elimination of Versailles as a competitor for cultural hegemony. The resulting "incessant rubbing" that Balzac pointed to in *La Fille aux yeux d'or* turned Paris into a hothouse, a forcing ground for talent where, as James Fenimore Cooper remarked, great men were so common that one did not even bother to turn around in the street to take a look. Such was the effect of the concentration of talent in both time and space, Goethe explained to the astonished Eckermann. Paris was the key to the excitement of French literary culture and the high achievement of its writers, "not the Paris of a dull, lackluster time, but the Paris of the nineteenth century, in which, during three generations, men like Molière, Voltaire, Diderot, and others have kept up such a current of intellect (*Geist*) as cannot be found twice in a single spot in the whole world." With its intense rivalries, its concentration of writers ambitious of success, and its constant exchange of ideas, Paris created a coherent literary life impossible to realize in Germany, where the dispersion of writers made literature a far more solitary pursuit.[48]

After a century of salons and cénacles, of duels and polemics, Paul Valéry summarized the literary consequences of this intense sociability and the antagonisms it fostered. In France, he observed, intellectual development hardly occurs in isolation, without reference to regnant taste, opinions, and fashion: "One must be either for or against." The tensions of such a contentious intellectuality have traced the course of French literary culture. "Almost every great work [of French literature]," noted Valéry, "is answered by another great work." French literary history seems less marked by individuals than by groups or by pairs in opposition. The critic Albert Thibaudet contended that its most characteristic figures are not individuals—Dante, Shakespeare, Cervantes, Goethe—but complementary and antagonistic pairs—Montaigne-Pascal, Pascal-Voltaire, Voltaire-Chateaubriand. Even Molière, the exception Thibaudet cites to prove his rule, does not dominate French literature as Shakespeare and Cervantes dominate English and Spanish literature. The mid-seventeenth century was not the Age of Corneille or Racine or Molière but the Age of Corneille *and* Racine *and* Molière and La Fontaine and Bossuet and more. It was, as Voltaire convinced his contemporaries, the Age of Louis XIV.[49]

The Age of Louis XIV, the Enlightenment, the romantic generation, the belle époque, l'entre-deux-guerres—collective terms tend to prevail in French literary history, one more sign that literature and literary culture are more than a question of books and their authors. As Renan noted in the mid-nineteenth century, books are only one manifestation of a cultivated mind. In France in particular they are part of a larger culture in which an elite public has always played an important role. The close ties between the two, between those who write and those who read, create one of the moving forces of the *esprit français*. Although most of the social and cultural integration of the ancien régime had been lost by the nineteenth century, an educated public remained to make literature then, as in the past, more than literary.[50] The ties of literature to this public also tell us why in France more than elsewhere literature and society seem to go together, why French literature is a privileged social document, why it should have been a Frenchman who so stridently proclaimed literature the expression of society.

The clearest appreciation of the special status of French literature we owe, however, to Matthew Arnold:

More than any modern literature, [French literature] has been in the most intimate correspondence with the social life and development of the nation producing it. Now it so happens that the great place of France in the world is due to her eminent gift for social life and development, and this gift French literature has accompanied, fashioned, perfected, and continues to reflect. This gives special interest to French literature, and an interest independent of the excellence of individual French writers, high as that often is.[51]

To trace Arnold's "intimate correspondence" back to the ancien régime is to realize the peculiar ways French writers have been defined by their literary culture. To trace it forward to the twentieth century is to confront a nation splintered by war and occupation, by intellectual as well as political turmoil—divisions that lead an intellectual elite to question the very foundations of French literary culture.

6

From Philosophe to Prophet

The "writer" in France is something other than a man who
writes and publishes.

Paul Valéry,
"Pensée et art français"

Valéry's observation bespeaks the uncommon sense of purpose inscribed in the traditions of French literary culture and
perpetuated by its institutions.[1] Most writers, in France as
elsewhere, are content to write and to publish. But French
literary culture enjoins the writer to do more, to impose literature on the worlds without. Their success in doing so, in
taking the writer beyond the world of writers and the concerns of aesthetics, is responsible for the exemplary status of
a Voltaire, a Victor Hugo, a Jean-Paul Sartre, "public" writers
who translated the private affairs of literature into the public
arena of culture and society. Public personae, virtually cultural phenomena in their own right, these writers speak
from, to, and for their times as others do not.

Other writers, "private" writers, take another tack entirely,
setting themselves and their work against French literary culture and its instrumental conception of literature. In refusing
the definitions and the values of French literary culture, private writers reject the fusion of the literary and the extra-
literary and insist on the inviolability of literature as an end
in itself. By accepting, even glorying in, the specialization
that literature became over the nineteenth century, private
writers strive to isolate the literary object and themselves
from extraneous pursuits and distractions.

For the paradigmatic private creators of French literature,
we can surely find no better examples than Flaubert and

Proust. Their commitment to art transformed aestheticism from a literary creed into a distinct mode of being. Both saw in art the only salvation possible for contemporary man, the one sacred object in a profane and intrusive world, an ideal admitting no competitors. Flaubert's correspondence is usually read less for the personal life it details than for the aesthetic problems it confronts: indeed, Flaubert's life *was* those problems. Participating in French literary life yet curiously apart from it, Flaubert retreated to his Normandy home so often that he came to be known as the hermit of Le Croisset. Proust's even more dramatic retirement to the legendary cork-lined room signaled a desperate strategy to exclude everything that might deflect his purpose from the one thing that mattered—*A la recherche du temps perdu*. That neither Flaubert nor Proust—no more than their predecessors or successors—succeeded in defining the separate nature of literature except by the example of their own work stresses the significance of their attempts to do so.

Because literature also communicates, retreat can never be absolute. Compromise is unavoidable. Both men published their work, Proust using his own fortune to do so, and Proust quite happily accepted the Prix Goncourt in 1919 for *A l'ombre des jeunes filles en fleurs* in spite of the acrimony involved and accusations made. Compromise takes many forms. Flaubert had to acknowledge that the artist who wanted to think like a god had to live prosaically like a bourgeois, which he and Proust most emphatically did. Inevitably, Flaubert and Proust exhibit the profound influence of the very culture they were fleeing—one need consider only the acute sense of language each cultivated to comprehend the extent to which these private creators were marked by the concerns and values of French literary culture. But private they remained. The inevitable concessions do not negate the essential definition of the private author as an "internal émigré" who dissents from the sense as from the sensibility of French literary culture and who rejects the model of the public writer in whom that culture is most fully realized. In almost every respect French literary culture works against the private creator who, turning inward to focus literature ever more intensely upon itself, must rely on inner resources and a personal sense of art and the aesthetic. By contrast, the public writer, inclined to prize breadth of scope over intensity of focus, finds in that same literary culture reinforcement for personal commitment.

As the public writer projects literary culture, so too he affects that culture. His role in the continuing process of adaptation to social change and its incorporation into literary culture defines the exemplary writer as both agent and recorder of change. Every generation elects literary spokesmen for just this purpose. In perpetuating tradition these figures reinforce the continuity of French literary culture even as they modify that tradition and that culture. Sensitivity to cultural tradition coupled with receptivity to social change makes French literary culture an especially valuable historical barometer and makes its exemplary figures exceptional vehicles for studying the ways in which a society calls upon its past to interpret the present. In the dialectic of cultural tradition and social change over the past three centuries in France the exemplary writer has been a key figure. Voltaire the philosophe, Victor Hugo the prophet, and Jean-Paul Sartre the intellectual were public writers by virtue of their decision to act in and on society through the written word. They became exemplary figures because their own and subsequent times recognized that testimony and acknowledged its relevance.

I

Jean-Jacques writes only to write, and I write to act.
Voltaire, letter, 15 April 1767

The public writer emerges in the eighteenth century, a creature of the social, political, and intellectual ferment that was the Enlightenment.[2] The public writer does not simply bear witness to his times—every writer does as much; he consciously confronts his times and contests his society. By an appeal to individual judgment over institutional authority the public writer makes a case before a public of peers. The first instance in French literary history of such a radical redefinition of literature and the writer is Pascal's *Provinciales* (1656), which translated the arcana of a convoluted theological dispute into terms comprehensible to a lay public of *honnêtes gens*. But *Les Provinciales* stands apart, in Pascal's career and in the seventeenth century. Pascal's fundamental pessimism could not sustain the intervention in social affairs that characterizes the public writer, and the century of Louis XIV offered no institutional platform from which the writer could speak and be heard. But the eighteenth century encouraged an independence of thought and action that made the public writer possible.

The representative figure of the Enlightenment was the philosophe, and the representative philosophe was certainly Voltaire—a man of ideas rather than theories, an incredibly prolific writer who ranged over the entire spectrum of literature and beyond, making every genre his own. With an energy that matched his interests and a longevity—he died in 1778 at the age of eighty-four—that allowed him to draw on both to good effect, Voltaire's work and career fixed the model of the public writer for generations, a model that was perhaps his most important legacy to the nineteenth century. As the literary culture that developed over the nineteenth century incorporated many elements of the aristocratic culture of the ancien régime, so also the public writer who came to incarnate that literary culture descended directly from Voltaire.

Although in some sense every age is transitional, caught between the legacy of the past and the agenda of the future, the Enlightenment is a special case. It clearly points to modern times, but it does so from an age generally consigned to the distant past. The equilibrium Voltaire maintained between the contending forces of old and new made him the exemplary personage of the Enlightenment, the philosophe par excellence. Traditional enough to reach his contemporaries and be acclaimed by them yet modern enough to undermine their assumptions and reach beyond, Voltaire reflected the concerns of his public even as he created new images and definitions of self and society.

The twentieth-century reader is likely to find Voltaire's allegiance to the past especially striking. The works of his own that he esteemed most—the plays and the poetry—seem stilted to us, lifeless imitations of seventeenth-century classical models. But, the pejorative adjectives excepted, imitations are precisely what Voltaire expected of himself and his contemporaries—continuations of a glorious tradition, realizations of formulas both tried and true. Voltaire's taste, like that of his public, was firmly grounded in the principles and practice of the seventeenth century and, by extension, in the still more traditional precepts of the ancient classics. *Le Siècle de Louis XIV* (1751), Voltaire's most important historical work, warned his contemporaries just how difficult it would be to surpass the masterpieces of the previous age. "Nature," he observed, "seems to be resting."³ Like Voltaire, the eighteenth-century writer could do no better than to emulate.

New aesthetic impulses would come from others, from Diderot and his *drame bourgeois*, from Rousseau and his *Confessions*. The Voltaire who wrote *Le Temple du goût* and who showed such distress at Shakespeare's evident lack of good taste sought no reordering of the aesthetic hierarchy. No French writer, least of all Voltaire, could condone Shakespeare's casual coupling of the sublime and the grotesque. Gravediggers and a prince did not belong in the same play, much less the same scene: *Hamlet* must be censored. Characteristically, the most popular eighteenth-century translation of Shakespeare, by an epigone of Voltaire, altogether eliminated this and other offensive incongruities. Jean-François Ducis's *Hamlet* (1769) and *Roméo et Juliette* (1775) did away with the gravediggers and Friar Laurence, replaced the ghost of Hamlet's father with an antique funerary urn, moved duels and deaths off stage, and generally adapted Shakespeare to classical unities and *bienséances*.⁴ Abbé Prévost's translations of Richardson made similar accommodations to French taste.

Yet Voltaire did as much as anyone to subvert that aesthetic hierarchy. Traditional models did not apply to the *conte philosophique*: there were none. For all its fidelity to the glories of the past, *Le Siècle de Louis XIV* proclaimed a new kind of history, one that situated the conventional parade of kings and wars in the larger context of civilization. What came to be known as cultural history commenced with Voltaire's *Histoire de Charles XII* of 1731 and the *Siècle de Louis XIV* twenty years later. Nor were Voltaire's aesthetic notions as rigid as might appear on first reading. The depreciation of Shakespeare's "barbarisms" was the opinion of Voltaire's century, the appreciation of Shakespeare's beauties very much his own. Moreover, Voltaire made his *Lettres philosophiques* (1734, also known as *Les Lettres anglaises*) into a veritable course in English literature and a lesson in comparative cultural analysis. English literature is not really worse; it is different because English culture has its own distinctive values and perspectives and conventions. English poetry would not do for France. Like the English garden, the English *génie* rejects the constraints on which French genius and French gardens thrive. Transplantation will not work. The historian's discernment gave the writer's preferences an appropriate explanatory cultural context.[5]

Voltaire's sense of order and respect for tradition were not solely aesthetic in nature, for they were as basic to the man and the philosophe as to the writer and the critic. Not by chance did Voltaire name the golden age of French letters for its ruler rather than for any of the writers who so gloriously illustrated that reign. Great as these men were, their greatness served the monarch by ensuring his still greater glory. Louis XIV reciprocated by providing a context in which the arts could flourish. Voltaire's own career illustrates the continued relevance of traditional patterns of advancement through patronage and frequentation of the great. No revolutionary, Voltaire served as royal historiographer and gentleman of the chamber for Louis XV and was the honored guest of Frederick the Great. Voltaire was the quintessential bourgeois parvenu, intent on moving up the social ladder, not tearing it down.

Always, however, Voltaire's example is more nuanced than a first reading suggests. Temperamentally and philosophi-

cally unsympathetic to any revolution, Voltaire's constant re-
ferral to and praise of the English system of government implied support for the social change that he could not advocate
outright, as did his championing of justice and the campaigns
to right such social wrongs as the condemnation of Jean Calas
for heresy.[6] The career makes an even stronger case for a "radical" Voltaire. Like any bourgeois accepted into aristocratic
social circles, Voltaire weakened the social barriers he had
transgressed much as *Candide* and *Le Siècle de Louis XIV* undermined established aesthetic categories. Voltaire's example
was still more insidious because he broke even those rules by
which other bourgeois, and notably other bourgeois writers,
abided. He found no need, as Beaumarchais did, to buy his
way into the nobility. Voltaire went much further, in effect
decreeing his own aristocracy, the parallel aristocracy of talent
to which so many nineteenth-century artists would lay claim.
Having been banished from the court of France and having
banished himself from the court of Prussia, Voltaire set up
his own court at Les Délices outside Geneva and subsequently at Ferney, just across the border in France. There he
received the emissaries of intellectual Europe like the prince
that he had in fact become. Indeed, his triumphant return to
Paris in the last year of his life was worthy of royalty.

A great space, social and political and chronological, separates the M. de Voltaire of 1778, patriarch of Ferney and philosophe triumphant, from the François-Marie Arouet of a half
century earlier, who suffered assault, imprisonment, and exile at the whim of the great who chose to take offense at his
writings.[7] No wonder he complained about the esteem accorded writers in the early eighteenth-century England that
he came to know during his exile. More clearly than any of
his contemporaries, Voltaire's career charted the emergence
of a new kind of writer along with a new assessment of
literature and its possibilities. The eighteenth-century
philosophe already exhibited the acute consciousness of superiority characteristic of the nineteenth-century writer, for
Voltaire redefined the relationship of the writer to society by
equating the writer's prestige with that traditionally accorded

A bust of Voltaire was "crowned" during the performance of his play *Irène* at the Comédie-Française on 30 March 1778. The writer himself had been acclaimed in person at the premiere on his first visit to Paris after thirty years of exile. Voltaire's "apotheosis" set an example that would be followed a century later, in 1881, in elaborate celebrations of Victor Hugo's own ascendancy. (Photograph courtesy of the Bibliothèque Nationale)

literature. Although the ancien régime always acknowledged literature as such, Voltaire's personal ascendancy did much to force the recognition of the man of letters. The writer spoke with new authority.

Recognition, leading as it did toward cultural authority, redefined the bond between the writer and his audience. From deferential courtier the writer metamorphosed into the assertive spokesman of French society, who pressed claims for equality and superiority. Voltaire was no romantic seer imbued with the mission of saving humanity, nor was he the prophetic Rousseau preaching to his contemporaries. But neither was he the Molière of the century of Louis XIV whose golden rule was to please his public of *honnêtes gens*. Voltaire's tone was different because he habitually spoke from a sense of his own superiority and a consciousness of the writer's significance. Typically, he rebuked Addison for edulcorating one of his plays to cater to the expectations of his audience.[8]

Voltaire saw that the role of educator particularly suited the writer. The Enlightenment made literature the most general medium through which knowledge could be diffused. Literature comprehended vast territories of science and included erudition of all sorts; it was an intellectual endeavor that subsumed and facilitated every other. The literature of the eighteenth century sometimes gives the twentieth-century reader the impression that the philosophes, and Voltaire in particular, sought to be encyclopedias unto themselves. With his knowledge of literature—French, classical, Italian, and English—and of philosophy, history, theology, mathematics, and science, Voltaire felt compelled and fully authorized to speak on every front. He even went so far as to replicate some of Newton's experiments, and as he explained Shakespeare, so he presented Newton both in his general disquisition on English society and culture and, subsequently and in greater detail, in the *Eléments de la philosophie de Newton* (1738).

By virtue of these encyclopedic pretensions the writer could claim the role of educator as peculiarly his. The role was not new: literature had never abjured the Horatian dictum of *utile et dulce*. But to this general utility traditionally assigned to literature the Enlightenment added the urgency of explicit social concerns. The writer transformed into a social critic had new responsibilities. The *esprit critique* became a veritable *esprit de combat* in the hands of Voltaire, who in his later years took up one cause after another. Polemics constituted a way of life, and of writing. In virtually all of his nondramatic prose Voltaire took on one enemy after another, religious, philosophical, literary. Because he saw himself in an embattled minority, criticism became for him an integral function of life as well as of literature.

"Every *honnête homme* should try to be a philosophe—without bragging about it." Abiding by his own prescription, Voltaire the philosophe remained very much Voltaire the *honnête homme*, which meant that his learning never degenerated into pedantry, nor his polemics into vituperation. Voltaire escaped these extremes through an acute aesthetic sensibility—what the ancien régime meant by "taste"—that informed everything he wrote. From the beginning taste was a constant preoccupation, offering Voltaire a principle of literary conduct much as reason provided a philosophic foundation. The coherence implicit in these comprehensive notions of taste and reason enabled Voltaire to mold everything he touched into a distinctly Voltairean whole. The taste and reason that presided over Voltaire's work and made literature the characteristic vehicle of the Enlightenment reinforced, as it explained, the unique relation of literature to language. Was not French the language of reason and civilization? What better vehicle for the defense of reason than the language whose very structure embodied those principles to be defended? What better medium for educating men to style and beauty than the language defined by its elegant precision?[9]

For a half century and more, Voltaire steadfastly defended reason and taste. His plays and poetry, his essays and tales, his histories and criticism, his voluminous correspondence—all show the philosophe in action. In *L'Ingénu* (1767), written late in his career, Voltaire shows the philosophe in the making. Around the protagonist of this tale coalesce the themes and tensions that run through all of Voltaire's work. The model for the philosophe Voltaire presents in this work, however, sets *L'Ingénu* apart as a highly stylized bildungsroman of the public writer Voltaire had become.[10]

L'Ingénu belongs most obviously to the tradition of social satire from an outsider to the society scrutinized. In this case, the stranger is a Huron Indian who lands on the shores of Brittany one day in 1689. L'Ingénu, like Candide, is a *naïf*, innocent in the ways of the world he is made to encounter. But l'Ingénu is no Candide. Though untutored in the mores and manners of civilized society, he is strong-minded and strong-willed, even aggressive in pressing his opinions and desires. His innate reason and good taste expose the inconsistencies, the incongruities, and eventually the corruption rampant in the century of Louis XIV. The clear implications for the century of Louis XV led the ever-prudent Voltaire to move the setting back a century and publish the tale anonymously in Geneva with a Dutch imprint, all the while denying authorship; even so, the work was banned in France.

The satire begins gently. The Bretons who adopt the foundling are good-hearted and scarcely less naive and ignorant than he. L'Ingénu's baptism affords Voltaire yet another opportunity to point out with great glee the many discrepancies between biblical injunctions and current Christian practice. A literal reader of the Holy Word, l'Ingénu insists on circumcision and a river baptism. But when l'Ingénu's Breton fiancée is forced into a convent ("a sort of prison where girls were held captive, horrible thing") and l'Ingénu himself thrown into the Bastille, the satire turns acerbic. The touch remains light—Voltaire could not write with a heavy hand—but the aim is sure as Voltaire takes on his old enemies, one after another, the Church, the Jesuits, the Jansenists, to denounce the inanity of theological disputes, the abuse of power, the corruption of society. Only the good offices of Mlle de St.-Yves, his pretty fiancée, effect l'Ingénu's release from prison, and she, full of remorse, dies of shame.

The society that forces dishonor upon Mlle de St.-Yves as a price for her "every generous action," "sells misfortune and happiness," and lets l'Ingénu languish in prison is not only unjust but also blind to its own best interest. Dead or in prison, the individual can be of no use to society, and use is one of the watchwords of *L'Ingénu*. Voltaire's philosophe makes himself of use, and almost all of Voltaire's criticisms are related in one way or another to derogation from this standard of utility. Superstition, theological dogma, and metaphysical doctrine are profoundly useless because they obscure reality and thereby hinder social progress. Voltaire holds no brief for the disputes of Pangloss and Martin in *Candide* and denounces even more emphatically the injustice, the suffering, and the disservice to society caused by intolerance upheld by the power of social institutions. The Huguenots fleeing France after the revocation of the Edict of Nantes deprive the king of "useful subjects" and make him enemies through their service in foreign armies. L'Ingénu himself has served France well in repulsing an English attack on the Breton coast and deserves better than the Bastille: "I want to be useful: give me a job and rewards." Mlle de St.-Yves argues for l'Ingénu's freedom on the basis of his past and future services to the Crown.[11] That this society refuses these services is perhaps Voltaire's most devastating criticism.

L'Ingénu rapidly outdistances the noble savage whose sallies are so amusing because he always does what he wants and says what he thinks. "He listens only to nature," exclaims his astonished cell mate. Yet the voice of nature will not suffice. Voltaire is no simpleminded advocate of natural law, and l'Ingénu early on, precisely because he is reasonable, accepts positive, or man-made, law as necessary in a complex, populous society. Because reason, though a natural faculty, can "progress," l'Ingénu must be educated. Nature must be "perfected." The year-long incarceration in the company of a learned Jansenist priest allows Voltaire to give his incipient philosophe the proper instruction: mathematics, physics, astronomy, philosophy, ancient and modern history, classical and contemporary literature. Free of the prejudices instilled by a perverted education, l'Ingénu "sees things as they are" and makes astounding progress in all the sciences and especially in the most important of all, the science of man. By the time he quits prison, "l'Ingénu is no longer an ingénu." "He is no longer the same man—his behavior, his tone, his ideas, his mind—everything is changed." Our hero himself acknowledges that although he was once no more than a "savage," he has been virtually metamorphosed "from a brute into a man," and as Europe is superior to America by virtue of the knowledge and arts that endow society with a past and a future as well as a present, so too this educated man is superior to the *naïf*. Nature and civilization join forces to make l'Ingénu an "intrepid philosophe."[12]

"Intrepid philosophe"—what better epithet for Voltaire

himself? This identification gives *L'Ingénu* a positive cast lacking in the better-known *Candide*. The few years that separate *Candide* (1759) and *L'Ingénu* (1767) marked Voltaire's transformation from social critic to activist philosophe. During these years Voltaire took up one cause after another, putting his prestige on the line and his talent to the service of victims of religious fanaticism and political injustice. The most famous of these cases involved Jean Calas, a Protestant executed as a heretic and parricide. Voltaire's campaign of letters and publicity succeeded in clearing Calas's name and reinstating his family's civil rights.[13] *L'Ingénu* registers these and similar successes. The greater work, *Candide* speaks to the human condition. The more positive work, *L'Ingénu* speaks to the conditions of the individual in society. The tempered optimism of *L'Ingénu*—Voltaire proposes the motto "Misfortune is good for something"—corrects the tempered pessimism of *Candide*—"All well and good, but we must cultivate our garden." Although much can be said on the subject of Candide's garden, it is certainly neither the "earthly paradise" from which Candide is expelled at the beginning of the tale nor Eldorado, which he quits of his own accord. *Candide* leaves the reader with an overwhelming sense of human limitations in an incomprehensible and capricious universe. *L'Ingénu* ends with an "intrepid philosophe" and a sure sense of what can be accomplished within these limitations. Such was the credo of the philosophe and the faith of the public writer.

II

A writer ought to look at himself as a teacher of men.
De Bonald, quoted by
Balzac in avant-propos
to the *Comédie humaine*

The comprehensive reach of literature joined to the will to make literature relevant to every inquiry constituted Voltaire's legacy, which the nineteenth century alternately accepted and rejected, magnified and countered. By defining the writer as philosophe and the philosophe as *littérateur,* Voltaire set a pattern for the public writer to emulate and his private counterpart to oppose. By pitting the heirs of Voltaire against those of Rousseau, French literary culture simultaneously pulled in one direction—toward the public writer—and pushed in another—toward the private artist.

The same self-consciousness that turned the private writer inward and motivated a withdrawal into self and art pointed the public writer outward in a search for new fields of literary purpose. The expansion of the market and the multiplication of literary institutions stimulated literary activities as never before and situated the writer within an increasingly complex network of institutional and intellectual relations. By giving an aesthetic definition to an existential rejection of society—represented most forcefully by Rousseau—the emergent literary culture of the nineteenth century altered the very meaning of dissent. The aestheticisms of mid-century set apart the private writer, who rejected the public writer's definitions of the situation and of literature. Flaubert's unfinished novel *Bouvard et Pécuchet* makes what is probably the ultimate argument against the public writer, against the pretentions to encyclopedic knowledge and to anything resembling effective action in the world. This devastating critique of the nineteenth century takes its two hopelessly mediocre, though curiously sympathetic, protagonists from agronomy to politics, from art to science, in a gradual exposure of intellectual and cultural impotence. The novel indicts the entire century and the illusions it fostered.

Bouvard et Pécuchet demonstrates that aesthetic opposition to bourgeois society signaled more than a general disaffection from prevailing literary mores. Antagonism often focused on and was directed against the public writer—but one significantly different from his eighteenth-century predecessor. The nineteenth century transformed literary relations in two ways, by giving intellectual support to the aesthetic dissent of the private writer and by providing the public writer with an institutional platform. The philosophe of the ancien régime became the prophet of the nineteenth century, who in turn prefigured the literary intellectual of the twentieth century.

As writers adapted to the changing literary context, the model of the public writer bequeathed by Voltaire began to appear inadequate even to those who shared Voltairean ambitions and conceptions of literature. The century was new, and according to myth the French Revolution had wiped the slate clean. Should not the writer too have license to start anew? To make a new literature? Voltaire's obeisance to the past, his evident allegiance to the century of Louis XIV, his sense of having come too late, at the end of a tradition, were themselves elements of a perspective and a rhetoric that no longer obtained. The nineteenth-century writer made new and more pressing claims. He spoke from an assurance that was also new, from a confidence of horizons to widen, possibilities to exploit. Where Voltaire's confidence and prestige had been singular because personal, that is, based on his own achievements and experience, the nineteenth-century writer's certainty was more collective, based on his status as a writer and his connections to an ever-widening network of literary institutions.

Until Victor Hugo at mid-century and after, no literary figure commanded the exemplary status that had been Voltaire's. Despite the greater and more numerous opportunities in literature and in politics, no single individual imposed the public writer and his values with the same force as the philosophe. Of the writers prominent early in the nineteenth century Chateaubriand came the closest. (After all, the adolescent Victor Hugo vowed to be Chateaubriand or nothing!) Born in 1768, François-René de Chateaubriand was a child of the eighteenth century in reaction against it. Although he shared the philosophes' conception of literature as a means to a public social end, he chose a contrary aim. Chateaubriand the believer intended his writing to serve the Church rather than to combat it; Chateaubriand the aristocrat desired to stabilize the monarchy instead of criticizing it. A second difference was Chateaubriand's political career: member of the Chambre des Pairs, twice minister and twice ambassador,

Chateaubriand played a minor but notable role in the political institutions of the Restoration.

Finally, however, the political career ill served the public writer. As an actor in the political system, Chateaubriand, like Lamartine subsequently, contradicted Voltaire's image of the public writer opposed to the established regime. Chateaubriand remained an opponent within the framework set by political parties; defeated, he withdrew without contesting the rules of the game. The younger Chateaubriand, it is true—significantly during the segment of his career singled out for literary pursuits—had crossed Napoleon and had made much of his opposition to the ruler he saw turning into a tyrant. But Chateaubriand's grievances, like those of Mme de Staël, were finally too personal to rally an important public. His anti-Napoleonic pamphlet, *De Buonaparte et des Bourbons* (1814), came late—just before Napoleon's first fall from power—and was too obviously self-serving to have the resonance of Voltaire's disinterested campaigns for justice.

Like other aristocrats, Chateaubriand considered politics both the privilege and the duty of his social station. Literature was a domain somewhat apart. The *Mémoires d'outre-tombe* draw a clear distinction between his three careers, as traveler, as writer, as statesman.[14] He prized them equally, or so he claimed, yet in his own mind they did not fuse so much as they succeeded one another. Traveler during the Revolution, writer during the Empire, and statesman during the Restoration, Chateaubriand associated each career with a political regime. Politics did not extend his literary interests; it followed them. Certainly literary repute did not hurt Chateaubriand's political fortunes. On the contrary, his literary works were the original basis of his celebrity. But they did not supply the ideological vehicle they had provided for Voltaire.

The public writer of the nineteenth century was not a politician enmeshed in institutions and legislation but a prophet imbued with the mission of saving society through literature. The social and intellectual dislocations of the French Revolution had much to do with both this arrogation of leadership to the writer and the penchant for social planning that characterized an entire era. Social romanticism was the literary manifestation of an impulse that prompted utopian thinkers like Saint-Simon and Pierre Leroux, as well as the founder of sociology, Auguste Comte.[15] It reinforced the pride instilled by aestheticism and by the writer's conception of his own superiority. Unlike aestheticism, social romanticism enjoined the writer to enter the world rather than to withdraw from it. As a consequence, nineteenth-century public writers were thinkers intent on reconceptualizing social life and prophets committed to social change.

Balzac offers one of the most striking examples of these literary ambitions, an example all the more striking for his failure to achieve the status he coveted. Balzac certainly made grandiose claims. He compared himself to the great thinkers and statesmen of modern times, to Napoleon, to Cuvier, and to O'Connell, the Irish political leader, and vowed to complete with the pen the work Napoleon had begun with the sword: the bringing into being of a modern world.[16] The celebrated expression of de Bonald—that literature is the expression of society as language is the expression of man—is the most appropriate motto for his own work. The *Comédie humaine* is very much the expression of Balzac's society, the society of postrevolutionary France, a fictive society so real and so modern that Marx and Engels took it as a textbook of sorts.[17]

Balzac's recourse to science to legitimate the *Comédie humaine* was also resolutely modern. Inspired by the work of Geoffroy Saint-Hilaire, Balzac used the parallel between zoological and social species to supply a basic structure and coherence. "Archaeologist" of social structure and "nomenclator" of the professions, Balzac set himself the goal of popularizing the "astonishing facts" of modern science.[18] Perhaps the most conspicuously modern gesture of all was his choice of the novel as the genre on which to build his career. Other prominent men of letters wrote novels—Chateaubriand, Lamartine, Hugo, Vigny—but none before Balzac staked their claims so single-mindedly on this parvenu genre. Until the 1830s the novel was the poor relation in the literary pantheon, all too frequently contemned for insignificance or immorality or both. In opting for the novel Balzac assumed the task of redefining the literary hierarchy and promoting a genre as well as his own works. This enthusiastic embrace of a modern literature only makes Balzac's fundamental conservatism all the more striking. No writer was more solidly anchored in tradition, political, literary, intellectual, social. Though patronage no longer represented an alternative for the writer in the nineteenth century, Balzac sometimes acted as if it did. Like his predecessors during the ancien régime, Balzac courted the great, submitting one novel to the Académie française for a prize (he lost) and presenting himself twice as a candidate to the Académie itself.[19]

As a scientist, as a historian, Balzac studied society; as a writer of "decided moral and political convictions," he prescribed for its ills. Beyond the analyst of society lay the intellectual committed to social change. For both Balzac and Voltaire, sheer range of knowledge inspired the writer to be a leader of humanity, a "teacher of men" whose "absolute devotion to principle" made him "equal, perhaps superior to, the statesman." As he put it himself, "Machiavelli, Hobbes, Bossuet, Leibniz, Kant, Montesquieu are the knowledge that statesmen apply."[20] To Voltaire's image of the public writer the nineteenth century added the urgency of political commitment. Balzac had a political program in mind as Voltaire did not: the *Comédie humaine,* he proclaimed, would illustrate "the great principles of order, politics, and morality," and he would rely specifically on the "twin principles," the "eternal Truths of Religion and Monarchy." He could do better than the historian, Balzac declared, because he was freer to present the "better world," the "ideal" that the novel should be. *Le Médecin de campagne* and *Le Curé de village* turned Balzac's principles to the task of social engineering. Both novels, and on a smaller scale *Le Lys dans la vallée,* are Balzacian utopias, societies organized around the principles he preached with such fervor.[21] The consequent disjuncture between the ultraconservative politics of the man and the radical implications of his work has struck and disconcerted readers ever since, especially Marxists (though Victor Hugo was one of the first to see Balzac as a "revolutionary writer" whether he willed it or not, whether he knew it or not).[22] However else it may be explained, this disparity manifests the conflict between past and present, between tradition and modernity—a conflict central to the public writer who must articulate the ambiguities and ambivalences of an era.

That Balzac failed to achieve the status he so earnestly sought is clear. He saw himself as a public writer, yet he never played the public role that had been Voltaire's in the eighteenth century and that would be Hugo's later in the nineteenth century. The question is why. Political conservatism is too easy an answer. One important reason was, simply, time. Balzac died at fifty-one, too young to have achieved the solidly established, uncontested reputation from which to launch a public persona. He was celebrated during his lifetime (notorious might be a better word), but his "glory" remained problematic for some time.[23]

A second consideration lies in the nature of Balzac's creativity. Although temperament and conviction fitted Balzac to the role of public writer, his obsession with his own work hindered the translation from literary to extra-literary. The famous anecdotes are revealing—Balzac brushing aside a friend's troubles to concentrate on the really important problems posed by the marriage of Eugénie Grandet, Balzac on his deathbed calling for Bianchon, the ubiquitous doctor of the *Comédie humaine*. It was not an idle boast that he carried an entire society around in his head. *La Comédie humaine* was, as Balzac proclaimed it, a society with "its own geography, its genealogy and its families, its places and things, its persons and its facts; its coat of arms, its nobles and bourgeois, its artisans and peasants, politicians and dandies, its army, in a word, its world!"[24] The real world must have paled in comparison. In the end Balzac put the philosophe into the novel as author, as narrator. The public personage envisaged by Balzac took his rightful place within the *Comédie humaine*, not without.

III

To love is to act.
Victor Hugo's
last words

Contemporary intellectual currents incited the writer in early nineteenth-century France to just the action in the world Voltaire had advocated to convey literature beyond the aesthetic. The rapidly expanding literary market continued to multiply opportunities as well as pressures—in the more effective means of communication it put at the writer's disposal, in the larger audience it captured, and in the more diverse intellectual concerns it accommodated. But neither pressure nor opportunity nor concern made the public writer what he was. What he was, and what Chateaubriand, Balzac, and others lacked, becomes clearer when these writers are set against the nineteenth-century writer who magnified the Voltairean model and redefined the public writer as prophet. Where others had failed to fuse poetics and politics, Victor Hugo succeeded. By making the literary and the political a function each of the other, Hugo brought the philosophe into the nineteenth century, clothed him in modern vestments, put him in a modern pulpit, and gave him a modern congregation. Hugo was metamorphosed into the symbol of France—the France of the Third Republic, tied to a revolutionary past purged of its terrors. Hugo's extraordinary popularity and prestige made him the ideal symbol of an age that reached to new constituencies even as it perpetuated traditional patterns and assumptions.

Hugo realized the hopes and aspirations for commitment in and through art because he was able to translate literary repute into political presence. The poet, dramatist, and novelist became Victor Hugo the prophet. His literary reputation, to begin with, was immense. By the 1840s Hugo had been at the center of French literary life for a quarter of a century. He had been a topic of conversation in literary circles as early as 1817 when the Académie française bestowed a "Mention" on the precocious fifteen-year-old poet whom Chateaubriand is supposed to have called "the sublime child." No other writer was so closely identified in the public mind with the heroic (and sometimes mock-heroic) enterprise of romanticism, for it was Hugo who led the romantic brigades into battle and brought them forth victorious. Election to the Académie française in 1841—the first of his generation—and a peerage in 1845 ratified the victory and made it official.

What gave Hugo such authority? How could he speak for an entire literary generation, indeed almost for literature itself? The sheer scope of Hugo's literary production offers a partial answer. In an age that was turning literature into a specialized discourse, Hugo adamantly refused intellectual borders and literary boundaries. Faced with the increasing divisions of literary labor, he ranged ever more widely, excluding nothing from his purview. To be sure, other writers ventured beyond a single genre, but Hugo's epic imagination and prodigious mastery of language took him into every literary domain: he was a poet in the traditional vatic sense of the term.

Whatever Hugo touched he refashioned in the image of his own poetics. By the 1840s he had a literary reputation as a successful revolutionary, leader of the insurgents who had stormed and toppled the citadel of neoclassicism. Lamartine's *Méditations poétiques* (1820) signaled literary transformations to come, but Hugo's preface to his (unperformed) play *Cromwell* (1827) sounded the battle cry, and the turbulent premiere of his *Hernani* in 1830 secured the triumph of this avant-garde. The audacity of the attack was all the greater because unlike Balzac, who sought to create a new literature through a "new" genre, Hugo confronted the ancien régime directly in its most traditional and prestigious, hence most fervently defended, genres: poetry and the drama. Like every other revolution, romanticism created its own myths. Hugo was at the center of both myth and reality, the stuff of which legends are made.

Hugo figured so prominently in the legends of romanticism because he was in the thick of every battle, and battle is

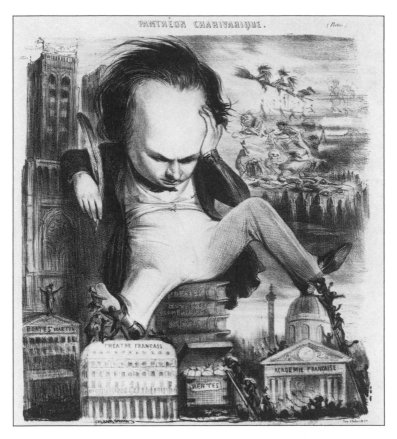

The writer as colossal figure is a favorite French theme. As the title indicates, *Le Charivari*, the journal in which this caricature by Benjamin Roubaud appeared in 1841, had already put Victor Hugo in its pantheon. Hugo (always recognizable by his "forehead of genius"), pen in hand and astride Paris, perches on a tall pile of his own books. One elbow rests on the cathedral of Notre Dame, the setting for his novel *Notre-Dame de Paris* in 1831, one foot on the Théâtre Français where *Hernani* triumphed in 1830, and the other on the Académie française, which Hugo entered in 1841. The bags of money being carried up the ladder and deposited in the coffer marked *Rentes* make it clear that this genius did not inhabit a garret! (Photograph courtesy of the Musées de la Ville de Paris, SPADEM © 1986)

certainly the appropriate term for the struggles. The prefaces written between 1827 and 1831 are rife with metaphors and images of combat, of oppression, and of (Hugolian) liberation. Hugo advocated "taking a hammer to theories, poetics, and systems" and "tearing away the old plaster that masks the face of art." In these heady days of freedom "no more rules, no more models" constrain the creator. Art must be free: "It has nothing to do with borders, handcuffs, or gags" but lets you loose in "the vast garden of poetry where there is no forbidden fruit." The jumble of metaphors betrays the urgency of change, the imperative need to break fractiously with the past and to define literature in resolutely modern terms. The old society had been cast off; what about the old literature? Hugo called for a new one. As "a new society, with a new people" nineteenth-century France required, and deserved, a new literature.[25]

Like the new society that it expresses and sustains, this new modern literature is—must be—free. "Liberty in art, liberty in society," should be the goal of every writer, the banner that rallies youth and age alike, the guiding principle of the century that justifies Hugo's striking formulation of romanticism as "liberalism in literature." Hugo was prepared for the July Revolution that came only a few months after this ringing preface to *Hernani* and the triumph of the play itself. July 1830, he predicted soon thereafter, would prove a date no less important for literature than for politics.[26]

Revolutions need revolutionaries, and Hugo enthusiastically cast himself in the role. Unlike Voltaire, he proclaimed, indeed trumpeted, his revolutionary intentions, accepting every accusation. His poetics were a poetics of revolution that reached into the very heart of language. His poem "Réponse à un acte d'accusation" (1854) expressly identified Hugo's transformation of French literary language with the French Revolution. It was Hugo who "blew a revolutionary wind on the dowager Académie and its squadrons of rigid alexandrine verse"; it was Hugo again who put a revolutionary's red cap on the old dictionary, declared war on rhetoric ("besieged and destroyed the Bastille of rhyme"), and invoked the Marseillaise ("To arms, prose, and verse!").[27]

From the beginning, from the *Odes royalistes* of 1819 and *Le Conservateur littéraire*, the journal started with his brother in the same year, Hugo's work shows an unmistakable sense of the broad political and social context of literature and literary activity. This orientation became progressively more marked and Hugo's pronouncements increasingly more emphatic during the 1820s. The preface to *Cromwell* presents a full-blown (though scarcely original) sociological explanation of the parallel development of literature and society. But as Hugo came to realize in the next few years, literature is more than a social product; it is also a social act, destined to impress the very society of which it is so obviously an expression. The writer's social mission follows logically from, and is indeed an extension of, his literary interests. After justifying his new aesthetic by an appeal to a postrevolutionary society in need of a postrevolutionary literature, Hugo turns the tables by making that same literature a vehicle of further social progress. Even in his supposed adherence to the aestheticism of art for art's sake, Hugo told Baudelaire many years later, he had always believed in art for the sake of progress, and the prefaces bear out the contention.[28] Art must always "correspond to the needs of society," and the writer must reject the temptations and consolations of nature in favor of the active life, the commitment required in this century where "each one of us owes himself to every one."[29] Literature, in short, must be turned to account to produce a new society even as society had been invoked to create a new literature.

The writer's task is to prepare the future—a better future. Visionary utopian, he renders the future vividly present; "sacred dreamer," he "illuminates eternal truth."[30] Upon the writer devolves the duty of leadership. The theater in particular represents the privileged vehicle through which the writer could "take charge of souls." A source of "counsel and of order," the theater has a mission that is at once "national, social, human."[31] The drama gains its especial importance from its ability to reach the masses and to expose the illiterate to the elevated lessons of literature. No longer restricted to the *honnêtes gens* whom Voltaire could address as equals, the writer's audience henceforth includes *la foule, le peuple,* all those ignored and disdained by earlier writers, whom the poet undertakes to shepherd, to guide, to teach.[32] Democratization of the audience—a fact of nineteenth-century literary life—became for Hugo an article of faith. He addressed the masses and he wrote about them as well: in the most celebrated of his novels, *Les Misérables* (1862, but began in the 1840s); in *Quatrevingt-Treize* (1874); and as early as *Le Dernier Jour d'un condamné* (1829), *Claude Gueux* (1834), and his play *Ruy Blas* (1838).[33]

The mission of the modern writer was specifically literary as it had not been for Voltaire and the Enlightenment. The philosophes used literature because it was convenient to do so. The much-vaunted clarity ascribed to the French language and the conception of writing that derived from the obligation to clarify made eighteenth-century French prose the ideal instrument for the application of reason to human affairs. The nineteenth century saw things differently. By jettisoning the rules, the *bienséances,* and the unities and opening literature to new realities, writers redefined the relationship between literature and language. A vast distance separates Voltaire's clear, direct mastery over language from Hugo's sense of being inhabited by language or his notions of a mystic communion with words. The correspondence Hugo drew between the French Revolution and his own French language revolution derives from an even more comprehensive correspondence between the word and the world. Like the prophet, Hugo spoke a language that tied him, and by extension his readers, to the divine: "words are the Word, and the Word is God."[34]

Hugo's politics were at one with his poetics. The political role he played, like the political figure he came to incarnate, in its triumphs no less than its limitations, was conditioned by a higher sense of mission. These were not politics delimited by political institutions. For while Hugo had access to institutional political forums at various times in his career, he took his stands outside, and usually against, those institutions of which he was nominally a part: the Chambre des Pairs after his 1845 peerage, the Assemblée nationale in 1848 and again in 1871, the Sénat in 1876. He was, however, by temperament and by design an ineffectual legislator, lacking any notion of parliamentary strategy and antipathetic to the compromises such strategy entails. His tempestuous resignation from the 1871 Assemblée nationale showed his distance from anything resembling practical politics. Impassioned speeches had little effect in the legislature: notwithstanding Hugo's eloquent pleas, amnesty was *not* granted to convicted members of the insurrectionary Paris Commune, and the death penalty was *not* abolished (it was abolished in 1981). Hugo was at his best presiding at the international peace congresses of 1849 and 1869, beseeching stays of execution for individuals (John Brown, for example) or pardons for political prisoners and pleading the case of the downtrodden—whether in *Les Misérables* or in stirring speeches or in calls to the Germans to desist from attacking Paris.[35]

Hugo's revolution of language was also a politics of words, of words that were "omnipotent," "living beings" endowed with a past, a present, and the future to which they were dedicated by the poet ("Suite" à la "Réponse à un acte d'accusation"). These words were themselves acts. This characteristic Hugolian political poetics was nowhere more clearly marked, or more magnificent, than in his self-imposed exile during the eighteen years of the Second Empire, from Louis-Napoleon Bonaparte's coup d'état in December 1851 to Napoleon III's defeat and abdication in September 1870. Originally a supporter of Bonaparte, Hugo moved to the left and to opposition. By July 1851 a coup d'état seemed likely, and Hugo was already at work on *Napoléon le Petit*. Hugo himself was untouchable, but his two sons were imprisoned and their journal was shut down by government order. Hugo quit Paris under cover in December, and for eighteen years, from Brussels and from the Channel Islands, first Jersey and then, after expulsion from Jersey, Guernsey, the poet excoriated France: in *Napoléon le Petit* (1852), in *Histoire d'un crime* (1851, published in full 1877–1878), in the poems of *Les Châtiments* (1853). Both in and outside of politics, Hugo had no political program. In 1871 he condemned the Commune as he had denounced the Empire, but he defended the Communards, even offering them asylum in his home. For Hugo 1871 was *L'Année terrible;* he reproved the oppressors and pitied the victims regardless of politics. He did not plot the overthrow of the empire; he sustained the ideal of a republic that would realize his vision of freedom and fraternity. "When liberty comes back to France, so shall I," he declared, refusing the amnesty offered him by the government in 1859.

Less important than the fact of Hugo's many connections to politics was the mode of those connections. The political commitments over almost the whole of his career tend to obscure the underlying ambiguity of Hugo's relation to politics and, by extension, to society. The specific positions he advocated counted for less than the ideal of commitment that he dramatized in both word and deed. Hugo's voice was not that of the rationalist philosophe, firmly grounded in the present. His was the call of the prophet, eyes fixed on the future and a world beyond this one. The apocalyptic tone, the appeal to faith over reason, the exhortations to moral righteousness, the dramatic intensity and verbal excess—all these traits that mark the prophet and Hugo as well place him beyond politics, beyond history, beyond reason. Characteristically, Hugo's finest hour was the most dramatic, the exile during which he spoke to France as a Frenchman—from a distance. Duty as a writer meant dramatization of higher truths. From the rocky promontory facing the coast of France, Hugo hurled anathema upon his errant homeland and called upon the chosen people to forswear false imperial gods and return to the paths of republican virtue.

The ambiguity no less than the drama of Hugo's position is nowhere more evident than in *Quatrevingt-Treize,* the novel written at the very beginning of the Republic that Hugo had defended with such zeal. *Quatrevingt-Treize* recounts a (fictitious) episode in the counterrevolutionary insurrection of royalists and peasants in Brittany and the Vendée that pits the marquis de Lantenac, leader of the insurgent royalist forces, against his great-nephew, Gauvain, leader of the revolutionary army, in a struggle in which, as Hugo stresses again and again, no quarter could be given nor mercy shown. The conflicting conceptions of the Revolution amplify and complicate the oppositions that structure *Quatrevingt-Treize*—republic-monarchy, revolution-feudalism, medieval château-modern guillotine, old-new, Paris-provinces.

Hugo sets Gauvain's vision of society as "nature sublimated,"[36] a humane, merciful, and profoundly just society, against the implacable justice advocated by Cimourdain, a former priest and tutor to Gauvain, envoy of the Committee of Public Safety to Gauvain's army. Yet in moments of crisis each of these men sacrifices his duty to history to the moral and affective imperatives of a higher order. Lantenac saves three small children from certain death in the burning château, knowing full well that his capture and execution will destroy the counterrevolution; Gauvain betrays the Revolution and France by setting Lantenac free, even though he is well aware of the immense destruction and suffering that Lantenac will wreak; and Cimourdain, after casting the deciding ballot condemning Gauvain to death for treason, shoots himself as the blade of the guillotine descends on the only person he ever loved.

There is no denying that *Quatrevingt-Treize* confronts history at its most dramatic.[37] Revolution, arguably, is the ultimate historical event. Individuals have taken the initiative to make their own history and to decree the possibility of significant change and indeed progress. At the same time revolution brings the horrors of violence, and Hugo chose to take the French Revolution at its most horrific: 1793 and the Terror. He justifies 1793 not by avoiding the horrors but by invoking the new society these terrible events will bring. "The visible work is ferocious, the invisible work is sublime." The tumultuous meeting of the Convention "was producing civilization. It was a furnace of passions but also a forge. In this vat where terror bubbled, progress fermented." History is assimilated into nature, and the Terror becomes a cleansing storm, a great wind delivering civilization of a great plague. As "the horrors of the miasma" explain the "fury of the wind," so the monarchy explains the Revolution. In another striking organicist metaphor the guillotine turns into a "sinister tree" growing out of the very earth, "watered by centuries of sweat, tears, and blood." The future will arise out of this earth like the sun that rises on Gauvain's execution, and it is a future made possible by the "terrible year" 1793. It is relevant to this future that the three small children taken hostage and then freed by the marquis de Lantenac have been adopted by a battalion in Gauvain's army: as their innocence guarantees the Revolution, so the Revolution guarantees their future.[38] In its defense of the First Republic, *Quatrevingt-Treize* offers important symbolic support to the Third.

"Every century has its work, today civic duty, tomorrow humane." This humanitarian vision of a better world saves the Revolution, but a vision it remains, for both Hugo, writing in 1873 at the birth of the Third Republic, and his character Gauvain, speaking in 1793 from the First Republic. Theirs is "the republic of the ideal," a republic that listens to poets, not politicians. "I am not a politician," Gauvain ripostes to Cimourdain's accusations of utopianism, and Hugo elsewhere likens him to a prophet. Like Hugo himself, Gauvain is a visionary who looks to another world, a world where man will be "transfigured," where the earthworm will become a butterfly, freed from the chains of the terrestrial. "Man is not made to wear chains but to open wings." The motif of ascension figures the attraction of the divine and its literal and symbolic superiority over the history made by mankind.[39]

For finally history does not count. Individual action alone defines, justifies, or condemns the individual. The assimilation of historical events to forces of nature, the organic metaphors, the explicit dissociation of Gauvain from politics, and

his association with the prophet absolve the individual of historical responsibility. One does not fight a tempest; one waits
for it to pass. "What does the storm matter so long as I have
my compass? What do events matter so long as I have my
conscience?" Hugo emphatically places Gauvain beyond the
reach of the storms of history. That Gauvain, like Lantenac
and Cimourdain, betrays his cause does not really matter.
The moral act alone counts; the "human absolute" super-
sedes the revolutionary one. However detestable his politics,
however ruthless his conduct, Lantenac is "transfigured" by
the sacrifice of both his life and his cause for the three children. Gauvain undergoes an even more spectacular transformation. At the scaffold, with his "sublime and ineffable"
smile and the halo made by the sun around his whole body,
Gauvain resembles a "vision," an "archangel": the entire
army, transfixed, begs his pardon. Even the inexorable Cimourdain, by his suicide, acknowledges the primacy of the
individual over the historical. His soul and Gauvain's,
"tragic sisters, flew off together, the darkness of the one
mixed with the light of the other," in the ultimate transfiguration, an ascent into the realm that reconciles the irreconcilable.[40]

So too Hugo's own work reconciles the irreconcilable and
fuses the characteristic dramatic antitheses into an equally
characteristic and dramatic synthesis. Gauvain asserts that
the poet's "lyre" serves "to put everything in harmony." To
maintain this harmony, within *Quatrevingt-Treize* as without,
Hugo simultaneously made commitments and withdrew
from them, engaged in and disengaged himself from the political and the social. The triumph of the Third Republic notwithstanding, Hugo mostly kept his distance, no longer
geographical but psychic. He remained committed to "the
republic of the ideal," governed by love, whence all paths led
to God. Hugo did not advocate policies, he preached a gospel
of mercy, of solace, of love. "To love is to act," the last words
Hugo wrote, sum up his vision of the universe and his—the
prophet's—role in it. Unlike Voltaire, who "wrote to act,"

Hugo conceived of writing as itself the ultimate creative act: "words are the Word, and the Word is God."[41]

It was entirely fitting that Victor Hugo should become a prophet with great honor in his own country, a legend in his own century. So strong was Hugo's religious aura that Romain Rolland's devoutly Catholic mother wanted him to bless her son.[42] He did not present a program for the Republic, but he articulated its ideal, its faith in the future, in democracy, in liberty, in prosperity. Neither the Republic nor its citizens stinted in marking their gratitude for the powerful symbols Hugo provided. Admiration, adulation, and official ceremonies of all sorts filled the fifteen years between Hugo's majestic return to Paris in 1870 and his death in 1885 when two million French followed him to his final resting place in the Panthéon.[43]

Hugo's canonization by the Third Republic resembled Voltaire's apotheosis a century earlier—even to the similar images, Hugo in attendance at a performance of Saint-Saëns's "Hymne à Victor Hugo" recalling Voltaire's glorification at the Comédie-Française premiere of his play *Irène*. The official gestures of recognition were also parallel. The more fragile the union, the more ostentatious the gratitude of governments in search of stability. In naming the street where Voltaire died after the philosophe and in transferring his ashes to the Panthéon, the First Republic gave itself an instant and impeccable ancestor and acquired a sorely needed legitimacy. The Third Republic placed busts of Voltaire in city halls across France and in Paris gave his name to the boulevard Voltaire, which, like the persona of Voltaire himself, makes the symbolic connection between the place de la République and the place de la Nation. The same Republic named the avenue Victor-Hugo to celebrate the poet's eightieth year and upon his death orchestrated a grandiose lying-in-state under the Arc de Triomphe and solemn burial in the Panthéon.[44] "Aux Grands Hommes la Patrie reconnaissante"—the inscription on the Panthéon could not be more appropriate. The country *was*

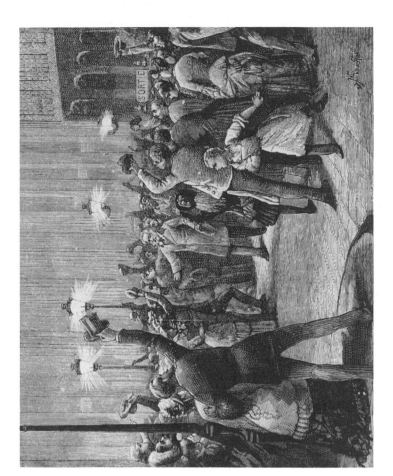

Victor Hugo arrived in triumph at the Gare du Nord in September 1870 after eighteen years of (mostly) self-imposed exile. Hugo symbolized republican resistance to Napoleon III, and his return to France celebrated the end of the Second Empire. French troops had just gone down to ignominious defeat at the hands of the Prussians in the battle of Sedan. (Photograph courtesy of the Musées de la Ville de Paris, SPADEM © 1986)

The spectacular official funeral of Victor Hugo, 1 June 1885. Past crowds of 2,000,000 or more, the brightly bedecked Garde Républicaine escorted the hearse down the Champs-Elysées, where the body had lain in state the night before, to the Panthéon, where the writer was interred. Hugo already had made his own comment on all this pomp by stipulating a pauper's coffin. The writer who made antithesis a basic aesthetic principle must have savored the contrast. (Photograph courtesy of the Musées de la Ville de Paris, SPADEM © 1986)

grateful, immensely so, for these great men who transcended partisan politics to embody the very ideal of the Republic. Voltaire and Hugo became "universal" republicans to whom almost everyone in the republic could assent, figures so politically charged yet so apolitical that they could serve as symbols not simply of a government but of the nation.

7

The Writer as Intellectual Hero

I have only one passion—light.
Emile Zola, "J'accuse"

The twentieth-century public writer is the intellectual, a
very different creature from the philosophe and the prophet,
though clearly of the same lineage. When the conditions that
allowed a Voltaire or a Hugo to speak for his age disappeared,
the public writer faced a dilemma: how to address and how,
in addressing, to represent a whole culture in a time marked
by ever greater intellectual and literary specialization. The
fragmentation of literary life is already apparent by the end
of the nineteenth century with Emile Zola. Squarely in the
tradition of Voltaire and Hugo, Zola's courageous stand in the
Dreyfus affair showed the public writer at his best. Yet Zola
never became the personage that his two predecessors had
been; he never became the same symbol of nation or culture.

The ingredients certainly were there. Zola's reputation in
the 1890s, like Hugo's before, gave him the moral authority
to speak out on issues that reached beyond the literary. He
was probably the best known contemporary French author,
a "serious" writer whose name and work were associated
with the "new" literature of naturalism much as Hugo's had
been identified with romanticism. In 1893 the twentieth volume of the Rougon-Macquart novel cycle had brought to a
conclusion Zola's vast "social and natural history of a family under the Second Empire." The novelist immediately
launched into the series Les Trois Villes (Lourdes, 1894; Rome,
1896; Paris, 1898), which was followed immediately by an
even more ambitious cycle, the Quatre Evangiles (Fécondité,
1899; Travail, 1901; Vérité, 1903, and the never-completed Jus-

tice). Like Hugo, Zola had been elected president of the Société des gens de lettres, although he had not received the ultimate consecration of the Académie française. Many objected to naturalism in general and to Zola in particular. Proust's duchesse de Guermantes refers nastily to the author of the *Rougon-Macquart* as the Homer of the cesspool. Others shared the opinion, if not the wit. François Mauriac recalled from his childhood in a very conservative, very Catholic family that a chamber pot was called "un Zola."[1] Zola's work remained controversial on social as well as aesthetic grounds, and his intervention in the Dreyfus affair made him more controversial still.

Zola's identification with the lower classes did nothing to dissipate the controversy. The creator of the Rougon-Macquart novels could boast of bringing *le peuple* into literature—not simply the exceptional and exceptionally virtuous individual like Ruy Blas or Jean Valjean but characters more representative of the working classes, like the washerwoman Gervaise in *L'Assommoir* or the miners in *Germinal*. Zola's vision of humanity and his compassion for the disinherited naturally allied him with all those fighting for truth and justice, and his combative temperament—"I am attacked, therefore I still am"—made him eager to do battle. And so Zola took up the cause of Dreyfus as he had taken up the cause of naturalism and the naturalists, of Manet and the impressionists.[2] A missionary zeal inspired these "campaigns" (Zola's term) and the novels as well, especially the later ones. Fiction was the manifesto of the public writer Zola had so consciously become. Involvement in the Dreyfus affair meant more than a political stand. It was, as Zola himself insisted, the logical consequence of everything he had ever done—or written.[3]

The dramatic possibilities of the Dreyfus affair were bound to attract the novelist. Zola admitted that the "poignant drama" and the "superb characters" of the affair had impressed him first; the "pity, faith, passion for truth and justice" came later.[4] Zola's act was easily as spectacular as Hugo's exile because his actions dramatized an already explosive situation. On 13 January 1898 Zola published a letter to the president of the Republic in a Parisian daily newspaper. His strategy in "J'accuse," as the letter came to be known, was to reopen the Dreyfus case by provoking his own trial for defamation of character (his citation of the relevant statutes made his intention clear and a trial unavoidable). He was tried within a month, was ordered to pay damages and condemned to imprisonment, was tried again after an appeal, and was condemned again. Eventually pardoned in a general amnesty, Zola was fully vindicated only after his death in 1902. Dreyfus was rehabilitated in 1906. Two years later, somewhat reluctantly and well after the fact, the nation showed its gratitude by transferring Zola's ashes to the Panthéon.

In the themes he stresed and the key words he used, Zola echoed Voltaire and Hugo, animated, as they had been, by "a single passion—light." Like his predecessors, Zola acted "to hasten the explosion of truth and justice." Like Voltaire, he fought in the name of reason; like Hugo, he defended liberty and revolution to bring down the old world and prepare the new.[5] Even so, despite his undeniable courage and despite the honors he received—a street in Paris and a place in the Panthéon—Zola failed to attain the exemplary status of the philosophe or the prophet. The designations no longer applied. The years between Hugo's death and the Dreyfus affair a decade later had redefined what it meant to be a public writer. The twentieth-century intellectual "stood against" in a different way.

Zola's stand in the Dreyfus affair was not his alone. The action he took and the articles he wrote in defense of Dreyfus identified Zola with a dissident group in French society that set itself against the government by placing the rights of the individual over the concerns of society. That Dreyfus was innocent necessarily called into question the integrity of the army; their actions and their writings gave the Dreyfusards' dissidence a distinct political coloration. For the Republic born of ignominious defeat scarcely a quarter century before, attacks on the army amounted to a betrayal of country. Because he distinguished between army and country, Zola's opposition was sectarian; Hugo's opposition to the Second Empire, in contrast, was total and unconditional. Hugo's refusal to admit compromise, to accept, for example, the pardon offered by Napoleon III, greatly simplified the ideological and political issues at stake. By remaining wholly outside the political system that he denounced with such fervor, Hugo escaped "playing politics" altogether. He joined no groups, fomented no revolution, planned no coup d'état. Hugo rose above politics into a mythic world largely of his own creation.

Circumstances were different for Zola. His participation in the Dreyfus affair was part of a collective defense that worked within the political system of the Third Republic. Unlike Hugo, Zola did not contest the government, still less the republic. He made use of that government and its republican institutions, taking advantage of a relatively free press to diffuse 300,000 copies of "J'accuse" and counting on laws that guaranteed a public trial. Zola carefully presented the unjust condemnation of Dreyfus as an aberration from the true Republic of 1789 and its principles of liberty and justice. "We have to know," Zola declared to the jury at his own trial, "if France is still the France of the rights of man, the France that gave liberty to the world and should give it justice." Zola did his utmost to ally himself with republican tradition, intending his defense of Dreyfus as a restoration of original, republican purity. "The sons of France who love their country" were "duty bound in this hour of danger" to "enlighten it, to save it from the errors of blind passion."[6] In the tones of a biblical prophet, Zola exhorted French society to abjure error and return to virtue.

But at the turn of the century the prophet's was the voice of the past. Because the Dreyfus affair brought about a confrontation of groups rather than individuals, it transformed the public writer's commitment. In contrast to Voltaire, who single-handedly created the Calas affair, Zola participated in a campaign that reached far beyond the individual. Dreyfus himself, "the accident" that started the affair, represented "all those who have been oppressed, all those who have suffered."[7] Zola did not create the Dreyfus affair, he associated himself with it—and late at that. Even though Hugo was not

the sole opponent of the Second Empire, the form his opposition took, the proud, visible, and solitary exile, emphasized
the singularity of the gesture. Hugo and Voltaire offered individual resistance to collective authority; Zola joined a collective resistance that owed its existence to others. Only two
days after *L'Aurore* published "J'accuse," it printed a less ex-

This print, aptly entitled "The Age of Paper," captures the intercon-
nection between the newspaper, public reading, and the café in
Paris at the turn of the century. The rods affixed to each paper mark
them as the property of the café. The issue of the moment is Zola's
"J'accuse," published two weeks previously. (Photograph courtesy
of Roger-Viollet)

plosive but even more significant manifesto in support of Dreyfus whose 104 signatories were immediately dubbed "le parti intellectuel."

The Dreyfusards were then the first official "intellectuals." But of course intellectuals in the broad sense of individuals committed to the life of the mind and to acting on that commitment come from the political Right as well as the Left. The Dreyfusard Ligue des droits de l'homme, founded in 1898, was soon countered by the anti-Dreyfusard, ultrapatriotic Ligue de la Patrie française. The pattern of group and counter-group, manifesto and counter-manifesto characterizes French intellectual and literary life to the present day. Zola's passionate espousal of Dreyfus's innocence was echoed by Péguy, Mallarmé, Proust, and Anatole France and countered, equally passionately, by Barrès, Pierre Loti, Paul Bourget, and Heredia, among many others.[8] Barrès or Péguy (who moved into the conservative camp a few years after the Dreyfus affair) would exemplify the early twentieth-century intellectual almost as well as Zola, just as Camus or Malraux, to mention only two names, might serve in place of Sartre in the discussion below. Zola and Sartre stand apart from their fellow intellectuals not because of their political positions but because they dramatized those positions so forcefully, using all the resources at their disposal.

The prominence of intellectuals is not unique to France. As has been noted time and again, intellectuals are a twentieth-century phenomenon, creatures of contemporary life in reaction against it. The increasingly complex needs of modern industrial and postindustrial society require increasingly complex expertise, whence, for example, the expansion of higher education, which has attempted to respond to those needs. Yet knowledge alone does not make the intellectual. Applying what one knows is not living the life of the mind. The self-conscious espousal of that holistic life of thought directly challenges the fragmentation inherent in specialized knowledge: conflict is inevitable. Modern society, which approves and indeed requires specialization, must oppose the intellectual, who acknowledges no limits. In pressing claims to speak to and for all society, in setting themselves as the consciousness and conscience of society, intellectuals cast themselves in the role of outsiders, critics of society not because they consistently adopt any given ideological position, but because they refuse the jurisdiction of society and its circumscription of intellectual and moral authority. Intellectuals are, in sum, a modern variety of the public writer, and indeed, more strikingly than their counterparts elsewhere, intellectuals in France are *literary* intellectuals. Neither philosophe nor prophet yet a bit of each, the literary intellectual brought the public writer into the twentieth century.

I

The world was using me to become language.
Jean-Paul Sartre, Les Mots

What has it meant to be a literary intellectual in the twentieth century? No example is more telling than that of Jean-Paul Sartre, who was surely the exemplary intellectual of the twentieth century. Others were greater thinkers or better writers; others may have had greater impact on literature, on intellectual life, on society. But Sartre realized the fusion of these many domains in the persona of the public writer. Like Voltaire and Hugo before him, Sartre spanned most of his century: born in 1905, he died in 1980 after forty years as a celebrated, and notorious, figure on the literary and intellectual scene. His reputation was great, his production voluminous and varied—a novel and short stories in the 1930s, novels and plays in the 1940s and 1950s, and the autobiography of 1964, in addition to the more strictly philosophical work and the political essays, both general and topical. Sartre also favored the theater for the exploration of philosophical, moral, and social dilemmas, and like the earlier philosophe and prophet, Sartre the intellectual was a literary critic who ranged widely, from critical studies of contemporary authors like Camus, Dos Passos, Sarraute, and Genet to extended examinations of two of the most important figures in French literary history, Baudelaire and Flaubert.[9]

Sartre's ambitions were boundless. His avowed intention

to "bear witness to everything" impelled him beyond literature. He plunged into the arts, including the new art of film,
a passion of Sartre's as both a child and an adult; he pursued
a broad spectrum of other intellectual interests, the most important among them philosophic and psychoanalytic theory;
and finally, he aspired to the social and political commitment
that became for him what it had been for Voltaire and Hugo,
the sign of the public writer. These extra-literary concerns
went with literature. The Sartrean intellectual considered all
of these involvements, intellectual no less than social, a function of the unique capacity of literature to subsume every
intellectual endeavor. "We shall call on every literary genre,"
Sartre proclaimed in his editorial présentation of *Les Temps
modernes* in 1945, "to familiarize the reader with our ideas; a
poem or a novel, more than a theoretical work, can create a
favorable climate for their development."[10] True to his program, Sartre chose a short story by Richard Wright for the
lead article of this inaugural issue.

Sartre set the public writer as the model for *all* writers, not
only the elect few: commitment defines literature and social
responsibility the writer. For the writer is not merely an intellectual who happens to write. Others are intellectuals "by
accident"; the writer is the quintessential intellectual, superior by virtue of an occupation that confronts the contradiction between the particular and the universal.[11] The writer
lives, and writes, within this contradiction.

The urgent commitment attached to literature and the total
responsibility demanded of the writer marked the intellectual
as a public writer of a special sort. A descendant of the philosophe and the prophet, the intellectual was obliged to confront modern society and its discontents. Most immediately,
the intellectual had to contend with the intellectualization
and the politicization of a literary culture already notable for
its intellectuality and political concerns. In the twentieth century as earlier, the public writer aspired to subsume these
divisions and to address society as a whole. But the twentieth
century made such unity impossible. Sartre came as close as
any writer, but the tensions that made the writer the essential

intellectual also prevented him from achieving the cultural consensus attained by the philosophe and by the prophet. As Sartre himself noted more than once, the philosophe might plausibly think that he spoke not for a class, the bourgeoisie, but for all of society; even the illusion of such representation was denied his literary descendants. A product of, as well as a reaction against, the fragmentation of literary life, the intellectual strove for a comprehensive perspective beyond his powers—whence the feelings of isolation, the guilt, and the sense of frustration.

The intellectual himself was often a specialist.[12] Unlike the pragmatic philosophe—for example, Voltaire, who dismissed what he considered idle speculation—the intellectual commonly situated himself in relation to a system and a theory; Sartre certainly did. He was a philosopher in the modern sense of the term. Like the philosophe as well as the philosopher, the intellectual faced the problem of translating theory into effective social action. The great attraction of the Soviet Union for intellectuals, particularly in the 1930s, had much to do with the promise it held out of integrating principles and practice, the promise, in sum, of joining philosopher and philosophe.

Sartre's personal conception of intellectual work further segregated the intellectual specialist. Heavily influenced by German philosophy and a year in Berlin, Sartre created a particular style for his philosophic and critical writings that in its deliberate difficulty challenged French philosophy, French literary criticism, and the French language itself. Like Ronsard, accused by Boileau of speaking Greek and Latin rather than French, and like Rousseau, condemned by Voltaire for a foreigner's disregard of the French language and hence of France, Sartre was criticized for writing in some strange Teutonic dialect incomprehensible to the *honnêtes gens* habitually addressed by French philosophy. From Descartes to Bergson, French philosophy shared the prejudices of French literary culture against specialization and the technical vocabulary associated with it.[13] Sartre took just the opposite view, believing instead that the aim of philosophy was "to forge concepts that grow steadily and cumulatively weightier."[14] Thus laden with concepts, the language of philosophy can only be cumbersome and all but impenetrable—the antithesis, but by design, of the concision, the clarity, and the elegance ascribed to standard literary French.

A sense of the intellectual's isolation suffuses Sartre's early literary works. *La Nausée* (1938) is a meditation on the nature of intellectual activity, which concludes in defeat. Roquentin, the character whose diary constitutes the novel, is trying to write, if rather desultorily, a monograph on a minor historical figure. Eventually overcome with the visceral nausea of existence and the futility of intellectual enterprise, he abandons the biography. He dreams of writing another, very different, work that would perhaps justify his existence, but the conditional tense so dominates this terminal daydream of *La Nausée* that the reader is not very sanguine about its realization. Society offers no more hope. Roquentin rebuffs meaningful contact with the inhabitants of Bouville while his one protracted liaison recedes into the past, as lost as his research. The narrator of the short story "Erostrate" parodies this isolation. "Men," this would-be anarchist and unrepentent misanthrope observes, "should be seen from above." All things considered, he says, he should have spent his life on a seventh-floor balcony, finding symbolic support for the moral superiority he vaunts but knows he does not have.[15] The spectacular project of killing five strangers on the street and committing suicide with the remaining bullet points to the intellectual's sense of isolation and paralysis. For Erostrate cannot execute the project as planned: throwing away his gun with "his" bullet in it, he waits to be taken.

"Erostrate" projects the intellectual's ambivalence. The failed protagonist is simultaneously disgusted by those who "touch" him in the street, and who thereby impinge on his existence, and obsessed with the need to impress those same strangers with his own presence. As in *La Nausée* the impossibility of communication blocks effective human relations. At the same time that existence afflicts and sets the intellectual apart, it weighs upon the individual acutely conscious of and tormented by an isolation that he must overcome to act effectively, to attain the clarity and force of action. One's very body becomes a hindrance: "Why do we have to have bodies?" Lulu laments in "Intimité," dreaming of pure relations unsullied by physical demands and compromises. Lucien in "L'Enfance d'un chef" also rejects the "revolting intimacy" of sex, finding his solution and his identity in the anti-Semitism that gives him a sense of being "pitiless and pure," like "a steel blade." That Roquentin uses almost the same language to describe his ideal book—it would be "beautiful and hard, like steel"—casts further doubt on both the validity and the possibility of this kind of book.[16]

None of these characters, with the possible exception of Roquentin, is an intellectual, and all are in bad faith. Nonetheless these early works betray an anguished consciousness of self and society that separates the intellectual from the less introspective prophet and philosophe. Voltaire, Hugo, and their epigones rarely agonized over their roles as public writers. One would search their works in vain for any real doubts about the exercise of intellectual authority. The philosophe and the prophet derived their spiritual leadership logically from talent, and they saw themselves as part of what Balzac called the "aristocracy of talent." In much the same way political leadership had "naturally" devolved on the aristocracy in the ancien régime and on the upper classes thereafter. But for the modern intellectual, self-consciousness came close to inhibiting action. Mathieu in the trilogy *Les Chemins de la liberté* agonizes over the use he makes, or ought to make, of his existential liberty—the word appears again and again, especially in the first volume, *L'Age de raison*. Hugo proclaimed liberty; he did not worry about it. A century later, Hugo's enthusiasm and self-confidence disappeared in the constant self-criticism of the intellectual (which once moved Valéry to the acerbic comment "The species complains; therefore it exists").[17]

This isolation made literature even more crucial for the intellectual than for his predecessors. In an age of ever-greater specialization, hence fragmentation, literature re-

mained a general medium, able to move beyond the caste of
those whom Simone de Beauvoir so aptly called the Manda-
rins to the traditional public of *honnêtes gens*, updated for the
times. By using literary works to translate problems of the
specialist into a general discourse, the public writer palliated
the isolation of the intellectual. The philosophical and critical
works—*L'Etre et le néant*, *Saint-Genet*—contained "literary"
passages, although Sartre generally preferred to distinguish
the difficult, conceptually weighty language of philosophy
from the other languages he used, the language of prose and
of the theater. There is little doubt that the literary side of
Sartre's work, and most notably his drama, was responsible
for the vogue of existentialism among those who never
turned a page of *L'Etre et le néant*, not to mention the works
of Heidegger on which Sartre drew so heavily. Though Sartre,
beginning in the 1950s, wrote less and less literature, more
and more philosophical, social, and political works, most of
his readers probably considered literature his *raison d'être*.

II

We are the most bourgeois writers in the world.
Jean-Paul Sartre,
Qu'est-ce que la littérature?

Literature in the twentieth century was not the solution it
had once been. Its definitions and its institutions undermined by the same forces dividing the rest of French society,
literature became part of the problem it had once claimed to
resolve. The philosophe and the prophet had triumphantly
affirmed the rights of literature and the privileges of the
writer; the intellectual questioned both. The certitudes of
the eighteenth and the nineteenth centuries became the
questions of the twentieth. Meanwhile, nineteenth-century
trends continued their work of transformation. The expansion of the market that so revolutionized the literary scene in
the nineteenth century affected the twentieth century as well.
Most recently in the 1960s, French publishers and booksellers

began to cultivate new and different publics: inexpensive paperback editions, modern techniques of production, more aggressive marketing, and diversified offerings made French publishing far more heterogeneous than ever before. At the same time journals proliferated along with publishing houses in a multiplication that countered the mergers of older publishing firms with venerable established houses like Gallimard and Hachette. New genres or subgenres like detective novels and science fiction gained prominence in the market and a certain measure of respectability.

Like literary institutions themselves, the definitions of literature diversified. Intellectual currents turned truths into uncertainties. Issues that had once been beyond question, giving the public writer the confidence to speak out as he did, became questions. Phenomenology attacked the traditional stability of literature at its base by destroying the literary object. Placing the definition of reality in the eye and, in the case of literature, in the interpretation of the beholder compromised the authority of the text and its creator. The author's intended meaning became only one of many possible meanings, the author only one of many creators. The text itself became elusive: does a text even exist outside an interpretation? It should come as no surprise that the "deconstruction" of a literary work at times took precedence over the construction, the interpretation over the creation, the critic over the author. By the 1980s, much literary criticism was rebelling against its subordinate status as handmaiden to literature to proclaim instead its separate (and equal?) existence. Indeed, the distinctions between literature and criticism or between genres no longer necessarily obtain. Sartre's own studies of writers, from Baudelaire to Genet to the monumental unfinished work on Flaubert, are characterized by difficult convoluted language, excessive length, and torturous reasoning. The relation of Sartre's writing to the work or person of Flaubert is sometimes tenuous: one reads *L'Idiot de la famille* for Sartre rather more than for Flaubert.

The promotion of literary criticism was only one element in a general challenge to literary truths that had once appeared self-evident. In the 1920s and 1930s the surrealists, in a noisy break with centuries of French prose defined by clarity and logic, made one of the most explicit attempts to divorce artistic creativity from rational thought. But if the surrealists were among the most vocal opponents of this tradition, they were hardly alone in playing on the indeterminate status of literature. The self-reflexive novel and the self-referential nature of literature were not new to the twentieth century—one can find examples in the eighteenth century, in Diderot's *Jacques le fataliste,* and even in the sixteenth century in Cervantes's *Don Quixote.* The concepts of literary self-referentiality and reflexivity, however, were very much of this century, testimony to a self-consciousness and a concomitant loss of faith in literature. When writers themselves no longer affirmed their possibilities but like André Gide proposed the writer as counterfeiter (*Les Faux-Monnayeurs,* 1926), the public writer stood on a shaky platform indeed.

Marxist perspectives eroded what remained. Reinforced by the indigenous French line of sociologically oriented critics from Mme de Staël through Taine and Lanson, Marxist criticism subjected literature to the same constraints affecting the rest of society. Literature appeared more and more class bound, less and less universal. The intellectual became aware of the constraints imposed by a particular position in a particular society. Irremediably bourgeois, the writer emerged as one figure in a divided French society and, as writers themselves may have suspected, an increasingly irrelevant one at that. The French writer had always been removed, in education and often in sympathy, from those over whom he claimed ascendancy. The patent elitism of French literary culture and the clearly privileged status of the writer in France had long supplied the foundation for the "aristocracy of talent." The philosophe and the prophet accepted and even exploited these superiorities as their due. The intellectual wrestled with his conscience over their implications.

Sartre's work and career embraced all of the tensions inherent in the simultaneous rejection of French literary culture and the necessary subjection to it. On the one hand, Sartre refused the individualistic assumptions from which the public writer originally drew his definition of self and mission. On the other hand, like most intellectuals, he knew himself to be the product and the vehicle of this individualism. Sartre could rail against, but he could not deny, the literary culture that elected him the exemplary intellectual of twentieth-century France. Insofar as he wrote to influence readers and succeeded in doing so, Sartre had to accede to the public writer's assumption of leadership. Despite insistence on the equality of all men, Sartre specifically cited Voltaire and Zola as models of the commitment he required of the writer and, reservations notwithstanding, even recognized the leadership Victor Hugo represented.[18]

Sartre repudiated French literary culture with such passion because he was so much a part of it. Throughout the 1920s at the Ecole normale supérieure and the 1930s in various lycée teaching posts Sartre thought of himself as an individual opposed to society, and especially to the bourgeoisie, but disinclined to turn that opposition into action. Communism was for those who needed it, and Sartre, the bourgeois intellectual, could not see that he had any such need. Typically, he approved of the Popular Front without supporting it. Sartre was a "right-thinking" leftist who failed to translate conviction into commitment. Sartre in the 1930s wrote *against* the bourgeoisie, which was also his subject, and *against* the bourgeois reader, who was also his reader. The short stories "La Chambre," "Intimité," and particularly "L'Enfance d'un chef" as well as much of *La Nausée* heap scorn on the bourgeoisie, its way of life and of thinking, its bad faith.[19]

If the style of these works was striking in its originality and brutality, the criticisms were familiar enough and so was the perspective from which they came. The author remained aloof from his subject, fundamentally uninvolved, the omniscient chronicler who retained his superiority. Sartre doubted everything, he tells us in *Les Mots*, except his own mission to present that doubt. He was Roquentin and he was Roquentin's judge.[20] The war confronted Sartre with a palpable enemy of a different order than the bourgeoisie. His situation in the army and subsequently under the occupation required a different course of action and a different conception of the individual, the writer, and literature. With the realization that he too belonged to the collectivity and that his writings committed him willy-nilly, Sartre entered the "socialistic" stage of his life.

Consciousness of the many ties linking him to all men everywhere drastically shifted Sartre's critical perspective. No longer the "outsider" attacking the bourgeoisie from afar, he became the "insider," acquiescing in his own essential complicity in these attacks. The detached censure of the bourgeoisie in Sartre's early works gave way to an intensely personal denunciation of the literary culture he knew so well. *Les Temps modernes*, the journal founded by Sartre and close associates after the war, was intended to redefine what it meant to be a writer, to counter French literary culture and what Sartre saw as its tradition of bourgeois irresponsibility. The writer whom Sartre judged so fiercely had been neutralized by this culture. Kept safely apart from the world by the twin ideologies of aestheticism and scientism, as useless as a bird in a gilded cage, the contemporary writer, his language increasingly debased, produced "trinkets of sonorous inanity."[21] A couple of years later, *Qu'est-ce que la littérature?* (1948) elaborated the program of *Les Temps modernes* into a full-scale defense of literary commitment and a full-fledged indictment of French literary culture.

To construct his new writer, Sartre had first to destroy the old, and this destruction entailed a devastating critique of French literary culture. It is true that much of the discussion is couched in general terms. The first three sections of *Qu'est-ce que la littérature?* pose the most basic questions: What is writing? Why write? For whom does one write? The general questions receive more particular answers, and the final section as well as most of the preceding one—two-thirds of the book—deals explicitly with the French writer and the social, historical, and intellectual context of French literature. After following the writer's passage from the ancien régime to the ostentatious rupture with the bourgeoisie in the nineteenth century (an analysis distended to monstrous proportions twenty-five years later in *L'Idiot de la famille*), Sartre turns to the writer in 1947, to the French writer of 1947, "the only one who has remained a bourgeois" through and through, even unto the "bourgeois-ified" language he must use.[22] Despite satire and even comedy in Sartre's work—*La Nausée*, the short story "Intimité," and most obviously *Les Mots*—the reader does not expect to find comedy in a work proposing so serious a topic as the nature of literature. Yet the last chapter of *Qu'est-ce que la littérature?* on the contemporary writer in France opens with a mordant, and funny, exposé of French literary culture, which Sartre turns upside down and inside out, his indignation momentarily tempered by a sardonic humor, his harsh judgment mitigated by the collective pronoun that implicates him along with everyone else.

Familiar traits identify this collective portrait of French literary culture sketched in the exaggerated strokes appropriate to satire. Excessive, the characterization yet rings just true enough to compel recognition. To emphasize the quintessentially bourgeois nature of the French writer, Sartre invokes "unbourgeois" writers elsewhere, whose very different relations to their literatures and their societies accentuate the uniqueness of the French situation and the omnipresence of the bourgeoisie. First is the American writer, who is likely to return to ranch or workshop between books, who dreams of fraternity instead of glory yet writes in solitude, remote from any milieu even vaguely literary. Nothing about this existence is bourgeois, and indeed Sartre is unsure that a bourgeoisie worthy of name even exists in America. English writers, on the other hand, isolated in their clubs, belong to a caste apart: no one takes them very seriously. Finally, in Italy, where the bourgeoisie never counted for much in any case, writers are needy, underpaid, and forced to inhabit dilapidated palaces they can afford neither to heat nor to furnish.

"Therefore," Sartre concludes after his breathtakingly rapid literary tour, "we French are the most bourgeois writers in the world."[23] The French writer is so tied to bourgeois institutions and so impregnated with bourgeois culture that literature is not the personal act it can be for other writers but an object; it is no longer a means but an end, a "national property" consecrated with pomp and circumstance, stamped with the proper institutional seal of approval. Well before setting pen to paper, the French writer—Sartre's "we" is at once personal and general—knows all about literature from school; he knows that a poem is meant to progress through magnificent illustrated editions to hardbound editions of classics "whose clean smell of wood pulp and ink seemed the very perfume of the Muses." Literature is thus destined to reenter the classroom whence it came, where it will supply future generations of students with texts for that ultimate of French literary exercises, the *explication de texte*.[24]

The literary milieu appears equally circumscribed, so small and so concentrated that twenty-four hours and a little luck suffice for "an American in a hurry" (no one else, apparently, would bother) to get everyone's opinion on the burning issues of the day, twenty-four hours for an expert cyclist to circulate a petition or for a rumor to return, distorted, to its point of origin. If the American or the cyclist should chance to miss anyone on his rounds, he need not despair. After all, "everyone" turns up at the same gatherings, in the same cafés, at the same concerts, even, on properly literary occasions, at the British Embassy. To be sure, every now and again someone will make the startling gesture of retiring to the country with appropriate media fanfare; boredom soon sends the exile back to Paris. Even "regional" writers do their writing in Paris, Africans as well. Literature itself provides the model for every literature and every career. Every writer's route is marked out in advance. No surprises disrupt the orderly progress from obscurity to fame: everything is *already* written in books.[25] Structurally almost self-contained and ideologically self-sustaining, this very bourgeois literary culture has turned French writers into a modern clerisy, insulated by tradition and privilege against the incursions of society. The esprit de corps that characterizes these modern clerics reinforces the isolation inherent in the writer's condition and blinds the individual to the more fundamental involvement of the writer *as writer* in society.

The Parisian café is a complex literary forum, one that encourages personal expression, political reconciliation, and public policy all at once. Here the café unites a present and a future Nobel Prize winner, François Mauriac and Jean-Paul Sartre. Mauriac's guarded gaze conveys the distrust of one who had criticized him severely. The voluble Sartre's politics were also considerably to the left of Mauriac's own. Yet literary and ideological differences notwithstanding, the two writers joined forces in 1957 to protest ongoing French military action in Algeria. Sartre and Raymond Aron would effect a similar public reconciliation in 1979 to launch an appeal for the Vietnamese "Boat People." (Photograph courtesy Agence France-Presse)

The satire of this esprit de corps in *Qu'est-ce que la littérature?* was only one element in Sartre's attack on aestheticism and its attempts to separate the literary object. By removing literature from the confusions of external realities, aestheticism removed the writer from society. Sartre, of course, wished to place the writer squarely in the midst of society.

Accordingly, his permanent concern with defining what the writer was and, more important still, what the writer should be led Sartre to reserve special attention and particular vehemence for the private writer. His ideal of literary commitment condemned the private writer fully as much as it proclaimed the public writer. For every page on Voltaire or Zola or anyone else who "measured his responsibility as a writer" Sartre devoted dozens to the discussion of Flaubert, Goncourt, Proust—those who abdicated this responsibility and hid behind the illusions fostered by aestheticism. The private writer opposed every value that Sartre advocated: he refused involvement, disclaimed even the traditional *utile et dulce* justification for literature, and glorified the solitude modern society imposed on the writer. The private writer was not another author with whom Sartre chanced to disagree; he was the enemy whom Sartre wrote to repulse. The arch enemy was Flaubert, aestheticism incarnate, the private writer par excellence, symbol and source of the ills afflicting modern literature. Accountable for silences as well as words and deeds, the private writer was derelict in his avoidance of public issues. Flaubert was party to the bloody repression of the Paris Commune in 1871 because he did nothing to prevent it. He wrote not one line in protest, and for this Sartre held him culpable. Then too Sartre contemned the bourgeois writer who affected to despise the bourgeoisie, the "talented rentier" who could literally afford to remain distant from the more distasteful aspects of bourgeois society.[26]

Even more fundamental than either of these admittedly incriminating accusations was the private writer's espousal of aestheticism in the first place. All other literary evils originated in this ideology, which justified indifference to the social context, disguised irresponsibility as commitment, and presented retreat from the real as devotion to the ideal. By focusing literature on itself, aestheticism turned literature from its original and, in Sartre's view, still primary function of communication. Flaubert's insistence on the novel as a purely aesthetic object augmented the prestige of the genre—and diminished its effect. Poets, too, frequently insisted on the autonomy of the aesthetic object. But, although Sartre charged Baudelaire with the same unconcern he found in Flaubert, the aestheticization of poetry presented a lesser danger, for Sartre did not expect commitment of poetry, which he placed "outside language."[27] That prose must communicate, however, must be one reason Sartre, in his endless search for the meaning of literature, returned again and again throughout his career to Flaubert the novelist. The monumental study of Flaubert, which occupied Sartre for decades and covers several thousand pages, belies the derisive dismissal of the "talented rentier."[28] *L'Idiot de la famille* attempts to settle accounts with the nineteenth century and to exorcise the ghosts it bequeathed to the twentieth.

That this legacy was pernicious became obvious with Proust, whose work revealed even more clearly than Flaubert's the intellectual foundations and literary consequences of aestheticism. In Flaubert, Sartre attacked the bourgeois individualism that was both a cause and an effect of the ideology of art for art's sake. With Proust, Sartre identified the intellectual source of that ideology, which he located in the *esprit de géométrie*—Sartre's term is *esprit d'analyse*—characteristic of the bourgeoisie: "The legend of the poet's irresponsibility . . . originates in the *esprit d'analyse*." Because this analytic mind conceives of reality atomistically as so many equal, discrete elements, it cannot apprehend crucial inequalities. Because it insists on a universal human nature, the analytic mind cannot perceive the different social natures of individual human beings. This is where Proust led literature astray. By crediting the notion of a human nature outside of society, Proust made himself "the accomplice of bourgeois propaganda." Just as the writer of the Enlightenment projected his own experience as a bourgeois and presented reason as a universal value and the analytic mind as a universal tool, so Proust universalized into general "laws" his own idiosyncratic experiences as a homosexual and a bourgeois.[29] Sartre's insistence that sentiments are always defined by the particulars of class, sex, nation, and milieu and by their reciprocal influence required him to refuse Proust as he rejected Flaubert: both writers

were woefully and disastrously inadequate to the task the
contemporary writer must fulfill.

III

I was born from writing.
Jean-Paul Sartre,
Les Mots

Again and again Sartre confronted literature. He never
ceased to ask what it was all about, never failed to scrutinize
even those assumptions that seemed self-evident. The problems posed by *Qu'est-ce que la littérature?* like the polemics in
which it engages are crucial to an understanding of Sartre's
exceptional stature as a literary intellectual. What is literature? What—if anything—can the writer do in society? The
questions recur frequently, from *La Nausée* to the studies of
Baudelaire, Genet, and Flaubert and from *Qu'est-ce que la littérature?* through occasional journalism. Sartre the writer took
care to test the speculations of Sartre the philosopher against
the realities peculiar to literature and literary culture. The
major philosophic and ethical concerns that directed Sartre's
work—the existence and use of freedom, the definition of the
self, the necessity of commitment—possessed resonance for
the individual who wrote, as every writer did, "from a need
to feel essential in the world."[30]

In exploring what it meant to be a writer, Sartre came at
literature from every possible direction, historical, sociological, psychological, political. These investigations are so interesting beyond themselves because of the many modes in
which Sartre treated his subject: the polemics of *Qu'est-ce que
la littérature?*, the satire of *La Nausée*, the psychoanalytic-
existential discourse of *L'Idiot de la famille*, and, most striking
of all, the ironic view of self in *Les Mots*. This most idiosyncratic of works, which is neither chronicle nor confession and
which does not even take the "hero" as far as adolescence, is
not an autobiography in any usual sense. Moreover, Sartre
never wrote the sequel to which he alludes in the final pages.
Yet *Les Mots* is a finished work, a study of the writer to add

to *Baudelaire, Saint-Genet,* and *L'Idiot de la famille* and an examination of French literary culture to put with *Qu'est-ce que la littérature?*

Sartre's title warns the reader what not to expect. *Les Mots* will not recount one more childhood of one more writer. It bears no resemblance to the literary memoirs or autobiographies of writers who come to mind most readily, even those who explore childhood in some detail and depth. *Les Confessions* and *Les Mémoires d'outre-tombe* tell us of Rousseau and Chateaubriand, men who eventually became writers. *Les Mots* presents an individual "born of the written word." Nor does *Les Mots* depict any agonizing Proustian search for a vocation. The words that determined the writer's vocation first determined the child's identity: "When I said 'me,' it meant the me who wrote" (130). The child linked the power of words to his own power through the mastery of language—a mastery that enabled him to answer the questions posed in *Qu'est-ce que la littérature?:* what is writing? why write? for whom does one write? The answers are, of course, wrong because the child acquired false notions of literature, which the adult must repudiate: he learned the definitions of French literary culture. Extending *Qu'est-ce que la littérature?,* *Les Mots* traced "The Situation of the Writer in 1947" (the title of the last chapter) back to the child/writer of 1914 and to the revelation of the literary culture behind the writer's words and behind his faith in their powers.

What is writing? The power of words came from their reality. Indeed, for the child, words *were* reality. Having "discovered the world through language," he naturally "took language for the world" (154). Looking at a tree, he would wait for its real leaves to appear in the guise of an adjective or phrase. "Karlémamie," the collective epithet for his grandparents, "threw its shadow on the thing" (33). "The intimate union of the four syllables evoked the perfect harmony of the individuals" (32). Discord disappeared in a word; the family triumphed. "Suspect and sinning, ever on the brink, my grandmother was held back by an angel's arm, by the power of a word" (33). To be a writer, the child later decided, meant

above all to "impose names" in an act that was at once creation and possession (154). The world used him to become
language (183).

Words were endowed with life as people and places were
not. "Absorbing the Word," the child was sure of "discovering
language in its natural state, without men" (50–51). Books
took the place of nature in this childhood, and the writers he
frequented and came to know so intimately took the place of
the brothers and sisters the child did not have, of the friends
he was too timid to seek out. They replaced too the family he
was trying to escape. Appropriately enough, this child without a father or siblings taught himself to read over the saga
of an orphan, Hector Malot's interminable novel *Sans famille,*
which he already knew by heart. Books had been his dolls
and constituted his real family. Writers were peers. Like the
child they had endured trials and tribulations, and like him
they had been rewarded, with a place in the illustrious tradition of Prophets and Saints of literature.

Why write? As words gave the individual possession of reality, so books, tangible evidence of a sacred presence on
earth, gave the writer his place in society. Well before he was
able to read, the child had learned to "revere" books and to
regard his grandfather's study as a "sanctuary," a "temple"
filled with "sacred objects," which his usually awkward
grandfather handled with "the dexterity of a priest saying
Mass" (63, 37). Not surprisingly, the child tended "to confuse
literature with prayer" and proved "as zealous as a new convert" in learning to read and recite the Saints and Prophets
from Hesiod to Hugo (151, 53, 54). Faith in literature shaped
more of a religion than the Catholicism in which the child
received perfunctory instruction. It was, moreover, a faith
untroubled either by the ostensible disagreement between his
Protestant and rabidly anticlerical grandfather and his con-
ventionally pious Catholic grandmother or by their covert indifference. Serene, unassailed by doubt, the writer would be
the Christian the child could not be, one who not only accepted this religion but "took vows" and, in a Proustian metaphor, determined to build "cathedrals of words" (210, 155).

Literature as religion supplies the constitutive metaphor for this work that charts the "true" birth of a writer. If, as Sartre claimed in *Qu'est-ce que la littérature?*, artists are driven by the desire to feel necessary in the world, the writer's mandate to save humanity solved the problem: a benighted populace obviously required illumination, needed a savior. Writers, the child discovered jubilantly, were feted and acclaimed, so many signs that they were needed. But a savior was more exalted than a hero. He was a martyr, destined "to defend the populace against itself and its enemies" (152). The written word became "a solemn high Mass" bringing "the benediction of heaven" (152). The child chose to write neither for his neighbors nor yet exclusively for God, but "for God, with a view to saving [his] neighbors" whose "insufficiency of being" required the intercession of saints (153, 152). Essential, he was no longer the "supernumerary" child, the traveler with no ticket to give the conductor (86, 87). Writing gave him a ticket in this world and in the next, for in saving others he saved himself. Good books merged with good works. The writer was necessarily among the elect, but his books were testimony for all to see of his right to a place among the Saints and Prophets, his friends and peers.

The exalted life of a hero and martyr was by definition a solitary one. The missionary kept his lonely vigil above two billion men, his moral advantage translated into physical superiority. Making a virtue of necessity, the child saw himself as not simply alone but above his fellows, on an "airy island" of privilege, on his "perch," his natural habitat a seventh-floor Paris apartment with a view over the roofs, where he breathed the "rarified atmosphere of belles-lettres" (167, 53, 116, 153, 53). Not that he placed himself superior to others. He simply wanted to live in "the ether among the airy simulacra of Things." The adult recognized that no matter how hard he tried to descend, "out of habit," he continues to live in the air (54). Without this "capital illusion of the world stretched at [his] feet," without his "symbolic seventh-story" vantage point, Sartre knew that he never would have written a line (54).

Where there are heights, there must also be depths. Paradise created a purgatory beneath it; the select company of Saints and Prophets presupposed the damned. The lofty world of literature into whose mysteries the child was initiated by his grandfather had, as its counterbalance, another world altogether where he ventured on his own. This fantastic world of cloaks and daggers and exotic adventures offered the exquisite clandestine pleasures of "real reading," "outside the sanctuary" under the table or in his room (163). Not the plays of Corneille or the novels of Flaubert but *Cri-Cri*, *L'Epatant*, *Les Trois Boy-scouts*, *Le Dernier des Mohicans*, with their garish illustrations; their fierce Indians, dashing cowboys, and intrepid explorers; their helpless young girls in distress—these works gave infamous joys "unworthy" of the "prophetic child" just as the "bad words" swarming in the "lower depths" of vocabulary were not for a properly raised child (70). The child was conscious of leading "a double life," keeping "bad company" and "spending vacations in the brothel," deserting Mérimée's pure heroine Colomba for "a painted woman," whom he enjoyed in the full knowledge that his "truth remained in the temple" (66, 67). After all, "the Holy Spirit only appreciated truly *artistic* writing" (157). One could scarcely ask for a more vivid demonstration of the inherent elitism and tyranny of French literary culture than this opposition of grandfather, properly scandalized by these dreadful rags he found his heir apparent reading, and grandson: the grandfather's cult of the dead, his preference for passages over entire works (the better to teach with), and the exaltation of the French language against the boy's adoration of the "magic boxes" where evil was punished and virtue rewarded. The child's own reading "gave him back to his childhood" by taking him out of the temple (64).

For whom does one write? So centered on himself were the child's notions of writing and literature that it never even occurred to him that "one could write to be read" (152). He did not want readers; he wanted people under obligation to him, able to applaud his powers and to reflect his glory. Writing was in consequence an intensely selfish activity. Claims to the contrary were so much dust in the eyes, patent evidence of one more of the child's many "impostures," of one more inauthentic self. To be sure, the writer-knight dedicated himself and his works "to protect the species" (144). In truth, however, "his only business was salvation"—his own (209, 214). Like his grandmother metamorphosed into a funeral stone, the child born once of the written word would be born again in a reverse transubstantiation in which the flesh would be made word. He would write to "carve a glorious body in words." On the shelves of the Bibliothèque Nationale, twenty-five volumes, eighteen thousand pages, and three hundred engravings (including a portrait of the author) would attest to his presence; his bones would become "leather and cardboard," his "parchment flesh" would "smell of glue and mold," and through sixty kilos of paper he would take his place, reborn, a "whole man" at last (163, 164).

Such glory was not heaven's alone. Society acknowledged for its own the "mandate" of the writer on whom its institutions bestowed "earthly immortality" (140, 144, 145, 193, 209, 210). Posterity was the writer's true public, a great-grandnephew or a grandnephew who would be moved by reading about his ancestor's exemplary life. The signs of glory were everywhere, on the Bibliothèque Nationale shelf reserved for his works, in articles in the Larousse encyclopedia and obituaries in the newspapers that recounted the letters of gratitude and appreciation sent by perfect strangers, the monument in his home town, the streets bearing his name. It was only logical for this child to assume that he too was destined to be buried in the Père Lachaise cemetery beside so many illustrious colleagues or perhaps even in the Panthéon. He too would have "his" avenue in Paris, "his" streets and public squares in the provinces and even abroad (143, 175, 149, 175).

IV

Atheism is a cruel enterprise.
Jean-Paul Sartre,
Les Mots

The gods of *Les Mots* are false, the answers they give are wrong, the writer is another imposter. The powers attributed to words and to literature provoked a succession of false personages—family savior, epic hero, writer-martyr, celebrated dead author, all of whom the author of *Les Mots* rejects as inauthentic. Yet these characters are essential to Sartre's career. An account of the birth of a writer, *Les Mots* takes its place with Sartre's biographical studies of Baudelaire, Genet, and Flaubert and a projected study of Mallarmé. The project is the same, and in all four cases Sartre the biographer takes the same path through childhood: the child is father to the man undoubtedly; he is assuredly father to the writer. In *Les Mots* Sartre asks himself the same question he puts to the other writers: how and why does an individual become a writer? What circumstances, social and psychological, lead to such a crucial decision? Sartre was convinced that what an individual writes subsequent to the initial primordial decision to write is far less interesting (because it is far less important) than the decision itself. His conviction helps explain why he never produced a sequel to *Les Mots* that showed the writer writing and why, unable to get Flaubert even to *Madame Bovary,* he never finished *L'Idiot de la famille.*[31]

Les Mots recounts the birth of a writer—the wrong kind of writer, the writer imbued with self-importance and the precepts of French literary culture. Like *Qu'est-ce que la littérature?,* *Les Mots* does battle with this literary culture, its absurd valuation of literature, its equally absurd anachronistic definition of the writer. In the twentieth century of the First World War and the Russian Revolution, the twentieth century of Gide's revolutionary *Les Nourritures terrestres,* "a man of the nineteenth century imposed on his grandchild ideas current in the 1830s." This grandfather faced the past, "lived off the dead," having ceased to read after the death of Victor Hugo (he reread favorites on occasion) (56, 58). Although a Dreyfusard, he never mentioned Dreyfus—or Zola. Through the outdated notion of culture taught and incarnated by his grandfather, Sartre denounces the public no less than the private writer: *both* originate in the egocentric universe of the bourgeoisie. He ridicules the bad faith of the public writer through his grandfather, "a man of the nineteenth century, who, like so many others, like Victor Hugo himself, took himself to be Victor Hugo" (23; cf. 148, 149). The "so-called imperious mandate" received by the child in ostensible humility and then taken up in arrogance was only more of the same, one more imposture to add to the series. But Sartre also attacks the aestheticism of the private writer, the "ferocious religion, . . . the old bile" of Flaubert, the Goncourt brothers, and Gautier, which "poisoned" the child with an "abstract hatred of mankind" and "infected" him with more pretensions than ever (151). For more than thirty years these illusions would afflict the writer with a "lucid blindness" (210).

The history of a writer's birth implies another birth of another writer, the author of *Les Mots* who has repudiated the persona sanctioned by French literary culture. This implied author, the "real" Sartre, has found new answers to the basic question, what makes a writer?[32] This other, superior, writer exists in the reader's familiarity with Sartre's career (one is unlikely to read the memoirs of an individual one knows absolutely nothing about) and in the emphasis of *Les Mots* on the many "impostures" of this personage, on the "sleight of hand" that enabled him to believe, on the "mirage" of this culture, and on the assimilation of his belief to "madness" (47, 150, 176, 193, 212), "delirium" (193), and "neurosis" (193, 213). Denunciation of the false writer makes sense only if we know the "real" writer who has triumphed over a former, inferior, self. *Les Mots* is structured around a conversion, one that takes place offstage, but a conversion nonetheless. As the *Confessions* of Saint Augustine evaluate the life of the sinner by the lights of the Christian, *Les Mots* convicts the "ersatz Christian" from the point of view of the convert. In both cases later truth serves to explain and to illuminate previous error. Unlike the *Confessions*, however, which make Augustine's conversion central to the demonstration of God's glory, *Les Mots* assumes but does not tell of Sartre's conversion to the doctrine of commitment and the consequent transformation of his "mandate" into an occupation and a habit. What is left? he asks at the very end. "A whole man, made of all men, worth all of them and any one of them worth him" (214).

But *Les Mots* does not tell of a conversion. For Sartre is not a convert, he is an apostate. The exaltation of conversion has no place in this drama of lost illusions and faith denied: "Atheism," Sartre wearily observes, "is a cruel enterprise" (212). Of course *Les Mots* condemns these illusions of Sartre's childhood and does so all the more stridently because beyond the individuals, beyond the child and the grandfather, it attacks the class and the society that sustained them. Much like "L'Enfance d'un chef" twenty-five years earlier, *Les Mots* makes a full-scale assault on the bourgeoisie, its bad faith, its egocentrism, its rationalizations of self-interest. Unlike "L'Enfance d'un chef," whose protagonist is only reprehensible, *Les Mots* is a valediction too. There is an unmistakable, if muted, sense of loss for the illusions that allowed the child to exist and the writer to be happy (211) and for the love that made this childhood a paradise. The author of *Les Mots* is above all one who has sustained loss. Sartre speaks not of truth found or of glory revealed but of the "acids eating away deforming transparencies," of "seeing clearly" where he was once blind, of "waking up," of "recovering" from a "long bitter, sweet madness" (210–12). And Sartre mourns his malady. "How sad recoveries are; language is disenchanted; the heroes of the pen, . . . stripped of their privileges, have stepped back into the ranks" and have sent him "twice into mourning" (61). Or Sartre thinks of Proust's Swann, sighing over a life wasted on a woman who wasn't his type. Loss of illusion entails loss of direction. The disabused adult can laugh at his errors, for he now knows the impotence of literature. But he no longer knows what to do with his life. He has renounced his vocation only to remain in the Church. Swann marries Odette and Sartre keeps on writing: what else can he do?

Intending *Les Mots* as a "farewell" to literature, Sartre was more than a little discomfited when the work was hailed instead as a return to literature and a sign of *désengagement*.[33] The misunderstanding was not wholly the fault of the public, for *Les Mots* reaffirms the very rights of literature that it purports to denounce and reasserts, even as it seems to condemn, the mandate of the writer. This work that aims to undermine literature is on all levels a "literary" work, bearing all the signs of careful writing and rewriting. A short work—not quite two hundred pages—*Les Mots* occupied Sartre off and on for at least ten years, and Sartre himself emphasized the time he spent reworking the presentation, multiplying the levels of irony, making it mean more than it says. *Les Mots* is rife with literary allusions; references, both explicit and implied; pastiches; and parodies of Sartre's own works. It spoofs traditional genres, the classics of French literature, and Sartre's contemporaries. Parody, sarcasm, and irony mark the rupture with the past on a stylistic level and make *Les Mots* a work that perpetually questions both itself and literature. At the same time, the very attention to style and to literary forms reaffirms the past by incorporating the parodied works into a living present. The reader plays a familiar game, hunting down allusions, marking the pastiches, and relating this work to Sartre's philosophical treatises, to his fiction, to his critical studies—and to those of everyone else as well!

The search is eminently rewarding. In one form or another, and for the most part indirectly, *Les Mots* touches on virtually all of Sartre's major concerns—the nature of man, the possibility of freedom, the possibility of literature.[34] Even the reader who knows little of Sartre's work will have the pleasures of recognition; the critic well versed in the Sartrean canon will have those pleasures tenfold. Perhaps as much could be said of almost any autobiography, which must after all tell something about a life. Still *Les Mots* differs strikingly, from, say, the *Mémoires d'outre-tombe* in refusing to recapitulate the interests and events of a lifetime, in analyzing and dramatizing them instead. The protagonist is less a reconstruction of the child Jean-Paul Sartre (referred to only by his nickname, Poulou) than a construction of a personage to demonstrate and dramatize Sartre's theses about the writer in bourgeois society. The writer of French literary culture is a general type born of neurosis and illusion. Sartre acknowledged that "his" Flaubert was partially an invention required by his hypotheses and that *L'Idiot de la famille* was to be read as a novel—a "true" novel but a novel nonetheless.[35] Surely the same can be said of *Les Mots,* which reinforces the pretensions of literature even as it condemns them as illusory. The hyperbolic style underlying the parodies and the authoritative and intellectually authoritarian epigrammatic statements in which *Les Mots* abounds dramatize an otherwise ordinary childhood and transform an ordinary history of growing up into an epic quest for salvation. The quest fails ultimately, but its drama remains to inform the work and to keep us on the edge of our seats—no mean feat for an autobiography in which the end is necessarily known in the beginning. The counter-metaphor to literature-as-religion is social-life-as-comedy, its form, Sartre's stress on role, imposture, actor, and acting. The vocabulary of the stage exposes the inauthentic self produced by bourgeois society; it also points to the fundamentally dramatic nature of *Les Mots.*

The simultaneous denial and affirmation of the rights and powers of literature mark the essential ambiguity of *Les Mots* and attest to the difficulty, if not the impossibility, of burying the past. One may rid oneself of neurosis, but one can never be cured of one's self. Sartre's "mandate" has become part of his character, his "delirium" has left his head to become part of his very bones. The adult's apostasy cannot destroy the self produced by faith. Atheism is a cruel and also a long-term enterprise. Precisely because the fifty-year-old recognizes in himself all the traits of the child, Sartre must continually write against himself; the committed atheist must think systematically against himself, against the believer who remains hidden, disguised but definitely present. If existence is defined by opposition, as Sartre suggests, then the writer Sartre exists in and through oppositions—to bourgeois society, to its particularly noxious manifestation in French literary culture, and to the self in which that society and that culture were so perfectly realized. The Sartre who saw virtually every one of his childhood dreams come true, the writer whose career gave credence to every one of the child's illusions, the public writer who could easily have taken himself for a philosophe or a prophet was also the intellectual painfully aware of the paradoxical situation these honors created. It was fitting, and eloquent testimony to Sartre's literary achievement, that the Nobel Prize for literature was awarded him the year *Les Mots* was published; it was equally appropriate, and revelatory of his marked ambivalence toward literature, that Sartre declined the honor. One feels that Sartre would wish to have said of him what he himself said of his friend Paul Nizan: "In himself he cared only for his revolt: it proved that he resisted still."[36]

Such was the dilemma of the literary intellectual in the twentieth century whom Sartre enjoined to resist what could not be withstood, to practice a literature that long ago forswore its mission, and to live a culture that no longer compelled belief. Bereft of a mandate, the modern writer found the Word fractured into a babble of words, all jostling for place and precedence. The superbly arrogant claim of Victor Hugo that "words are the Word, and the Word is God" diminished for Sartre to "a contrary rustling of words" (211). Language lost the power to enchant, literature the power to save. No more was the pen the sword the child once took it for—the disabused adult knew too well how little power writers really have. What then *is* literature? What is writing? Why write and for whom? Disillusioned and disbelieving, the Sartre of *Les Mots* nevertheless recalled the younger, still hopeful editor of *Les Temps modernes*. For even if literature saves no one or nothing, it serves, a product of and for human beings to whom it holds up a "critical mirror." Sartre's achievement in *Les Mots* was to present just such a critical mirror not only to Jean-Paul Sartre the writer but also to the literary culture responsible for transforming that writer into the exemplary literary intellectual of the century.

Epilogue: Great Men, Grateful Country

To Great Men the Grateful Country
Inscription on the Panthéon

I

Jean-Paul Sartre's death in 1980 marked the end of an era and the end as well of a certain intellectual, cultural, and moral center in French society. No individual today exerts an intellectual force of such magnitude as Sartre's. Circumstances no longer encourage the same preeminence, derived from the accumulated prestige of several roles. Each one of Sartre's roles carried considerable authority; their union created the "total" and totalizing intellectual, subsuming professor and *littérateur*, philosopher and philosophe, ideologue and *moraliste*, iconoclast and traditionalist. It was his victory over the fragmentation of contemporary intellectual life and the synthesis of disparate elements that captured the French imagination.

Sartre's genius lay less in his explorations of one or another intellectual field than in his ability to dramatize the general relevance of the apparently arcane. Sartre magnified the writer by extending still further the notion of literature. Though less grandiose than Hugo's virtual apotheosis almost a century before, Sartre's funeral in April 1980 was an impressive rite of passage that ratified change even as it affirmed tradition. Much as Hugo's lying-in-state symbolized the Republic triumphant, painting over the cracks and fissures in the republican consensus that the Dreyfus affair would break wide open, Sartre's funeral marked something of an ideolog-

Jean-Paul Sartre's funeral, 29 April 1980. A new generation mourned in a style far removed from the strict comportment of the crowds that watched Victor Hugo's funeral procession. The veneration, however, was the same despite its informality, and these mourners conveyed intact the citizen's awareness of the French writer's unique cultural significance. (Photograph by Guy Le Querrec, courtesy of Magnum Photos)

JEAN PAUL SARTRE
1905 - 1980

The same scene in July 1985 is tranquil, but as the fresh geranium attests, Sartre is not forgotten. (Photograph by Priscilla Clark)

ical triumph. This highly charged ceremonial occasion asserted the unity of the Left so sorely lacking in the 1978 Socialist-Communist electoral coalition, thus prefiguring, or so it seems in retrospect, the spectacular election of François Mitterrand to the presidency a year later. Sartre himself would have been the first to point out what events have shown, namely, the illusory nature of that unity. In marked contrast to Hugo's serene identification with the Third Republic, Sartre found his *raison d'être* in his role as perennial gadfly and opponent of every institutional authority. His unshakable sense of commitment was always tempered by a distrust of power and a fundamental pessimism concerning the use of influence, his own foremost.

All of these contending forces made Sartre's funeral a splendid celebration of French literary culture, and it hardly mattered that Sartre himself had so often attacked this literary culture with great fervor. Every commentator acknowledged Sartre's place in the scheme of things, his paramount role in a literary culture bent on transforming the public writer into the exemplary intellectual. Parnassus replaced the Panthéon. The crowd of several thousand walking to the Montparnasse Cemetery testified to the significance of both the writer-intellectual and the literary culture from which that model came. The ceremonies addressed those grandnephews whom Sartre of *Les Mots* had designated as his true readers and from whose ranks, presumably, future public writers would be recruited.

Hence, even though Sartre did not receive a state funeral and was not buried in the Panthéon (he would have hated the idea), he was thoroughly "pantheonized." Once again the grateful country bespoke its appreciation of the great men who keep French intellectual powers before the world. France in its funeral enshrinement enthusiastically accepted the Nobel Prize and all the other honors refused so emphatically by Sartre himself. The daily newspapers splashed headlines across their front pages and followed up with editorials and extensive recapitulations of the life and the work. Commentary came from across the political and literary spectrum and addressed every aspect of the man: Sartre the writer, Sartre the ideologue, Sartre the militant, Sartre the philosopher, and a host of other Sartres. The expected paeans from the Left were matched by the Right, which was just as vocal, from the conservative bastions of the Académie française and the Church to the prime minister and the president of the Republic.[1]

To contemplate this outpouring is to confront once again the paradox of French literary culture and the tensions it sustains between public and private conceptions of literature. Those furthest from Sartre's views of the links between politics and literature scrupulously overlooked the militant and the ideologue, the better to eulogize the writer in good conscience. Sartre received praise for having written works that somehow transcended not only ideology but the man who wrote them. The process metamorphosed the author who so insisted on the collective nature of art, the individual who proclaimed himself at the end of *Les Mots* a man worth any man, and any man worth him, into a solitary creator, a latter-day romantic genius without peers. Unable to protest, Sartre was turned into the private writer he ever sought to repress.

Yet at the same time, and even for some of the same commentators, Sartre, like Voltaire and like Hugo, came to symbolize national pride. More regional or sectarian, American history offers no instance of a comparable identification of national consciousness with an intellectual or literary figure. Robert Lowell presents some similarities with Sartre in his assertive integration of the literary and the moral. Lowell's efforts in protesting the Vietnam War may even have been more forceful, more integral to his life and work than Sartre's earlier stand against the war in Algeria. But Lowell's death in the United States in 1977 was a strictly literary gathering. At his funeral the world of letters mourned one of its own. President Carter felt no call to comment or to eulogize. In Lowell, American literature lost a great writer; in Sartre, France lost the embodiment of French intellectuality and esprit. For a comparable expression of national loss in American history one must turn to political figures—in recent history to John and Robert Kennedy and to Martin Luther King, Jr.—and in these cases the political importance of the individuals, their relative youth, and the violence of their deaths had much to do with the outpouring of sentiment.

Changes have occurred. Sartre quit a literary world different from the one he had encountered in the 1930s. The most visible transformations touch individuals more than institutions. Today the leading roles in French literary culture no longer devolve exclusively on literary figures. The domain of the literary-minded is now invaded by what the French call the "human sciences," including virtually any more or less systematic inquiry into social and intellectual existence. The catalysts of French literary culture in the late twentieth century, the writers who settle and start debates, raise issues, and pose problems, are less often the poets, the novelists, or the *gens de lettres* than the historians, the anthropologists, the philosophers, the semiologists. In recent years Michel Foucault, Claude Lévi-Strauss, Louis Althusser, Roland Barthes, and Raymond Aron crowded into the limelight, not displacing Sartre so much as redefining the cultural context in which he moved. Less important than the men themselves—Althusser is inactive; Barthes died just before Sartre in 1980, Aron in 1983, Foucault in 1984; and Lévi-Strauss gave his last lecture at the Collège de France in 1983—is their collective presence and the shift that presence portends.

In Sartre the French lost a *maître à penser,* whose place has been filled not by an individual but by an institution, the university.[2] To be sure, the university scarcely constitutes a new factor in French intellectual life. Since the priorities shifted to research in the "Nouvelle Sorbonne" at the end of the nineteenth century, the university in France as elsewhere has been the locus of specialized intellectual activity. In comparison with the university today, however, the university of the early twentieth century stood apart from general intellectual life. The literary critic Albert Thibaudet, writing in the 1930s, claimed only somewhat facetiously that the rivalry of his writer friends on the Right Bank and his professorial colleagues on the Left Bank obliged him to live "bilaterally."[3] Hyperbole no doubt, yet we must understand the lack of communication to which Thibaudet adverted if we are to appreciate Sartre's originality in bringing the professor into the world of letters. Sartre kept what distance he could from state institutions, teaching in the lycée only until the income realized on his writing enabled him to resign. The public writers of today, by contrast, are more likely entrenched in the university system, which they use as a springboard to general intellectual life and to a broad, heterogeneous public.

This shift in the site of cultural authority undermines the impact of the literary figure, who speaks from individual experience rather than as the exponent of an intellectualized approach to experience. Whereas Sartre's fame originated in his literary works, the cultural celebrities of the 1980s first appear on the scene as savants, their authority derived from research that is subsequently translated into general intellectual discourse. Despite manifest attention to style and form, few of these writer-savants press specifically literary claims. One can of course point to Lévi-Strauss's marvelous *Tristes Tropiques*, with its echoes of Rousseau and Chateaubriand, and to Barthes's wide-ranging essays (and the novel he was rumored to be writing at the time of his death). But none of these works founded a career or launched a reputation. Rather, they set forth meditations on a distinct mode of knowing, and it is this specialized intellectual competence that legitimates general cultural authority.

As the professors move toward stage center, the literary figure stands in the wings. Whether by choice or circumstance, the best-known literary figures of recent years have not claimed the overreaching cultural authority of the public writer: Michel Tournier, J. M. G. Le Clézio, Marguerite Yourcenar, Marguerite Duras, Simone de Beauvoir, Claude Simon, Henri Michaux, Nathalie Sarraute, Michel Butor, Alain Robbe-Grillet, Philippe Sollers. The list of these diverse writers, by no means inclusive, still makes a telling point: none of these writers incarnates French literary culture as a whole or pretends to do so. Membership in the Académie française will move neither Marguerite Yourcenar from her residence in the United States nor Léopold Sédar Senghor from his home in Senegal. Though a member of the Académie Goncourt and of necessity an important actor on the Parisian literary scene, Michel Tournier leads a fairly reclusive life in the country. Other writers work from a sense of literature that precludes the role of public writer, their hermetic works standing in as much need of translation as any scientific treatise. Victims or celebrants of the specialization of literary and intellectual labor, such writers eschew altogether the communication required of a public writer, which the university stars of French literary culture today cultivate so successfully.

The resolve to engage the broader questions of culture and society can only be weakened further by the structuralist and post-structuralist modes of thought that have figured so prominently in the past two or three decades of French intellectual life. The great divergence among individual practitioners—philosophers, anthropologists, psychologists, semiologists, literary critics—should not obscure the common rejection of the larger-than-life ideal of the writer as genius. In effect, structuralism has demoted the writer promoted by romanticism a century before. The dominion of structures, whether linguistic, literary, intellectual, or social, reduces the individual to one element within these structures and displaces the object of inquiry from a percipient subject to impersonal relations. The philosopher looks for systematic relations, not an individual subject; the anthropologist looks for kinship structures, not members of families; the literary critic seeks the formal structures of a text, not the creator of a work. Rather than the unique creation of a uniquely gifted individual, the work of literature itself has become a product of various codes embedded in the text, which is subjected to the joint interpretation of writer and reader. Structuralist poetics gives the complex, highly sophisticated decoding or deconstruction of texts precedence over their construction, the interpreter ascendance over the nominal creator. Post-structuralisms, even as they attack the rigidity of structuralist formalism, only exacerbate these tensions. Interpretive strategies that negate trust in individual action and undermine confidence in the individual actor can only erode the charge of the public writer. Then, too, the disillusionment that followed in the wake of the euphoria and exaltation of May 1968 sapped the faith of French intellectuals who had hoped to legislate for humanity as well as for the French. The loss of faith attendant upon this "de-ideologization" is inimical to the stance that the public writer must take and the claims he must make. Certainly no one has replaced Sartre. No orientation, no movement, no school has focused literary and intellectual discussion in any way comparable to the *nouveau roman* and the *nouvelle critique* of the 1950s, 1960s, and early 1970s.

II

> Modern myths are even less understood than classical
> myths, even though we are devoured by myths. Myths
> press us everywhere, they serve for everything, they ex-
> plain everything.
>
> Honoré de Balzac, *La Vieille Fille*

If, then, Sartre has no direct heir, if contemporary thought
and literary practice discourage the *littérateur* from arrogating
moral and intellectual leadership, and if public writers are
today recruited more from the university ranks of historians
and philosophers than from among novelists and poets, what
of the literary culture Sartre so brilliantly exemplified? French
society in recent years seems to have altered considerably,
though appearances may be deceiving. Observers over the
past three decades or so invariably express amazement at the
enthusiasm with which the supposedly traditional French
have left off time-honored ways of doing and being. From
punk rock and *hypermarchés* to battalions of camping vans,
the Club Méditerrannée, and Disneyland soon to come, from
the decline in attendance at Mass to the disarray of the educational system and the disruption of the Paris landscape by
skyscrapers—wherever one looks, one is apt to find a different France from the country one remembers in even the recent past. French society has palpably "loosened" its traditional social and economic structures and the states of mind
from which these structures drew support. Then, too, one
must invoke the modernization of French society and the un-
precedented prosperity brought by the economic boom of the
1950s and 1960s. The French quit traditional ways in part
because of very real economic incentives to do so.

As French society presents a different face, so too the
world of books. The pace of the literary market has acceler-
ated over the past quarter century, effecting sometimes spectacular alterations in the ways books are produced and mar-
keted and in the circuit that links writer to reader via
publisher and critic. Publishing houses in France have
merged, much as they have in the United States, and the

resulting concentration of capital has created veritable empires of books and journals and an array of collateral enter-
prises. At the same time, new, small, and usually quite specialized houses have emerged to augment both the numbers
and the kinds of books published. Notwithstanding all the
talk about the "Americanization" of French publishing and
the complaints about *les best-sellers* and *le discount*, publishing
in France as elsewhere persists as something of a cottage in-
dustry, modernized in crucial respects but tied still to stub-
bornly individualistic artisans of the word—a rubric that includes not only writers, as one would expect, but, with
astonishing frequency, publishers, editors, agents, and booksellers as well.[4]

Le Comité des amis de Georges Dumézil
vous remercie vivement pour la part que vous avez bien
voulu prendre à la souscription ouverte pour lui offrir
son épée d'Académicien.

Cette épée lui sera remise au cours d'une réunion
à laquelle nous sommes heureux de vous inviter
et qui aura lieu

le mercredi 16 mai 1979 à 17 h 30
aux Éditions Gallimard 17, rue de l'Université

Invitation to the presentation of the academician's sword to Georges
Dumézil. The invitation invokes a ritual of French literary culture
that illustrates the ways a publisher may assume functions once associated with patronage. The "Comité d'honneur" organized by the
publisher Claude Gallimard invited contributions from colleagues
and friends. The presentation ceremony held at the offices of Éditions Gallimard transformed an individual honor—the election of
Professor Dumézil to the Académie française—into a cultural celebration by and for the circle around him.

In any event, social or economic change does not produce immediate cultural change. Only very slowly do new approaches to publishing or marketing books alter basic relationships to books or relations within the literary culture. Transformations in the larger society never simply transfer into culture; they must be translated first into cultural terms. Bound to certain institutions in the past and dependent on others in the present, a culture develops both with those social structures and against them. Insofar as its familiar modes of thinking, perceiving, and acting mediate the most cataclysmic of social forces, any culture tends to resist change. By infusing a sense of the past into the present, culture supplies an important means of confronting the new. What is often summarily dismissed as "cultural lag"—the very concept dismisses culture as a permanent laggard, forever out of step with social structure—bears witness to the force of this resistance and hence to the continuity culture embodies.

French literary culture presents a model of the complex relations that result from this disjuncture between culture and society. The culture of the ancien régime survived the social structures from which it originally drew support and supplied a counterpoint—indeed a counterculture—to the new society that arose over the nineteenth century. Memories of aristocratic milieux in an autocratic monarchy shaped aspirations in the disconcertingly bourgeois society of post-revolutionary France and incited writers to cast themselves as the aristocracy for modern times. So too the more properly literary culture born of this confrontation between the old and the new regimes in the nineteenth century survived the severe social, economic, and political dislocations of the twentieth century. Tributary still to the nineteenth century and to its social structures, this culture offers a remarkable instance of cultural continuity in the face of often precipitous social and economic change.

The force of this practice ensures that French literary culture will not disappear with Sartre, any more than it did with Hugo a century earlier. Now as in 1885, too much has stayed firmly in place, solidly anchored in literary tradition, on the one hand, and in literary institutions, on the other. For some time to come, it is safe to predict, the *esprit de géométrie* and the esprit de corps will set French literary culture apart. More open, less "Byzantine" than in days past, French literary culture today would nevertheless soon make Balzac or Hugo, perhaps even Voltaire, feel quite at home.[5] Regardless of the dislocations, tradition today permeates vast sectors of French society, and by no means the least important.

Despite the radical reforms of recent years, French education is nowhere near as "open" as the American system. Some time will pass before the *baccalauréat* degree becomes as common as the American high school diploma. Similar structures mark higher education as well, still more elitist in France than in the United States.[6] France cannot boast of anything like the extraordinary range of educational institutions found in the United States, and the United States has nothing like the rigorously selective, highly competitive *Grandes Ecoles*. A system of national examinations, especially one with a still-high rate of failure, cannot fail to instill an exceptional sense of hierarchy and, among those who succeed, an equally acute consciousness of success. The university proper has undoubtedly changed less than might reasonably have been expected from the fracas attendant on the reforms of 1968 and thereafter. With the purse strings still unloosed or drawn in the Ministry of Education, the French university by and large, like the whole of French education, adheres to the familiar patterns of centralization.

Similar tensions mark the very language. Responding to considerable pressure, the Ministry of Education accepted Breton and Provençal as foreign languages for the *baccalauréat* degree and a few years ago, in great consternation and after much deliberation, accepted a *baccalauréat* examination written entirely in Breton. Then in 1985 the Ministry of Culture reversed the linguistic policies set by the Convention in 1794 and set up a National Council for French Regional Languages and Cultures. But the Académie française continues to chastise institutions and individuals for incorrect usage of French, and the High Committee for the French Language, established in 1967 by Georges Pompidou, works assiduously to "universalize" the use of French, quite as the abbé Grégoire intended.

If cultural policy in the twentieth century has emphasized the diffusion and even the "democratization" of culture, the Socialist government of François Mitterrand supports cultural activities as did the ministers of Louis XIV, sometimes just as spectacularly.[7] Literary prizes flourish today as a century ago, from those awarded by the Académie des Jeux Floraux de Toulouse since the fourteenth century to the new prizes established without fail every year. Indeed, the increasingly obvious commercial stress of the market has, if anything, augmented the fixation on prizes. The increase in the number and diversity of books exacerbates competition and renders choice at the same time more formidable and more necessary. Prizes guide those choices by supplying yet another instance of criticism, a criticism all the more effective for combining the paraphernalia of modern advertising with the cultural authority of the group bestowing the award. Advertising alone cannot confer authority, and academic authority cannot by itself sell books, but their combination cannot be beaten. The Prix Goncourt sells more books than any other prize not simply because it receives the biggest promotion and the most attention from critics but also because it conveys the authority of tradition. That authority in turn completes the circuit by affecting the investment publishers will make in a given work, the attention media will pay, and, consequently, the response readers will give.

In the same way, popular literatures may actually strengthen conservative institutions and attitudes. In the classic instance of legitimation, new literatures work toward recognition whereas established institutions assimilate and thereby co-opt new literatures. Institutions must adapt if they are to survive, and they do so, even the Académie française, the most venerable symbol of everything traditional in French literary life, the "guardian of useful prejudices," as Renan put it. It may be, as one administrator remarked twice in the course of a single conversation, that "the Académie never

Claude Lévi-Strauss here wears the official uniform of the Académie française, unchanged since it was designed in 1801. The academician traditionally receives his sword as a gift from friends and colleagues but must bear the expense of the elaborately embroidered green uniform, plumed hat, and cape—35,000 francs in 1978 ($8000). Lévi-Strauss, the ethnologist who has spent a lifetime analyzing the myths and rituals of exotic peoples, surely meditates on his own participation in a familiar French rite of passage, the very essence of French tradition. (Photograph courtesy of the French Embassy Press and Information Division)

changes." It does move with the times, albeit with all deliberate speed. The prestige of the Académie rests on its fidelity to tradition, but that fidelity in turn allows the Académie to redefine the contemporary as classic. As this bastion of literary (and political) conservatism came at long last to accept the novel in the mid-nineteenth century with the election of Octave Feuillet and the cinema some years ago with the election of René Clair, so more recently the Académie gave its approbation to television by electing Alain Decaux, a popular historian appearing on television (1979); acknowledged the creative significance of women by voting membership to Marguerite Yourcenar (1980); and honored francophone literature by admitting Léopold Sédar Senghor from Senegal (1983). These elections may be of little moment. Probably, with the exception of the publishers concerned, they will exert little influence on literary institutions. Yet like Sartre's funeral the year before, Marguerite Yourcenar's ceremonious induction into the Académie française, with the president of the Republic in official attendance as protector of the Académie, was one of the rites of passage whereby French literary culture affirms tradition by acquiescing to change. In a sense every formal reception into the Académie does the same.

In other domains too the modern and the traditional complement rather than contradict each other. Whatever may be said about television in France, it surely operates as much with as against French literary culture. Mass media in France treat literature as French literary culture from the beginning defined it: as a public event. The extensive television coverage of Marguerite Yourcenar's reception by the Académie française did not fundamentally alter the meaning of the occasion. Mass media amplify, but they cannot in themselves devise, cultural attitudes. French television intensifies the concentration of literary and cultural institutions begun in the seventeenth century. "Media personalities" have been consecrated at least since the print media began actively to seek a broad, heterogeneous audience, and Sartre jabbed at the inveterate media mongering of writers in *Qu'est-ce que la*

Tradition compromises with innovation, and both are enhanced. Here Valéry Giscard d'Estaing, president of the Republic, greets Marguerite Yourcenar at her official induction into the Académie française in January 1981. To avoid the awkwardness that the bulky uniform would have presented for the first female Immortal, Saint-Laurent designed Mme Yourcenar's ensemble. In place of the traditional sword (the candidate having emphatically declared her preference for an umbrella), the new academician received a coin from the time of Hadrian, in commemoration of her most celebrated novel, *Hadrian's Memoirs*. (Photograph courtesy of the French Embassy Press and Information Division)

littérature?, which he wrote decades before television became a force to reckon with.

Television works with what it finds. "Apostrophes," the phenomenally successful television book commentary program, owes its longevity—1985 marked the tenth anniversary and the five hundredth show—in great measure to the personality, the enthusiasm, and the integrity of the host, Bernard Pivot. But "Apostrophes" has not become virtually a literary institution in its own right on the strength of personality alone. Pivot's *tour de force* has been to adapt the salon to the archetypal mass medium, to combine the elite and the popular. This salon is both exclusive—authors appear by invitation only—and open—we are all invited. And we accept the invitation because watching Pivot and his guests, most of us participate more directly than ever before in the rites and rituals of French literary culture. Pivot's own half-serious off-the-cuff explanation of his success—"The French like to talk a lot"—tells only half the story.[8] The French like to talk a lot, but to certain effect. We who faithfully turn on "Apostrophes" Friday evenings, watch reruns, and order videotapes for our French classes savor the sociability, the contentiousness, the love of conversation, the mixture of literature with politics and art, with science and scholarship, whatever. In short, we savor the spectacle of French literary culture on parade.

It was only to be expected, then, that Michel Foucault's sudden death in 1984 should be transformed into an event of national importance, though not on the scale of Sartre's four years before. As befitted the specialized intellectual that Foucault ever sought to remain, no parades marked the passing, and burial was a private ceremony in the provinces. Nevertheless, television and the newspapers treated the occasion in the broadest of terms. Like the commentators on Sartre, those who wrote Foucault's memorials invariably pointed to the integration of his life and work and commented on his characteristic style. The chorus enshrined Foucault as another exemplary French intellectual and a brilliant representative of French literary culture.

Thus does the France of the 1980s pledge its allegiance to a civilization built on and around words, a civilization in which literature draws attention and confers glory. Once again the United States furnishes the impressive contrast as a country where intellectual authority is geographically and institutionally dispersed. The literary theorist Julia Kristeva, herself a good illustration of the "star system" of French literary culture as well as of the growing importance of the university, discovered to her great amazement just how "loose," how diffuse, and how apparently unhierarchical American culture is: "No authority based on a more or less sacred Word holds in this polyvalent ethnic, historical, and ideological space. . . . For American civilization is not a civilization of words; it is a civilization of sounds, gestures, colors, numbers."[9] That American culture presents far greater sophistication than Kristeva's fascination with jazz and engineers allows is less pertinent than the country and the culture we see through eyes suddenly opened to a different reality.

Emblematic of this culture today, its assimilation of the traditional and the modern and its integration of literature and larger social concerns, is François Mitterrand. Elected president in 1981, Mitterrand became the first Socialist head of state in France since Léon Blum in 1936, and as in 1936 the sense of change was immense, coming as it did after more than two decades of Gaullist and neo-Gaullist conservative governments. But Mitterrand's connections to Léon Blum reach beyond political conviction to a profound attachment to literature and its traditions. Blum was the more active literary figure, but even his adversaries recognize in Mitterrand, author of twelve books (one written in the midst of his term as president), a "born writer." Mitterand is a politican whose least pronouncement bears the imprint of vast reading and a Socialist who has read more works of literature than socialist theory, a man for whom literature has always been a "privileged paradise." It is not surprising that some time before Mitterrand declared his candidacy for the presidency, a prominent literary figure confided that were he willing to resign as first secretary of the Socialist party, Mitterand would make a good candidate for the Académie française. And if Mitterrand did not win the election in 1981, a friend assured *Paris Match*, he would surely abandon politics and devote himself to writing.[10] It was eminently appropriate that Mitterrand chose for his official presidential portrait a photographer known for her portraits of writers and that the photograph itself shows him not only in a library of leather-bound tomes (de Gaulle and Pompidou had also been photographed in the presidential library) but seated and visibly occupied with an open book.[11] The president as Reader secures the country in Words, in a Literature that transcends partisan politics and intellectual quarrels. If this glorification partakes of myth, it is a myth integral to French literary culture, and indeed to France and to French culture. Here is an example of what Balzac meant by the modern myths that he saw everywhere, more pressing but even less understood than the classical ones.[12] French literary culture conveys these myths far beyond authors and their books to shape the expectations of readers, the aspirations of writers, and the convictions of many who have little to do with either.

III

And what of the larger culture beyond? Where does this particular culture fit in the whole of something we can identify as French culture? To return to the question posed in chapter 1, we do well in the late twentieth century to ask whether such distinctive national cultures exist at all. Those who claim they do not contend that mass culture has engulfed every other through media that cater to the lowest common denominator. Others assert that the French are getting more and more unlike each other rather than like, as minority groups break down whatever national consensus may have existed in the past. Both propositions deny the possibility of a distinct and distinctively French culture, and both, I think, are

This official presidential portrait implies that François Mitterrand reads France like the open book before him. The visible association with French literary culture guarantees continuity and the future of the country. The photographer is well known for her portraits of writers, and soon after taking this photograph she received the Legion of Honor. (Photograph by Gisèle Freund, courtesy of the French Embassy Press and Information Division)

wrong. Consideration of French literary culture in the present and the probable future helps explain why.

Difficult though it may be to construe, national culture surely represents more than a simple sum of constituent parts. Some of these parts—in this instance identifiable, more or less autonomous cultures within the larger society—contribute more than others to a national identity. In France literary culture is one of these. Sustained, legitimated, and promoted by a broad spectrum of formal and informal institutions, many of long standing, French literary culture is implicated in almost any definition of country. The strong institutional support, and especially the close links to the central societal functions of governance and education, places literary culture closer to the center of French society and farther from the periphery to which the modern world usually consigns literature and the arts. These connections ensure that literary culture in France will continue as something of a touchstone within French society as a whole.

There are other touchstones, other traditions and cultures in French society that also count for much in any determination of a national culture and sensibility. For an example by no means as frivolous as it might seem, we should look to French cuisine. Few would deny that cuisine has long played and still plays a vital role in French culture or that it inheres in the image of France cultivated at home and projected abroad. The parallels to literature are as striking as they are numerous. French cuisine, too, developed a culture around traditions inherited from the ancien régime; cuisine similarly demonstrates perdurability in the face of momentous change, exceptional resilience; moreover, a plethora of institutions sustains its values, norms, and ideologies, sustains, in short, culinary culture. And this culinary culture illustrates the interchange between the part and the whole, between the particular culture and the larger society. Cuisine, too, manifests all the contradictions that inhere in a basically elite practice in a democratic society.

Culinary culture has followed a familiar course in France. Like literary culture it evolved around a product once associated with the aristocracy and eventually forced to adapt to a bourgeois world and to the incertitudes of the open market. During the ancien régime haute cuisine was elaborated in and around the court. Pushed into the streets by the Revolution, suddenly unemployed chefs opened restaurants and brought theretofore aristocratic fare into the public domain. The nineteenth century saw the emergence of new modes of gastronomy, with new publics, new practitioners, and a slew of interpreters, notably journalists and critics. Culinary institutions multiplied to legitimate the new functions, roles, and ideologies.[13]

Even though it has come under heavy attack, the complex culture that coheres around these culinary institutions marks France still today. *Le fast food* speaks to a different culinary sensibility than either the *grande cuisine* of aristocratic, then bourgeois antecedents or the *nouvelle cuisine* that exercises the most imaginative contemporary chefs. Nevertheless, *les self-services*, *les McDonalds*, *les supermarchés*, and such notwithstanding, the traditions of French cuisine, the elevation of its artistic and intellectual components, influence the France of the 1980s. These traditions are fixed and hence perpetuated by many strong institutions that sustain culinary culture even as they feed into French culture more generally. It is an altogether fitting gesture for the minister of culture to establish, as he did in 1985, an Ecole nationale and a Centre national des arts culinaires.[14] In short, cuisine in France matters still.

And literature matters still. French literary culture manifests similar patterns of continuity and change and illustrates a comparable symbiosis with French culture generally. Behind and explaining these parallels or homologies lies the common predicament of elite practices in a democratic society. "Serious" literature, like haute cuisine, is practiced by and for elites (not inevitably the same ones), and each has suffered competition from other elite subcultures along with the even more devastating leveling tendencies inherent in a democratic society invaded by the mass media. Yet for all their patent fragility, these cultures not only survive but also flourish. Why?

One key to survival belongs to the distinctly national character of these cultures, the long and glorious traditions defined as quintessentially French in ways that more recent phenomena can never be. This is so partly because of the much decried "Americanization" of the mass media, that is to say, the homogenization effected by mass media everywhere, and partly because of the increasing economic interdependence of the whole world—whence the similarities of book production in France and other advanced industrial societies observed in chapter 1. Traditions count in older countries because they can be identified with a particular nation and its particular history. As countries lose the semblance of economic independence and as supranational forces compromise political autonomy, such traditions fortify a peculiar cultural identity.

The resistance offered by cultural traditions to the potential loss of national identity explains why particular cultures can be esteemed incontrovertible achievements of the entire country even by people who do not participate directly in them. Those among the French who will never think of haute cuisine for themselves or who have never read a word of Sartre or Hugo or Voltaire can nevertheless value associations with cuisine and with literature. One need not frequent the three-star temples of gastronomy to applaud the stars of French culinary culture or know the work of Sartre, Camus, Mauriac, Gide, or Claude Simon to take pride in their Nobel Prizes. Individuals with only the vaguest notion of the Académie française no less than its most vociferous critics can accept this secular institution as unmistakably and essentially French, which is why literature, like cuisine, will continue to matter in France.

These and other cultures in French society prosper in the main because they are part of what it means to be French. The particular points to and then comprehends the general. In the face of a relentlessly fragmented modern society, French literary culture provides a means to combat the anomie that fragmentation so often betokens. To define the ever more complicated world in which we find ourselves, most of us most of the time resort to synecdoche, that is, we take the part for the whole, finding it easier to identify and identify with particular cultures than with a society that remains distant, abstract, and, inevitably, imperfectly apprehended. The various cultures with which we connect focus experience and help us construe the meanings—our meanings—of culture and of country. In mediating thus between self and society, these cultures shape a sense of self in society. For this, finally, is what culture is all about.

Appendix A
Cultural Indicators

Book titles published annually (1973). According to the *United Nations Statistical Yearbook,* 52.2 book titles were published in France per 100,000 inhabitants (the total includes pamphlets); 39.7 titles per 100,000 inhabitants were published in the United States. In the eighty-one countries reporting, the number of titles per 100,000 inhabitants ranged from .9 to over 100, and over half (fifty-one countries) published fewer than 20 titles per 100,000 inhabitants. Of all titles published, those classified as "Literature" counted for 26.2 percent in France and 22.3 percent in the United States.

Book sales (1970). In France sales amounted to .24 percent of the G.N.P.; in the United States they were .28 percent.

Reading. Reading surveys are notoriously unreliable. In the most thorough comparative study of reading habits, the French, who averaged seven minutes per day reading books, did not differ greatly from Americans, who spent five minutes a day on books (Alexander Szalai, ed., *The Use of Time* [The Hague: Mouton, 1972], p. 580).

Support for writers. With about four times the population of France, the United States provides about four times as much in direct subsidies to writers. See my articles "Deux types de subventions: L'Assistance aux écrivains en France et aux Etats-Unis," *Bibliographie de la France* 24 (June 1976): 1232–42, and "Styles of Subsidy: Support for Writers in France and the United States," *French Review* 50 (March 1977): 543–49. The French government accounts for some 70 percent of the direct support available and the American federal government for some 20 percent of the subventions available to American writers.

Relative to population Great Britain offers to writers about as much direct financial aid as France and the United States, based on the Arts Council Report for 1976 and the *Writer's and Artist's Yearbook* (London: A. & C. Black, 1978), pp. 278–93 (£1 = $2). According to the comparative study of William Baumol and William Bowen, *The Performing Arts—the Economic Dilemma* (New York: Twentieth Century Fund, 1966), France and Great Britain spent $0.14 per capita on the performing arts. See also *The Promotion of the Arts in Britain* (London: Central Office of Information, 1975).

Prestige.   On a scale of 100, "auteur de roman d'avant-garde" ranked 55.7 in France as compared with 57.0 for "author" in the United States, 64.6 in Belgium, 66 in Poland, 70.6 in Israel, and 71.0 in Italy. Whatever the arguments against the Occupational Prestige Scale—and they are many—they presumably apply in one country as in another. See Priscilla P. Clark and T. N. Clark, "Stratification and Culture: The Position and Roles of Intellectual and Other Elites in France and the United States," mimeograph, 1974. The international scores are from Donald J. Treiman, *Occupational Prestige in Comparative Perspective* (New York: Academic Press, 1977).

Book publishing.   In keeping with the centralization of the French government and economy, book publishing is more highly concentrated in Paris than American publishing is in New York. Of the 371 French publishers with sales over $20,000 in 1971, 321 (81 percent) were in the city itself. Of the 1514 publishers in the *Annuaire des Professions* (1963), 1124 (74.2 percent) were in Paris, with 289 (19 percent) in the fifth, sixth, and seventh arrondissements alone. The *Census of Manufacturers* (1967) placed 42 percent of all American publishers in the Middle Atlantic region, these publishers accounting for 55 percent of sales. Telephone directories from the early 1970s list 194 publishers of books in Chicago, 423 in London, 584 in Manhattan, and 1514 in Paris.

Bookstores.   Bookstores are salient in Paris as they are not elsewhere. Telephone directories list 337 bookstores in Chicago, 455 in New York, 456 in London, and 1,239 in Paris. On a per capita basis, with close to the same number of bookstores—10,000 for France, 12,000 for the United States—France is ahead of the United States. But the United States makes up for its relative lack of bookstores (where books constitute the major item sold) with its 200,000 paperback outlets.

Bank Notes.   Writers accounted for five of the seven individuals on French bills in circulation in the late 1970s (Hugo, Voltaire, Racine, Corneille, Pascal). Both sides of the note show the portrait of the individual against a background related to incidents in his life. The Federal Republic of Germany uses portraits from famous German paintings. United States bills depict political figures: $1.00, Washington; $2.00, Jefferson; $5.00, Lincoln; $10.00, Hamilton; $20.00, Jackson; $50.00, Grant; $100.00, Benjamin Franklin; $500.00, McKinley; $1000, Cleveland; $5000, Madison; $10,000, Salmon P. Chase. Great Britain has the queen on the front of all bills while the reverse carries historical figures: £1, Newton; £5, Duke of Wellington; £10, Florence Nightingale or the British lion; £20, Shakespeare. In the 1970s Italian currency pictured Verdi and Marco Polo (L 1000);

Columbus (L 5000); Michelangelo (L 10,000); Leonardo da Vinci (L 50,000); Manzoni (L 100,000). French bills change fairly often, primarily to discourage counterfeiters. Napoleon was on the 100 franc note a few years ago, and the notes with portraits of Voltaire and Hugo have been replaced by coins. More recent issues added Berlioz, Maurice Quentin de la Tour, Debussy, and Montesquieu.

Stamps. Issues were examined for Great Britain (1840–1944), the United States (1847–1950), France (1848–1944), and Germany (1850–1944). Heads of state were invariably the largest single category (the only category for British stamps), places, events, and allegorical figures placing second. The patterns for German semipostals (special surtax added, designated for some specific governmental project or charity) had no writers; those for French had four (3.6 percent). One French semipostal did show "France aiding an intellectual."

Streets. As of 1957 men and (a very few) women of letters accounted for 332 (6.4 percent) of 5,218 Paris streets. By comparison, according to street maps only 2.1 percent of the streets in West Berlin were named after writers, 1.5 percent of those in East Berlin, 1.2 percent of those in Boston, 1 percent of those in San Francisco, 0.9 percent of those in Chicago and London, and 0.6 percent of those in Manhattan.

Journalism. *L'Express* allots to cultural and literary affairs (including advertisements) more space than its American counterpart, *Time Magazine.* Five issues of *Time* and *L'Express* were examined for 1973–1974 and five for 1977–1978. "Cultural" pages accounted for 24 percent of all pages (less advertising, letters to the editor) in *L'Express* and 16.1 percent of all pages in *Time.* Book and literary pages represented 12 percent of *L'Express* pages, 6.9 percent of pages in *Time.* Even more striking evidence of the greater resonance of books and literature (and/or the more pronounced elite character of *L'Express*) can be gauged by advertisements: in thirteen issues for 1978 *L'Express* had over three times as many book or book-related advertisements (with fifty-three) as *Time* (with sixteen). Moreover, almost half the *Time* advertisements were for *Time-Life* books or magazines, few or none of them even remotely literary, whereas forty of the *L'Express* advertisements (75 percent) were literary, most of them for novels. *Le Monde* and *Le Figaro* also carry advertisements for books, often on the first page.

Both journals stress their elite readership: in a 1976 study 35.5 percent of *Time* subscribers were managers or administrators; 27.2 percent had a master's or doctor's degree (*National Subscribers Study* [New York: Time-Life, 1976]). In 1974 26.3 percent of *L'Express* readers had upper-level management or administrative positions ("cadres supérieurs") (*L'Express*, September 16–22, 1974).

Television. During a sample week in 1976 three French stations showed relatively more cultural programs (8 percent of all hours) than the thirteen channels in New York City, including the Public Broadcasting Station (2.6 percent of all hours). The French stations also offered more literary and dramatic programs (3 percent of Paris program hours versus 1.2 percent of program hours in New York).

Residence. The association with universities has dispersed American writers throughout the country. Census data for 1970 showed 17.3 percent of 25,376 employed authors in New York City, 9.1 percent in Los Angeles, 8.1 percent in Washington, D.C., 2.9 percent in San Francisco, and 2.3 percent in Chicago. The more selective *Directory of American Poets, 1975* indicates that of 1536 poets, 24.5 percent (330) resided in New York City, but 13 percent (201) lived in California, 8 percent (127) in New York State outside New York City, and 6 percent in Massachusetts.

Appendix B
Measures of Reputation

Mentions of Nineteenth-century French Writers in
Selected Literary Journals

Author*	Total mentions			Rank in sample†
	Romantic	Parnassian	Naturalist	
Alexis			64	21
Balzac	528			1‡
Becque		1		—
Céard			5	74
Coppée		0		—
Daudet			36	—
Dierx		0		—
Dumas	56			25
Gautier	85			17
Glatigny		0		—
Goncourt, E. & J.			25	—
Hennique			0	—
Heredia		5		74
Hugo	222			9
Huysmans			27	—
Lamartine	94			15
Leconte de Lisle		12		47
Maupassant			129	11
Mendès		2		—
Mérimée	70			20
Musset	88			16
Nerval	172			10
Ricard		0		—

Mentions of Nineteenth-century French Writers in Selected
Literary Journals (*continued*)

Author*	Total mentions			Rank in sample†
	Romantic	*Parnassian*	*Naturalist*	
Sand	100			14
Stendhal	419			3
Sully-Prudhomme		3		—
Vigny	61			22
Zola			336	5
Total	1,895	22	624	
Mean§	127.3	2.7	69.2	

Source: W. T. Bandy, "A Statistical Analysis of Recent Nineteenth-Century Scholarship," *Nineteenth-Century French Studies* 7, nos. 1–2 (Fall–Winter 1978–1979): 1–3. Professor Bandy analyzed the authors mentioned in the *MLA International Bibliography* from 1969 through 1976 and generously provided the counts for the full sample.

* Total authors in study: 273.

† Total studies in sample: 5,587.

‡ Other writers among the top ten in the sample are Baudelaire, second, with 503 mentions; Flaubert, fourth, with 369; Chateaubriand, sixth, with 265; Mallarmé, seventh, with 245; and Rimbaud, eighth, with 224.

§ Mean mentions per author: 20.5.

The table above is constructed around a single indicator of reputation—the mentions of authors in eight issues of a single bibliography. Despite the caution that is in order given the evident limitations of the sample and the source, in fact the table does not upset but confirms most of what we sense about the survival of literary works.

First, though reputations rise and fall and sometimes rise again, literary history is written by and around authors taken to be great. In a total of 5,587 studies treating 273 French authors writing during the nineteenth century, 80 authors (29 percent) accounted for 95 percent of the studies, for a mean of 20.5 studies for each author mentioned. But compare even this mean with the number of mentions for the top ten authors or even the top twenty. Paul Alexis, ranked 21 with 64 mentions, is three times more celebrated than the average writer in the sample.

Second, the writer survives as an individual, not as a member of a group. In each of the groups one or two individuals stand out, Balzac and Stendhal among the romantics, Zola and Maupassant among the naturalists, Leconte de Lisle among the Parnassians.

Third, contemporary success, commercial or traditional, cannot assure survival—witness Leconte de Lisle and Heredia—although recognition is probably a prerequisite to survival—note the difference among the Parnassians. Traditional success, though it represents a solid entrenchment in valued literary institutions, if anything, seems to predispose to oblivion. The Parnassians fare much less well than the "outsider" naturalists.

Fourth, a look at the groups rather than the individual authors shows a clear hierarchy. The romantics, the most heterogeneous of the three groups, stand well ahead of the others with an average of 172 studies each. Even the least studied romantic author, Dumas with 56 mentions, almost triples the mean of 20.5 for the entire sample. With a mean of 69 studies the naturalists (counting the Goncourts as one) trail the romantics but outstrip the Parnassians (2.7 studies each).

The most notable triumph to be read in these rankings, however, is not that of an individual or an aesthetic but that of a genre—the novel. Four of the five top-ranked authors are novelists. The decline of the drama is almost as striking. Although many of the others tried their hand at drama, of the ten most "popular" writers in this sample, Victor Hugo alone was a dramatist of any stature. With five of the ten considered primarily poets, poetry holds its own, but no more. Among the romantics, the two novelists outdistance the others—and Victor Hugo was also a novelist.

Notes

PROLOGUE

1. For an account of the physical transformations of the Pantheon, see Jacques Hillairet, *Dictionnaire des rues de Paris*, 3 vols. (Paris: Minuit, 1963). Mona Ozouf traces the politics of the Panthéon during the Revolution and its failure as a locus of collective memory. It represents not a national past but a particular political tradition ("Le Panthéon: L'Ecole normale des morts," in *Lieux de mémoire*, ed. Pierre Nora [Paris: Gallimard, 1985], pp. 140–66).

2. "Le nom du vieux Hugo était par nous marié à celui de la République. Sa gloire était, de toutes celles des lettres et des arts, la seule qui fût vivante dans le coeur du peuple de France" (Romain Rolland, "Le Vieux Orphée," *Europe* [Paris: Rieder, 1935], p. 8). "Victor Hugo est notre religion," a student quoted by André Maurois, *Olympio ou la vie de Victor Hugo* (Paris: Hachette, 1954), p. 477. All translations are my own.

3. "Notre littérature n'est pas nos Champs-Elysées; elle est le domaine intangible, incorruptible, agissant, de notre valeur véritable et de l'aventure française en ce monde. . . . Il est decevant de voir ce que nous appelons l'histoire de France sue et rebattue dans tous ses détails . . . tandis que le Français a tout le loisir d'ignorer notre vraie histoire, celle de notre esprit et de notre langue, celle dont tout survit. . . . Le goût de la lecture . . . est l'instinct national le plus pur" (Jean Giraudoux, Préface to *Littérature* [1941] [Paris: Gallimard, 1967], pp. 6, 18).

4. "La littérature est l'expression de la société comme la parole est l'expression de l'homme" (Louis de Bonald, *Législation primitive* [Paris: LeClere, An XI (1802)], 2:207). The celebrated phrase originally appeared in an article on the Querelle des Anciens et des Modernes in the *Mercure de France* no. 41, An X (1802), and was appended as a footnote to *Législation primitive*.

5. For a review of the problems encountered in the sociology of literature, see my article "Literature and Sociology," in *Interrelations of Literature*, ed. Jean-Pierre Barricelli and J. J. Gibaldi (New York: Modern Language Association, 1982), pp. 107–22, and for the intellectual background, my "Sociology of Literature: An Historical In-

troduction," *Research in Sociology of Knowledge, Sciences, and Art* 1 (1978):237–58.

6. Edward Burnett Tylor, *Primitive Culture: Researches into the Development of Mythology, Philosophy, Religion, Language, Art, and Custom* (London: J. Murray, 1871), p. 1.

7. "Nous appelons culture tout l'ensemble ethnographique qui, du point de vue de l'enquête, présente, par rapport à d'autres, des écarts significatifs. . . . on voit que la notion de culture peut correspondre à une réalité objective, tout en restant fonction du type de recherche envisagée. . . . Dans la pratique . . . le terme de culture est employé pour regrouper un ensemble d'écarts significatifs dont l'expérience prouve que les limites coïncident approximativement. Que cette coïncidence ne soit jamais absolue . . . ne doit pas nous interdire d'utiliser la notion de culture; elle est fondamentale en ethnologie" (Claude Lévi-Strauss, "La Notion de structure en ethnologie" [1952], *Anthropologie structurale* [Paris: Plon, 1958], p. 325).

8. Cf. the definitions of culture reviewed by Michel de Certeau (*La Culture au pluriel* [1974] [Paris: Christian Bourgois, 1980], pp. 189–91) with those of Maurice Crubellier (*Histoire culturelle de la France, XIXe–XXe siècle* [Paris: Colin, 1974], pp. 1–23). Crubellier notes (p. 10) the marked resistance of the French to the ethnographic definition of culture.

9. M. M. Bakhtin, "Forms of Time and Chronotope in the Novel—Concluding Remarks" (1973), *The Dialogic Imagination* (Austin: University of Texas Press, 1981), p. 249, n. 17.

10. We are all creatures of the metaphors we use. Howard Becker, *Art Worlds* (Berkeley and Los Angeles: University of California Press, 1982), p. 370, is unusual in admitting to the metaphoric status of basic sociological concepts, by no means excluding his own "art worlds." Becker stresses the mostly conscious collaboration required of the "members" of an "art world" to produce any artistic product. Pierre Bourdieu's concept of "field" similarly presupposes the relative independence of cultural institutions. Bourdieu's metaphoric source in "magnetic field," with its poles of attraction and repulsion, gives a deterministic cast to his analyses, which see competing lines of force in a state of permanent tension ("Champ littéraire et projet créateur," *Les Temps modernes*, November 1966:865–906, and the recent summary "Le Champ littéraire," *Lendemains* no. 36 [1984]:5–20). By contrast, the term *culture* emphasizes the medium of individual and institutional action. "Literary culture" is looser and more pervasive than "literary field," the relations more diffuse than the concerted activity involved in an "art world."

11. T. S. Eliot, "Tradition and the Individual Talent" (1917), *Selected Essays* (New York: Harcourt, Brace & Co., 1950), pp. 3–11. Eliot later elaborated his ideal of criticism in "The Function of Criticism"

(1923), pp. 12–22. For a comprehensive consideration of tradition in social life, see Edward Shils, *Tradition* (Chicago: University of Chicago Press, 1981).

12. Other ethnologists besides Lévi-Strauss should be invoked as well, notably Clifford Geertz, whose term "thick description" designates the texture that the observer of culture must seek to convey ("Thick Description: Toward an Interpretive Theory of Culture," *The Interpretation of Cultures* [New York: Basic Books, 1973], pp. 3–30). See also Sherry Turkle's investigation of a "psychoanalytic culture" in contemporary France, *Psychoanalytic Politics: Freud's French Revolution* (New York: Basic Books, 1976), in particular chap. 8, "Psychoanalysis as Popular Culture," pp. 191–209; and the Epilogue for French "culinary culture."

CHAPTER 1

1. "'L'écrivain' en France est autre chose qu'un homme qui écrit et qui publie" (Paul Valéry, "Pensée et art français" [1939], *Oeuvres* [Paris: Gallimard-Pléiade, 1960], 2:1053).

2. Claude Lévi-Strauss, "La Notion de structure en ethnologie" (1952), *Anthropologie structurale* (Paris: Plon, 1958), pp. 325–26.

3. Appendix A (see pages 217–20) lists these indicators. For more detailed analyses, see my article "Literary Culture in France and the United States," *American Journal of Sociology* 84, no. 5 (March 1979):1057–77.

4. See the sophisticated review and extensive criticism of these arguments for the homogeneity of cultures by M. Gottdiener, "Hegemony and Mass Culture: A Semiotic Approach," *American Journal of Sociology* 90, no. 5 (March 1985):979–1001.

5. Theodore Zeldin, *The French* (New York: Pantheon, 1984), esp. pp. 44–50.

6. For Edmund Wilson's comment, see his *Upstate* (New York: Farrar, Straus & Giroux, 1971), p. 156; see also Jean-Paul Sartre, *Les Mots* (Paris: Gallimard-Folio, 1964), pp. 143, 175.

7. Although state control of television has loosened since the 1981 Socialist election victory, and two private stations now exist, the three principal French stations are administered by government appointees at least as mindful of what is appropriate as of what is popular. The relative prominence of cultural programs reflects a judgment that such subjects are eminently appropriate and unlikely to raise hackles in or out of government circles. Leftist critics of French television point to the "delicacy" with which the television stations treat—or ignore—sensitive topics. In 1969 Marcel Ophuls made for television his highly acclaimed but unflattering film about the Resistance, *The Sorrow and the Pity;* it was not shown on French

television until 1981. The similar incident concerning another film about the Resistance, *Terroristes à la retraite,* created a similar scandal in 1985, the station that had originally financed the film having second thoughts about its acceptability. De Gaulle's oft-cited preference for television as an instrument of social control is consonant with the strong administrative control.

8. Edmond Goblot, *La Barrière et le niveau: Essai sur la bourgeoisie française moderne* (1925) (Paris: Presses universitaires de France, 1967), analyzes the dual function of Latin and the *baccalauréat* degree. On the lycée curriculum, see the important article by Gérard Genette, "Enseignement et rhétorique du XXe siècle," *Annales: Economies, sociétés, civilisations* 21, no. 2 (1960):293–305, reprinted in G. Genette, *Figures* (Paris: Le Seuil, 1969). The Sophocles-Racine and Mme de Sévigné–Mme de Lafayette examples along with a long discussion of the examiners' expectations are given by Marcel Proust, *A la recherche du temps perdu* (Paris: Gallimard-Pléiade, 1954), 1:911–15; 2:353. The examination is for an unspecified "certificat d'études" and not the more exacting and more philosophically oriented *baccalauréat,* but similar subjects would have been treated in lycée classes. Proust's criticism is devastating: "Mais . . . il n'y avait, au fond, de stupides que des professeurs faisant adresser par Sophocle une lettre à Racine" (2:353).

9. John Andrews, *A Comparative View of the French and English Nations in Their Manners, Politics, and Literature* (Dublin: White, Byrne, and Marchbank, 1785), pp. 28, 30.

10. Henry Lytton Bulwer, *France* (London: Richard Bentley, 1834), 2:196, 185, 187, 213.

11. Ford Madox Ford, *A Mirror to France* (London: Duckworth, 1926), p. 30; Ernst Robert Curtius, *Essai sur la France* (Paris: Grasset, 1932), p. 204.

12. Allen Tate, "The Profession of Letters in the South" (1935), *Collected Essays* (Denver: Alan Swallow, 1959), p. 265. Tate tells of being able to use a letter of credit immediately in a small French town on his word that he was a man of letters.

13. Gertrude Stein, *Paris France* (1940) (New York: Liveright, 1970), p. 21.

14. Bertrand Poirot-Delpech, "Ah! être écrivain . . . ," *Le Monde,* 27 July 1979, p. 9.

15. "L'ambition littéraire dans notre pays va très souvent de pair avec l'ambition politique. . . . De nos jours encore, nombreux sont les dirigeants qui souffrent d'avoir dû, pour occuper les grands emplois, sacrifier—du moins le croient-ils—leur carrière d'écrivain . . . c'est presque une singularité, et on n'imagine guère M. Ford romancier, M. Schmidt historien, ni M. Brejnev philosophe" (Pierre Viansson-Ponté, *Le Monde,* 12 October 1976, p. 1). See also Curtius,

Essai sur la France, p. 159. Jean-Paul Aron notes the literary references sprinkled throughout Pompidou's press conferences and even
those of Giscard (*Qu'est-ce que la culture française?* [Paris: Denoël-
Gonthier, 1975], p. 28). One writer, Roger Nimier, hailed de Gaulle's
return to power in 1958 in literary terms: "Pour la première fois dans
son histoire, la France est gouvernée par un écrivain" (quoted by
Philippe de Saint-Robert, "Charles de Gaulle: Figure littéraire," *Les
Nouvelles littéraires* no. 2622 [9–16 February 1978], p. 7).
    16. Philippe de Saint-Robert, "Charles de Gaulle: Figure littér-
aire," p. 7, praises de Gaulle's press conferences, "où le style deven-
ait tout ensemble naturel et somptueux," although "dans l'écrit
proprement dit, une certain tension subsiste toujours quant à l'em-
placement de la virgule." Nor could anyone say of an American political program what was said of the Popular Front of 1936, that its
"'plateforme' publicitaire, idéologique et électorale . . . a été consti-
tuée comme le sommaire d'une prestigieuse revue littéraire" (François Nourissier, *Les Chiens à fouetter—sur quelques maux de la société
littéraire et sur les jeunes gens qui s'apprêtent à en souffrir* [Paris: Julliard,
1956], p. 71). The observation in the epigraph to this chapter is also
on p. 71.
    17. The statement, which came to be known as the "Declaration
of the 121" (the original number of signatories) provoked a series of
counter-declarations, more support and signatories for the 121, re-
prisals by the government against signatories who were civil servants (lycée and university professors, magistrates). The seriousness of the statement and the courage of the signers can be gauged
by the refusal of French newspapers to print the manifesto, which
first appeared in full in the *Manchester Guardian*, until prosecution
made it news rather than treason. Sartre was seldom reluctant to
use the authority bestowed on him. Hervé Hamon and Patrick Rotman, *Les Intellocrates: Expédition en haute intelligentsia* (Paris: Ramsay,
1981), p. 262, cite a study for the period 1958–1969 that shows Sartre
signing more manifestos (ninety-one) than any other French intellectual. Laurent Schwartz (seventy-seven) and Simone de Beauvoir
(seventy-two) came in second and third.
    18. Quoted in Leah S. Marcus, "Present Occasions and the Shap-
ing of Ben Jonson's Masques," *ELH* (English Literary History) 45
(1978):205. Between 1614 and 1627, nine such proclamations in-
veighed against spending legal holidays in London. The 1632 proc-
lamation was followed by a census and suits against 14 peers and
250 gentry who disobeyed (Lawrence Stone, *The Crisis of the Aristocracy, 1558–1641* [Oxford: Clarendon Press, 1965], pp. 397–98).
    19. Clifford Geertz argues that the Elizabethan progress diffused
the values and norms of the center to the periphery through the
charisma attached to the royal personage ("Centers, Kings, and

Charisma: Reflections on the Symbolics of Power," in *Culture and Its Creators: Essays in Honor of Edward Shils,* ed. J. Ben-David and T. N. Clark [Chicago: University of Chicago Press, 1977], pp. 150–71, reprinted in *Local Knowledge* [New York: Basic Books, 1983], pp. 121–96). On the cost of Elizabethan progresses and the burdens they imposed, see Stone, *The Crisis of the Aristocracy,* pp. 451–54.

20. See Albert C. Baugh and Thomas Cable, *A History of the English Language,* 3d ed. (Englewood Cliffs, N.J.: Prentice-Hall, 1978), chap. 9.

21. On patronage in England, see Guy Fitch Lytle and Stephen Orgel, eds., *Patronage in the Renaissance* (Princeton, N.J.: Princeton University Press, 1981); and Edwin Haviland Miller, *The Professional Writer in Elizabethan England* (Cambridge: Harvard University Press, 1959), pp. 101–28.

22. Margaret Barnard Pickel, *Charles I as Patron of Poetry and Drama* (London: Frederick Muller, 1936); Michael Foss, *The Age of Patronage* (Ithaca, N.Y.: Cornell University Press, 1971), treats primarily music and painting; A. S. Collins, *Authorship in the Days of Johnson* (London: Robert Holden, 1927), esp. chaps. 1, 3; John Harris, *Government Patronage of the Arts in Great Britain* (Chicago: University of Chicago Press, 1970); Janet Minihan, *The Nationalization of Culture: The Development of State Subsidies to the Arts in Great Britain* (New York: New York University Press, 1977).

23. Samuel Johnson, letter to Lord Chesterfield, February 1755, quoted in J. W. Saunders, *The Profession of English Letters* (London: Routledge & Kegan Paul, 1964), pp. 142–43.

24. Stone, in *The Crisis of the Aristocracy,* argues that unlike the Continental aristocracies, the English aristocracy was not cut off from the rest of the population and that the titular peerage and the upper gentry can be considered a single class. Looking at the eighteenth century, Leonard Krieger contrasts just this mingling of social groups in England with the greater separation in France (and the even more rigid separation in Russia) (*Kings and Philosophers, 1689–1789* [New York: Norton, 1970]).

25. On the patronage of the visual arts in early America, see Neil Harris, *The Artist in American Society: The Formative Years, 1790–1860* (1966; reprint Chicago: University of Chicago Press, 1982).

26. On the significance of law and lawyers for American literature in the early republic, see Robert A. Ferguson, *Law and Letters in American Culture* (Cambridge: Harvard University Press, 1984), chaps. 1–3.

27. John Quincy Adams, *Poems of Religion and Society* (1848) (New York: William H. Graham, 1850), Publisher's Notice and "Justice," p. 98. A close analysis of and claims for *Notes on the State of Virginia* as a *literary* text are made by Robert A. Ferguson, "'Mysterious obliga-

tion': Jefferson's *Notes on the State of Virginia,*" *American Literature* 52, no. 3 (November 1980): 381–406. Edmund Wilson discusses the sophisticated rhetorical style of Lincoln and makes an important case for Grant's memoirs as a literary masterpiece (*Patriotic Gore* [New York: Oxford University Press, 1962]).

28. Daniel Webster, "Adams and Jefferson" (speech at the commemorative service of 1826), *The Writings and Speeches of Daniel Webster,* 8 vols. (Boston: Little, Brown & Co., 1903), 1:300.

29. John Adams to Abigail Adams, May 1780, *Adams Family Correspondence,* ed. L. H. Butterfield et al. (Cambridge: Harvard University Press, 1963–), 3:342.

CHAPTER 2

1. "Les rapports qui existent entre l'état social et politique d'un peuple et le génie de ses écrivains sont toujours très nombreux; qui connaît l'un n'ignore jamais complètement l'autre" (Alexis de Tocqueville, *De la démocratie en Amérique* [Paris: Gallimard, 1961], 2 [1840], pt. 1, chap. 13, p. 65).

2.   Les Dieux eux-mêmes meurent
       Mais les vers souverains
             Demeurent
       Plus forts que les airains.
          (Théophile Gautier, "L'Art,"
             Émaux et camées [1852])

3. The very thought of being presented to the king led Rousseau to refuse the pension offered him for his opera, *Le Devin du village* (1752) (Jean-Jacques Rousseau, *Les Confessions,* bk. 8, *Oeuvres complètes* [Paris: Gallimard-Pléiade, 1959], 1:379–81).

4.   Grand Roi, dont nous voyons la générosité
       Montrer pour le Parnasse un excès de bonté
       Que n'ont jamais eu tous les autres,
       Puissiez-vous dans cent ans donner encor des lois,
       Et puissent tous vos ans être de quinze mois
       Comme vos commis font les nôtres!
             (Pierre Corneille, "Au Roi Pour
             le retardement du paiement de
          sa pension" [1665], *Oeuvres complètes*
             [Paris: Le Seuil, 1963], p. 885)

5. Antoine Adam, *Histoire de la littérature française,* 5 vols. (Paris: del Duca, 1962), 3:10–11, 235–36; 4:265; *Europe* no. 453 (January 1967) (on Racine); Jacques Donvez, *De quoi vivait Voltaire* (Paris: Les Deux Rives, 1949), p. 106 and passim; Jacques Proust, *Diderot et l'Encyclopédie* (Paris: Colin, 1967), pp. 105–10. Sources, types, and amounts of writers' incomes are given by John Lough, *Writer and*

Public in France from the Middle Ages to the Present Day (Oxford: Clarendon Press, 1978), chaps. 3, 4, 5. Alain Viala's rigorous study of the seventeenth-century literary field, *Naissance de l'écrivain* (Paris: Minuit, 1985), is an invaluable resource, esp. pp. 76–80 and the table comparing sources of earnings, pp. 305–16. Viala (chap. 2) distinguishes between patronage (*le mécénat*), moneys given in recognition of talent, and what he calls "le clientelisme," the payment of writers for rendering specific services. The two, in fact, as indeed Viala recognizes and demonstrates, overlap in practice. See also the older but still useful study by Maurice Pellisson, *Les Hommes de lettres au XVIIIe siècle* (1911) (Geneva: Slatkine Reports, 1970).

6.   Qu'on parle mal ou bien du fameux Cardinal,
Ma prose ni mes vers n'en diront jamais rien:
Il m'a fait trop de bien pour en dire du mal,
Il m'a fait trop de mal pour en dire du bien.
(Corneille, *Oeuvres complètes*, p. 872)

The successor put in charge of finances by Mazarin immediately canceled all royal pensions (though the move may have been initiated by Louis XIII himself) (Mark Bannister, "The Crisis of Literary Patronage in France, 1643–1655," *French Studies* 39, no. 1 [January 1985]:18–30).

7.   Timothy Murray analyzes patronage of the drama as a means for Louis XIII and Richelieu to "perform" their legal and literary authority. Both actually intervened in the organization of theatrical troupes, and Richelieu personally oversaw work for the Théâtre du Marais, solicited revisions of scripts that did not please, and even revised scripts himself ("Theatrical Legitimation: Forms of French Patronage and Portraiture," *PMLA* [Publications of the Modern Language Association] 98, no. 2 [March 1983]:171–72).

8.   Viala, *Naissance de l'écrivain*, chap. 1, documents the rise and fall of private academies during the seventeenth century, as the state took control and effectively stifled private initiative. Bannister, "The Crisis of Literary Patronage," demonstrates the shift in tone and content of dedications as "heroic virtue" became redefined as service to the state.

9.   "J'ai vu tant de gens de lettres pauvres et méprisés que j'ai conclu dès longtemps que je ne devais en augmenter le nombre" (*Mémoires pour servir à la vie de M. de Voltaire écrits par lui-même* [1759] [Paris: Emile Hazan, 1927], p. 64). "Rien n'est si doux," he adds, "que de faire sa fortune par soi-même."Although Voltaire is speaking particularly here of the inadequacies of patronage, the sentiment and the reasoning applied equally to the market. Because he had invested shrewdly, he could go on to boast that "après avoir vécu chez les rois, je me suis fait roi chez moi."

10. Fernand Cuvelier, *Histoire du livre: Voie royale de l'esprit humain* (Monaco: Editions du Rocher, 1982), p. 65.

11. See Robert Darnton, *The Literary Underground of the Old Regime* (Cambridge: Harvard University Press, 1982), pp. 1–121. Darnton stresses the passionate resentment of these lower, scorned ranks of the literary world, a resentment that fueled revolutionary fervor.

12. "Un homme de lettres . . . ne doit être animé quand il compose que de la vue du bien public. Le commerce qu'il fait de sa plume . . . rabaisse sa qualité à celle d'un négociant" (André Chevillier, *L'Origine de l'Imprimerie de Paris* [1694], cited by Pellison, *Les Hommes de lettres*, p. 78).

13. Dès que l'impression fait éclore un Poëte,
Il est esclave né de quiconque l'achète,
Et ses écrits tous seuls doivent parler pour lui.
        (Nicolas Boileau, *Satire IX* [1668], *Oeuvres complètes* [Paris: Gallimard-Pléiade, 1966], p. 53)

14. "Corneille est excellent, mais il vend ses ouvrages" (the poet Antoine Gaillard, quoted by Adam, *Histoire de la littérature française,* 1:514).

15. Travaillez pour la gloire, et qu'un sordide gain
Ne soit jamais l'objet d'un illustre Ecrivain.
Je sçai qu'un noble Esprit peut, sans honte et sans crime,
Tirer de son travail un tribut légitime:
Mais je ne puis souffrir ces Auteurs renommez,
Qui dégoûtez de gloire, et d'argent affamez,
Mettent leur Apollon aux gages d'un Libraire,
Et font d'un Art divin un métier mercenaire.
        (Boileau, *L'Art poétique,* chant 4, p. 183)

16. Marcel Reinhard, "Elite et noblesse dans la seconde moitié du XVIIIe siècle," *Revue d'histoire moderne et contemporaine* 3 (1953):23.

17. "Tous les jours à la Cour un sot de qualité / Peut juger à travers avec impunité" (Boileau, *Satire IX*, p. 53).

18. Domna C. Stanton presents the *honnête homme* as an artistic creation of the self (*The Aristocrat as Art: A Study of the "Honnête Homme" and the "Dandy" in Seventeenth- and Nineteenth-Century French Literature* [New York: Columbia University Press, 1980], esp. chaps. 1, 2).

19. The brunt of Viala's analysis in *Naissance de l'écrivain* is that such a consciousness did exist and that the seventeenth century saw the beginnings of a true literary field (in Pierre Bourdieu's sense of a semi-autonomous domain). Philippe Desan argues that poets in sixteenth-century France were already on the road to professionalization ("Ronsard's *Odes* as a *Curriculum Vitae*," in *Renaissance Studies,* ed. M. Horowitz [in press]). The question is one of degree—and

Viala acknowledges ambiguity as the principal feature of this first (incipient) literary field (p. 176).

20. "Sire, rien n'est impossible à Votre majesté; elle a voulu faire de mauvais vers, et elle y a réussi" (quoted by Charles Augustin Sainte-Beuve, "François I Poëte" [*Le Journal des savants*, 1847], *Oeuvres* [Paris: Gallimard-Pléiade, 1960], 2:564). In the fifteenth century the king was assumed to be able to turn *good* sonnets, although Sainte-Beuve doubted whether François I in fact did.

21.   Envain contre le Cid un Ministre se ligue.
        Tout Paris pour Chimène a les yeux de Rodrigue.
        L'Académie en corps a beau le censurer,
        Le Public révolté s'obstine à l'admirer.
                            (Boileau, *Satire IX*, p. 54)

22. "Je dis bien que le grand art est de plaire et que cette comédie ayant plu à ceux pour qui elle est faite, je trouve que c'est assez pour elle, et qu'elle doit peu se soucier du reste" (Molière, *La Critique de l'Ecole des femmes* [1663], *Oeuvres complètes* [Paris: Le Seuil, 1962], p. 210). On the cultural integration of aristocracy and bourgeoisie in seventeenth-century France, see the classic studies of Paul Bénichou, *Morales du Grand Siècle* (Paris: Gallimard, 1948), and Erich Auerbach, "La Cour et la Ville" (1951), *Scenes from the Drama of European Literature* (New York: Meridien, 1959), pp. 133–79.

23. For a discussion of controls and restraints, see, for example, Robert Mauzi, *L'Idée du bonheur au XVIIIe siècle* (Paris: Colin, 1965).

24. "Je ne me sens pas en état de tenir tête à Voltaire. Puis, l'animadversion des gens de lettres me paraît la plus dangereuse des pestes. J'aime les Lettres, j'honore ceux qui les professent, mais je ne veux de société avec eux que dans leurs livres, et je ne les trouve bons à voir qu'en portrait" (Louise Honorine, duchesse de Choiseul Stainville, letter to Mme du Deffand, quoted by Sainte-Beuve, "Madame du Deffand," *Causeries du lundi* [9 May 1859] [Paris: Garnier, n.d.], 14:226–27).

25. See Lough, *Writer and Public in France*, chap. 4, and Pellisson, *Les Hommes de lettres*, chaps. 2–5, on incomes in the eighteenth century. The proliferation of posts leads Lough (p. 230) to assert that Louis XV and Louis XVI did more for men of letters than Louis XIV. Darnton, *The Literary Underground*, pp. 1–40, details the exemplary career of J.-B.-A. Suard, a second-generation philosophe who cannily accumulated posts, gifts, and sinecures. Lough (pp. 233–34) fixes on Marmontel to make the same point.

26. Robert Darnton has explored some of the lower reaches of literary life in *The Great Cat Massacre and Other Episodes in French Cultural History* (New York: Basic Books, 1984), pp. 145–89, and *The Literary Underground*, pp. 1–70.

27. Madeleine Cerf, "La Censure royale à la fin du XVIIIe siècle,"

Communications 9 (1967):2–27. Censorship was exercised by the Crown, by the several regional parlements (the Parlement of Paris was especially active), by the Church, by the booksellers (la Chambre syndicale des Libraires), by the police, and by the inspectors of the book trade (les inspecteurs de la Librairie). The Crown alone intervened before publication.

28. Rousseau, *Les Confessions*, bk. 11, pp. 573–84.

29. "Le plus grand malheur d'un homme de lettres n'est peut-être pas d'être l'objet de la jalousie de ses confrères, la victime de la cabale, le mépris des puissants de ce monde, c'est d'être jugé par les sots" (Voltaire, "Lettres, gens de lettres, ou lettrés" [1765], *Dictionnaire philosophique* [Paris: Garnier, 1961], p. 273); Jean d'Alembert, *Essai sur la société des gens de lettres et des grands, sur la réputation, sur les mécènes, et sur les récompenses littéraires* (1753), *Oeuvres* (Paris: Belin, 1822), 4:337–73.

30. Alexis de Tocqueville, *L'Ancien Régime et la Révolution* (1856) (Paris: Gallimard, 1952), bk. 3, chap. 1, pp. 193–201. Assigning, accepting, or denying responsibility for the Revolution was a matter of controversy almost as soon as the Revolution settled. See also Lough, *Writer and Public in France*, pp. 246–47.

31. Ironically enough, given the republican French context, *droits d'auteur* are usually translated into English as "royalties" instead of the literal "rights of authors." Royalties in the modern sense as a percentage of sales did not become usual until the mid-nineteenth century or later, and even then (today as well) exceptions to the rules were probably as common as compliance.

32. These literacy rates are estimates only. For geographical and chronological detail and reflection on the meanings of literacy, see François Furet and Jacques Ozouf, *Lire et écrire: L'Alphabétisation des Français de Calvin à Jules Ferry* (Paris: Editions de Minuit, 1977), vol. 1. It would be wrong to see the triumph of literacy as beyond question. In the United States, despite official statistics from the Department of Health, Education, and Welfare, which counted 1.5 percent of the American population as illiterate, a recent Gallup poll (1978) found fully 15 percent of the population to be functionally illiterate. It is true that the basic requirements for literacy have risen over time as contemporary societies have become dependent on increasingly sophisticated print media. See Furet and Ozouf, p. 58, on residual illiteracy in France.

33. On this popular literature of the ancien régime, see Robert Mandrou, *De la culture populaire aux XVIIe et XVIIIe siècles* (Paris: Stock, 1964); Geneviève Bollème, "Littérature populaire et littérature de colportage au XVIIIe siècle," in Geneviève Bollème et al., *Livre et société dans la France du XVIIIe siècle* (Paris and The Hague: Mouton, 1965), pp. 61–92; and the classic study of Charles Nisard, *Histoire des*

livres populaires (Paris: E. Dentu, 1864). Literacy effectively killed this *littérature de colportage* in the last third of the century.

34. The *cabinets de lecture* played an important role in the extension of the reading public and in catering to its presumed tastes. See Françoise Parent-Lardeur, *Lire à Paris au temps de Balzac: Les Cabinets de lecture à Paris, 1815–1830* (Paris: Editions de l'Ecole des hautes études en sciences sociales, 1981), especially pp. 107–65.

35. See the important study of Georges May, *Le Dilemme du roman au XVIIIe siècle* (Paris: Presses universitaires de France, 1965).

36. By comparison the United States published 2,076 new titles in 1880 and an average of 5,001 between 1890 and 1900, less than half the titles published in France. In 1890 France published thirty-five new titles per 100,000 inhabitants in contrast to just seven titles for the United States. For detailed figures, see my "Stratégies d'auteur au XIXe siècle," *Romantisme* 17 (1977):92–102; and Christophe Charle, *La Crise littéraire à l'époque du Naturalisme—roman, théâtre, politique: Essai d'histoire sociale des groupes et des genres littéraires* (Paris: Presses de l'Ecole normale supérieure, 1979), pp. 92–102.

37. Balzac was wont to refer to Sue's *Le Juif errant* (The Wandering Jew) as *Le Suif errant* (Running Lard).

38. "Il n'y a pas une vertu qui ne soit doublée d'un vice. La littérature engendre bien les libraires. —Et les journalistes!" (Honoré de Balzac, *Illusions perdues*, *La Comédie humaine*, 12 vols. [Paris: Gallimard-Pléiade, 1976–1981], 5:369). "Il ne reconnaissait pas en lui [Doguereau] le libraire de la vieille école, un homme du temps où les libraires souhaitaient tenir dans un grenier et sous clef Voltaire et Montesquieu mourant de faim" (5:305); "Dauriat est un drôle qui vend quinze ou seize cent mille francs de livres par an, il est comme le ministre de la littérature" (5:370). "Il existe dans tout critique un auteur impuissant. Ne pouvant rien créer, le critique se fait le muet du sérail. . . . Aujourd'hui que tout va se matérialisant, la critique est devenue une espèce de douane" (Balzac, *Monographie de la Presse parisienne* [1843] [Paris: J. J. Pauvert, 1965], pp. 113, 115).

39. "Vous ne connaissez pas, messieurs, le mal que les succès de lord Byron, de Lamartine, de Victor Hugo, de Casimir Delavigne, de Canalis et de Béranger ont produit. Leur gloire nous vaut une invasion de Barbares. . . . Depuis deux ans, les poètes ont pullulé comme les hannetons" (Balzac, *Illusions perdues*, 5:368–69). See the whole tirade, pp. 366–69, on how a publisher works. On the other hand, Boileau was already complaining in the late seventeenth century about the excessive number of writers attracted by the market:

> Escrive qui voudra . . .
> . . . Delà vient que Paris voit chez luy de tout temps,
> Les Auteurs à grands flots déborder tous les ans:
> Et n'a point de portail, où jusques aux corniches,

Tous les piliers ne soient enveloppez d'affiches.

(*Satire IX*, p. 51)

40. György Lukács, "Balzac: Lost Illusions," *Studies in European Realism* (1948) (New York: Grosset & Dunlap, 1964), pp. 47–64.

41. Jean V. Alter, *Les Origines de la satire anti-bourgeoise en France*, 2 vols. (Geneva: Droz, 1966, 1970); César Grana, *Bohemian versus Bourgeois: French Society and the French Man of Letters in the Nineteenth Century* (New York: Basic Books, 1964), pt. 1; and my *Battle of the Bourgeois: The Novel in France, 1789–1848* (Paris: Didier, 1973).

42. Auguste-Hilarion de Kératry, "Les Gens de lettres d'autrefois," in *Paris; ou, Le Livre des cent-et-un* (Paris: Ladvocat, 1832–34), 2:395–422 (quotations from pp. 398, 418, 421).

CHAPTER 3

1. For greater detail on pensions and moneys earned, see John Lough, *Writer and Public in France from the Middle Ages to the Present Day* (Oxford: Clarendon Press, 1978), chap. 5; and P. Clark and T. N. Clark, "Patrons, Publishers, and Prizes: The Writer's Estate in France," in *Culture and Its Creators: Essays in Honor of Edward Shils*, ed. J. Ben-David and T. N. Clark (Chicago: University of Chicago Press, 1977), pp. 197–225.

2. Lough, *Writer and Public in France*, pp. 310–12; Benjamin Bart, *Flaubert* (Syracuse, N.Y.: Syracuse University Press, 1968), pp. 727–35.

3. The budget allocation for "Encouragements aux savants et hommes de lettres" ranged from a low of 73,042 francs in 1833 to a high of 373,536 francs in 1843, with an average from 1833 to 1880 of 221,000 francs (Charles Nicolas, *Les Budgets de la France depuis le commencement du XIXe siècle* [Paris: Berger-Levrault and E. Guillaumin, 1883], pp. 282–83; Félix Faure, *Les Budgets de la France contemporaine depuis vingt ans* [Paris: Guillaumin, 1887], pp. 248–49). For two examples in greater detail, see *Projet de loi pour la fixation des recettes et des dépenses de l'exercice 1862* (Paris: Imprimerie nationale, 1862) and *Projet de loi du Budget Général de l'exercice 1881* (Paris: Imprimerie nationale, 1880). Official pensions could come only from the Ministry of the Interior (see *Budget*, chap. 9, "Secours fixes et éventuels" and "Secours à divers frais"). But a note indicates that the moneys were mostly designated for those "personnes auxquelles les événements de 1851 ont porté préjudice" (*Projet . . . 1881*, p. 523). In 1862, the moneys were designated to "secourir certaines infortunes particulièrement dignes d'intérêt" (*Projet . . . 1862*, p. 253).

4. George D. Painter, *Marcel Proust*, 2 vols. (New York: Random House, 1959), 1:179, n. 1. Cf. Lough, *Writer and Public in France*, pp. 306–7, 310–13. A professional librarian related the underdevelop-

ment of French library resources to this habit of appointing un-
professional staff (Roger Pierrot, "Les Bibliothèques," in *Le Livre
français*, ed. J. Cain et al. [Paris: Bibliothèque Nationale, 1972], p.
202).

5. Painter, *Marcel Proust*, 1:179, 184, 187, 266.

6. Victor Brombert's notable *Intellectual Hero* (New York: Lipin-
cott, 1961), chap. 1, reviews writers' educational connections from
the end of the nineteenth century to the mid-twentieth century.

7. The Académie has received subsidies from the government,
through legacies over the centuries, and has considerable property
in its own right. According to a recent history, the government supplies approximately 1 percent of current operating expenses (Duc de
Castries, *La Vieille Dame du Quai Conti* [Paris: Hachette, 1978], p.
110). The first five hundred members of the Académie (1635–1906)
included three members of ruling families; twenty dukes; forty-eight
cardinals, archbishops, or bishops; fifteen prime ministers; and
forty-eight government ministers (Emile Cassirer, *Les Cinq Cents Im-
mortels* [Paris: Henri Jouve, 1906], pp. 210–12).

8. "L'idéal de l'Académie fut d'être la représentation de l'esprit
français" (Gaston Boissier, former secrétaire perpétuel of the Académie, quoted by Choucri Cardahi, *Regards sous la Coupole* [Paris:
Mame, 1964], p. 35).

9. "L'Académie française était seule considérée en France, et
donnait réellement un état. Celle des Sciences ne signifiait rien dans
l'opinion. . . . D'Alembert avait honte d'être de l'Académie des Sciences. . . . A l'Académie française *nous regardions les membres de celle
des Sciences comme nos valets*" (Jean Siffern Maury, conversation with
Joseph de Maistre, 1799, reported in Charles Augustin Sainte-
Beuve, "L'Abbé Maury," *Causeries du lundi* [23 June 1851], 4th ed.
[Paris: Garnier, n.d.], 4:283 [emphasis in text]).

10. "L'Académie . . . s'évanouit à l'idée d'une lettre de change
qui peut envoyer à Clichy. Elle est sans coeur ni pitié pour l'homme
de génie qui est pauvre ou dont les affaires vont mal. . . . Ainsi, . . .
ayez une position . . . et vous êtes élu" (Charles Nodier, quoted by
Marcel Bouteron, "Balzac et l'Institut de France," *Etudes balzaciennes*
[Paris: Jouve, 1954], p. 132).

11. "Ah! Princesse, vous ne savez pas quel service vous avez
rendu aux Tuileries, combien votre salon a désarmé de haines et de
colères, quel tampon vous avez été entre le gouvernement et ceux
qui tiennent une plume. Mais Flaubert et moi, si vous ne nous aviez
pas achetés, pour ainsi dire, avec votre grâce, vos attentions, vos
amitiés, nous aurions été, tous deux, des éreinteurs de l'Empereur
et de l'Impératrice!" (Edmond de Goncourt and Jules de Goncourt,
Journal [13 November 1874], 22 vols. [Monaco: Editions de l'Imprimerie nationale, 1956], 10:209).

12. François Coppée's comparison is cited by Rémy Ponton,

"Programme esthétique et accumulation de capital symbolique," *Revue française de sociologie* 1 (April–June 1973):202–20. Ponton's analysis builds on the categories of Max Weber, charisma in particular, itself a variation of the basic religious metaphor.

13. "Dans ce désert de Paris, Lucien trouva donc une oasis rue des Quatre-Vents"; "ces êtres supérieurs . . . portaient au front . . . le sceau d'un génie spécial" (Honoré de Balzac, *Illusions perdues, La Comédie humaine,* 12 vols. [Paris: Gallimard-Pléiade, 1976–1981], 5:320, 315). Atypically, Balzac's idealized cénacle does not subscribe to any single aesthetic but is definitely set against the market.

14. See Luc Badesco, *La Génération poétique de 1860* (Paris: Nizet, 1971), on what he aptly terms "revues de combat" in poetry.

15. "Pour avoir l'honneur de faire partie de la Société, il sera nécessaire d'être homme de lettres. Rien qu'homme de lettres, on n'y recevra *ni grands seigneurs, ni hommes politiques*"; "une académie vengéresse et consolatrice" (Testament d'Edmond de Goncourt, in Jacques Robichon, *Le Défi des Goncourt* [Paris: Denoël, 1975], p. 332 [emphasis in text]). The work also contains the statutes of the Académie Goncourt, members and prizes through 1974, and a detailed history. Much of the same material is judged negatively by Roger Gouze, *Les Bêtes à Goncourt* (Paris: Hachette, 1973).

16. The Société des gens de lettres, founded in 1838, represents different purposes. Neither a union nor a professional association, the Société was and is a protective association, collecting royalties, seeking more effective copyright laws, protecting members from plagiarism. Funds derive principally from members' fees, drawn in turn from royalties.

17. "La littérature, la production littéraire n'est point pour moi distincte ou du moins séparable du reste de l'homme et de l'organisation; je puis goûter une oeuvre, mais il m'est difficile de la juger indépendamment de la connaissance de l'homme même. . . . L'étude littéraire me mène ainsi tout naturellement à l'étude morale" (Sainte-Beuve, "Chateaubriand jugé par un ami intime," *Nouveaux lundis,* 22 July 1862 [Paris: Calmann-Lévy, 1892], 3:15). A satire written by one Laprade, who lost his chair at Lyon, appeared in 1861, making the obvious connection to censorship:

> Un jour viendra, ce jour rêvé par Sainte-Beuve,
> Où *les Muses d'Etat,* nous tenant sous la main,
> Enrégimenteront chez nous l'esprit humain.
> (Quoted by Albert Cassagne,
> *La Théorie de l'art pour*
> *l'art en France* [1906]
> [Paris: L. Dorbon, 1959], p. 95)

18. Victor Hugo, préface to *Marie Tudor* (1833), *Théâtre complet,* 2 vols. (Paris: Gallimard-Pléiade, 1964), 2:414.

19. "Nous avons . . . tenté une oeuvre de rapprochement, de conciliation, entre les deux classes placées aux deux extrémités de l'échelle sociale" (Eugène Sue, epilogue, *Le Juif errant* [1844–1845], 2 vols., rev. ed. [Paris: Librairie internationale, 1869], 2:321).

20. "Un écrivain . . . doit se regarder comme un instituteur des hommes"; "J'ai pris de bonne heure pour règle ces grandes paroles, qui sont la loi de l'écrivain monarchique aussi bien que l'écrivain démocratique" (Balzac, avant-propos to *La Comédie humaine*, 1:12, 13).

21. "Nous croyons à l'autonomie de l'art, l'art pour nous n'est pas le moyen mais le but" (Théophile Gautier, introduction to *L'Artiste*, cited by Cassagne, *La Théorie de l'art*, p. 137).

22. "Mille recettes de style et de forme agitées; . . . une discussion puérile et grave, ridicule et solennelle, de façons d'écrire et de règles de bonne prose . . . l'idée n'était plus que comme une patère à accrocher des sonorités et des rayons. Il nous a semblé tomber dans une bataille de grammairiens du Bas-Empire" (Goncourt, *Journal* [11 April 1857], 2:94).

23. "Le Beau n'est pas le serviteur du Vrai, car il contient la vérité divine et humaine. . . . Le poëte . . . doit réaliser le Beau . . . par la combinaison complexe, savante, harmonique des lignes, de couleur et des sons, non moins que par toutes les ressources de la passion, de la réflexion, de la science et de la fantaisie" (Leconte de Lisle, avant-propos to *Poètes contemporains* [1864] [a series of articles that appeared in *Le Nain jaune*], *Articles, préfaces, discours* [Paris: Les Belles Lettres, 1971], p. 159).

24. "Il n'y a de vraiment beau que ce qui ne peut servir à rien; tout ce qui est utile est laid . . . l'endroit le plus utile de la maison, ce sont les latrines" (Gautier, préface to *Mademoiselle de Maupin* [1834] [Paris: Garnier, 1966], p. 23).

25. "L'art et la science, longtemps séparés par suite des efforts divergents de l'intelligence, doivent donc tendre à s'unir étroitement, si ce n'est à se confondre. L'un a été la révélation primitive de l'idéal contenu dans la nature extérieure; l'autre en a été l'étude raisonnée et l'exposition lumineuse" (Leconte de Lisle, *Articles, préfaces, discours*, pp. 118–19).

26. "Quiconque est avec la science, doit être avec nous"; "*Le Roman expérimental* est une conséquence de l'évolution scientifique du siècle . . . il est . . . la littérature de notre âge scientifique" (Emile Zola, *Le Roman expérimental* [1880] [Paris: Garnier-Flammarion, 1971], pp. 60, 74).

27. "Il y a plusieurs morales. Il y a la morale positive et pratique à laquelle tout le monde doit obéir. Mais il y a la morale des Arts. Celle-là est toute autre" (Charles Baudelaire, *Les Fleurs du mal* [Paris:

Garnier, 1958], p. 255). Cf. Cassagne, *La Théorie de l'art*, pp. 226–261, on the definition of art as a higher morality.

28. "Car toute oeuvre de l'esprit, dénuée de ces conditions nécessaires de beauté sensible, ne peut être une oeuvre d'art. Il y a plus, c'est une mauvaise action, une lâcheté, un crime, quelque chose de honteusement et d'irrévocablement immoral" (Leconte de Lisle, *Articles, préfaces, discours*, pp. 159–60).

29. "On est très coupable, quand on écrit mal; en littérature, il n'y a que ce crime qui tombe sous mes sens, je ne vois pas où l'on peut mettre la morale, lorsqu'on prétend la mettre ailleurs. Une phrase bien faite est une bonne action" (Zola, "La Littérature obscène," *Le Voltaire* [1880], reprinted in *Le Roman expérimental*, p. 334).

30. "La dénigrer, mais tâcher d'en faire partie" (Gustave Flaubert, *Le Dictionnaire des idées reçues, Oeuvres* [Paris: Gallimard-Pléiade, 1952], 2:999).

CHAPTER 4

1. "La production littéraire se fait de jour en jour, plus énorme, plus menaçante. Le livre monte, déborde, se répand: c'est une inondation. Il s'échappe en torrent des librairies encombrées, croule en cascades jaunes, bleues, vertes, rouges, des étalages vertigineux. On ne se fait pas une idée de tous les noms arrachés des profondeurs de l'inconnu, que cette marée déferlante soulève un instant sur le dos de ses vagues, roule pêle-mêle . . . et rejette ensuite, en un coin perdu de la grève, où nul ne passe, pas même les voleurs d'épaves" (Octave Mirbeau, *Les Ecrivains–1ᵉ série, 1884–1894* [Paris: Flammarion, n.d.], p. 85).

2. Cf. Clifford Geertz, "Ideology as a Cultural System" (1964), *The Interpretation of Cultures* (New York: Basic Books, 1973).

3. Honoré de Balzac, avant-propos to *La Comédie humaine*, 12 vols. (Paris: Gallimard-Pléiade, 1976–1981), 1:12.

4. See the conclusion to my *Battle of the Bourgeois* (Paris: Didier, 1973).

5. "On lisait beaucoup alors dans les ateliers. Les rapins aimaient les lettres" (Théophile Gautier, *Histoire du romantisme* [1874] [Paris: Charpentier, 1877], p. 4). Georges Matoré has noted the contributions of the painters' milieu ("Les Notions d'art et d'artiste à l'époque romantique," *Revue des sciences humaines*, April–September 1951:120–37).

6. Pierre Martino, *Le Roman réaliste sous le Second Empire* (Paris: Hachette, 1913), pt. I, chaps. 3, 4, analyzes the interaction of literary and artistic "campaigns." See also Zola's study of Manet (1866) in

Mes haines (Paris: Charpentier, 1879), and René Dumesnil, *L'Epoque réaliste et naturaliste* (Paris: Tallandier, 1945), chap. 18.

7. The romantics are (in order of birth) Stendhal (Henri Beyle), Alphonse de Lamartine, Alfred de Vigny, Honoré de Balzac, Victor Hugo, Alexandre Dumas, Prosper Mérimée, George Sand (Aurore Dupin Dudevant), Gérard de Nerval (Gérard Labrunie), Alfred de Musset, Théophile Gautier. Biographical information was obtained from Dr. Hoefer, ed., *Nouvelle Biographie générale* (Paris: Firmin-Didot, 1865).

The Parnassians, identified by Rémy Ponton ("Programme esthétique et accumulation de capital symbolique: L'Exemple du Parnasse," *Revue française de sociologie*, 1 [April–June 1973]:202–20), are Charles-Marie-René Leconte de Lisle, Albert Glatigny, Léon Dierx, Sully-Prudhomme (René François Armand Prudhomme), Catulle Mendès, José María Heredia, François Coppée, Xavier de Ricard.

The naturalists include the six contributors to the joint publication *Les Soirées de Médan* (1880): Emile Zola, Paul Alexis, Joris-Karl Huysmans (Georges Charles Huysmans), Henry Céard, Guy de Maupassant, and Léon Hennique. To their number I have added three "elders": Henry Becque, Alphonse Daudet, and (counted as one) Edmond and Jules de Goncourt. See Pierre Martino, *Le Naturalisme français, 1870–1895* (1925) (Paris: Colin, 1945); Jacques Dubois, "Emergence et position du groupe naturaliste dans l'institution littéraire," *Le Naturalisme: Colloque de Cerisy* (Paris: Union Générale d'Edition-10/18, 1978), pp. 75–91; Rémy Ponton, "Naissance du roman psychologique: Capital culturel, capital social, et stratégie littéraire à la fin du XIXe siècle," *Actes de la recherche en sciences sociales* no. 4 (July 1975):66–81 (Ponton uses the naturalists as a basis of comparison); and Christophe Charle, *La Crise littéraire à l'époque du Naturalisme—roman, théâtre, politique: Essai d'histoire sociale des groupes et des genres littéraires* (Paris: Presses de l'Ecole normale supérieure, 1979), esp. pt. 2, chaps. 1, 2.

8. "J'ai d'abord posé un clou et d'un coup de marteau, je l'ai fait entrer d'un centimètre dans la cervelle du public; puis d'un second coup, je l'ai fait entrer de deux centimètres. . . . Eh bien, mon marteau, c'est le journalisme que je fais moi-même autour de mes oeuvres" (Emile Zola, quoted in Edmond de Goncourt and Jules de Goncourt, *Journal* [19 February 1877], 22 vols. [Monaco: Editions de l'Imprimerie nationale, 1956], 11:128–29).

9. "Oui, c'est vrai que je me moque . . . de ce mot *Naturalisme* et cependant je le répéterai sans cesse parce qu'il faut un baptême aux choses, pour que le public les croie neuves" (Zola, quoted in Goncourt, *Journal* [19 February 1877], 11:128). Edmond de Goncourt calls

realism a "mot drapeau" in the preface to *Les Frères Zemganno* (1879).

10. "On devait s'emparer des journaux, envahir les théâtres, s'asseoir dans les fauteuils de l'Académie, se former des brochettes de décorations, et finir modestement pair de France, ministre et millionnaire" (Théophile Gautier, *Honoré de Balzac* [Paris: Poulet, Malaissis, et de Broise, 1859], pp. 90–94).

11. Pierre Bourdieu refers to properly cultural (that is, noneconomic) resources brought to any social situation as "cultural capital" ("Les Trois Etats du capital culturel," *Actes de la recherche en sciences sociales* no. 30 [November 1979]:3–6).

12. Goncourt, *Journal* (19 February 1877), 11:128.

13. Octave Mirbeau, "La noblesse et la littérature," *Les Ecrivains*, p. 66.

14. Théophile Gautier, *Histoire du romantisme*, p. 101.

15. The patterns of recruitment to literary groups confirm the observations of Alfred Odin, who found that among 623 French *gens de lettres* from 1300 to 1830, those of aristocratic origin declined from 50 percent in the period 1330–1500 to 16 percent in the years 1776–1825 (*Genèse des grands hommes: Gens de lettres français modernes* [1895], discussed by Alain Girard, *La Réussite sociale en France* [Paris: Presses universitaires de France, 1961], p. 287).

16. "En élevant le roman jusqu'à vous, vous l'engagez; en lui reconnaissant des droits vous lui imposez des devoirs. . . . Plus d'une fois sans doute avant ces derniers temps, le roman avait pénétré dans cette enceinte . . . mais il ne s'y présentait qu'en s'effaçant dans la lumière d'oeuvres plus accréditées et plus imposantes, *et l'on peut dire qu'il y était plutôt pardonné qu'admis.* Malgré de grands exemples en effet, vous n'étiez pas encore assurés . . . que le roman s'offrît comme une forme légitime de notre littérature nationale (Octave Feuillet, inaugural speech at the Académie française, cited by Paul Bourget, "Le roman à l'Académie," *Trois Siècles de l'Académie française* [Paris: Firmin-Didot, 1936], p. 213 [emphasis in original]).

17. Pierre Bourdieu, "Le Marché des biens symboliques," *L'Année sociologique* 22 (1971):49–126.

18. "Zola, dans le triomphe [celui de *L'Assommoir*], a quelque chose d'un parvenu, arrivé à une fortune inespérée" (Goncourt, *Journal* [19 February 1877], 11:128).

19. See appendix B.

20. Jules Huret, *Enquête sur l'évolution littéraire* (Paris: Charpentier, 1891). The interviews originally appeared in *L'Echo de Paris*, 3 March–5 July 1891.

21. "Je crois que c'est une spécialité française que d'avoir des écoles qui sèment la terreur et qui se fondent sur la terreur, mais (et

ceci est vrai pour toutes nos écoles) finissent toujours par éclater en personnalités dont les fortes subsistent. Si on prend l'époque de Zola et le recueil des *Soirées de Médan*, on comprend ensuite que, dans ce recueil, seuls comptent Zola et Maupassant: le reste n'est rien. L'ensemble produisait bien sûr à l'époque une impression de terreur, parce que les naturalistes étaient aussi terroristes, mais à partir du moment où leur école s'est diluée et où chaque personnalité a repris son autonomie, ce sont ces personnalités qui ont changé ensuite la totalité du roman français" (Maurice Mourier, "Y a-t-il encore un roman français?" *Esprit*, May 1985:113).

CHAPTER 5

1. Edith Wharton, *French Ways and Their Meaning* (New York: D. Appleton, 1919), p. 80.

2. Alfred Odin's concern with the social forces that influence genius (see chap. 4, n. 15, above) led him to choose French men of letters born between 1300 and 1830 because the French literature not only supplied many important writers but also distributed those writers fairly evenly over time (*Genèse des grands hommes: Gens de lettres français modernes* [1895], discussed in Alain Girard, *La Réussite sociale en France* [Paris: Presses universitaires de France, 1961], pp. 280–92). The anthropologist Alfred Kroeber singled out French literature, which "from before 1100 on . . . manifests a continuity of performance unequaled in Europe" (*Patterns of Culture Growth* [Berkeley and Los Angeles: University of California Press, 1970], p. 236). Kroeber based his ratings on the conventional judgments of textbooks and encyclopedias. There is no doubt that French literature is striking in its continuity. Whether it is unique is irrelevant.

3. "Les Français n'ont point proprement d'ouvrage national, parce qu'ils ont une littérature toute nationale. Quand une littérature toute entière est l'expression d'une société, un ouvrage particulier ne peut être l'expression d'un peuple" (Louis de Bonald, "Pensées diverses," *Oeuvres* [Paris: D'Adrien LeClere et Cie, 1847], p. 379; Ernst Robert Curtius, *Essai sur la France* [Paris: Grasset, 1932], p. 190).

4. "Ce qui n'est pas clair n'est pas français. . . . Ce qui n'est pas clair est encore anglais, italien, grec ou latin" (Antoine Rivarol, *De l'universalité de la langue française* [Paris: Cocheris, 1791], p. 40). See also Ferdinand Brunot, *Histoire de la langue française*, 13 vols. (1905–1943) (Paris: Colin, 1966–1972), 8:839–64.

5. "Quoy que nos moeurs ne soient peut-estre pas plus pures que celles de nos voisins, nôtre langue est beaucoup plus chaste que les leurs" (Le Père Bouhours, cited by Brunot, *Histoire de la langue française*, 4:280–81).

6.   Enfin Malherbe vint, et le premier en France
       Fit sentir dans les vers une juste cadence:

D'un mot mis en sa place enseigna le pouvoir,
Et réduisit la Muse aux Règles du devoir.
  (Nicolas Boileau, *L'Art poétique* [1674],
    chant 1, *Oeuvres complètes* [Paris:
    Gallimard-Pléiade, 1966], p. 160)
De Bonald, "De l'éducation dans la société," *Oeuvres*, pp. 408–9.

7.   Aimez donc la Raison. Que toujours vos écrits
Empruntent d'elle seule et leur lustre et leur prix.

. . . .

Hastez-vous lentement, et sans perdre courage
Vingt fois sur le mestier remettez vostre ouvrage.
Polissez-le sans cesse, et le repolissez.
Ajoûtez quelque fois, et souvent effacez.
  (Boileau, *L'Art poétique*, chant 1, pp. 158, 161)

8. "La production du plaisir se fait par l'ordre et par la vrai-semblance"; and "j'aimerais presque mieux que l'on m'accusât d'avoir failli par connaissance que d'avoir bien fait sans y songer" (Jean Chapelain and Guez de Balzac, respectively, cited by Daniel Mornet, *Histoire de la clarté française* [Paris: Payot, 1929], p. 53). "Le style n'est que l'ordre et le mouvement que l'on met dans ses pensées," (Georges-Louis Leclerc, comte de Buffon, "Sur le style," *Oeuvres complètes* [Paris: Delangle Frères, 1827], 1:5).

9. "La méditation, l'étude, le travail . . . sont les Apollons . . . qui inspirent les uns [les poètes] et qui font les autres [les critiques]" (Guez de Balzac, quoted by Mornet, *Histoire de la clarté française*, p. 53). "Il est impossible qu'un poète ne contienne pas une critique" (Charles Baudelaire, "Richard Wagner et *Tannhäuser* à Paris" [1861], in *Critique littéraire et musicale* [Paris: Colin, 1961], p. 373). Sainte-Beuve observed "Cette faculté de vraie critique qu'elle [la France] a toujours possédée" ("Des jugements sur notre littérature contemporaine à l'étranger," *Revue des deux mondes*, 15 June 1835, in *Oeuvres* [Paris: Gallimard-Pléiade, 1966], 1:588).

10. "Vous autres, Anglais, vous ne vous soumettez à aucune règle, à aucune méthode; vous laissez croître le génie sans le contraindre à prendre telle ou telle forme; vous auriez tout l'esprit que vous avez, si personne n'en avait eu avant vous. Oh! nous ne sommes pas comme cela. Nous avons des livres; les uns sont l'art de penser; d'autres l'art de parler, d'écrire, de comparer, de juger, etc. etc. Nous sommes les enfants de l'art; quelqu'un de parfaitement naturel chez nous devrait être montré à la foire; enfin ce serait un phénomène" (Marie de Vichy-Chamrond, marquise du Deffand, letter, 17 May 1767, *Horace Walpole's Correspondence with Madame du Deffand*, ed. W. S. Lewis and W. H. Smith [New Haven: Yale University Press, 1939], 1:294).

11. "La France est peut-être le seul pays où des considérations de pure forme, un souci de la forme en soi, aient persisté et dominé dans l'ère moderne. Le sentiment et le culte de la forme me sem-

blent être des passions de l'esprit qui se recontrent le plus souvent en liaison avec l'esprit critique" (Paul Valéry, "Images de la France" [1927], *Oeuvres* [Paris: Gallimard-Pléiade, 1960], 2:1002). See also W. L. Wiley, *The Formal French* (Cambridge: Harvard University Press, 1967).

12. "Le génie français, c'est certainement le plus complet, le plus mesuré, le plus propre à créer une forme de culture intellectuelle qui s'impose à tous" (Ernest Renan, "L'Académie française," *Essais de morale et de critique* [Paris: Michel Lévy, 1860], p. 345).

13. W. C. Brownell, *French Traits* (New York: Scribner's, 1886), p. 86; Wharton, *French Ways and Their Meaning*, p. 59.

14. Matthew Arnold, "The Literary Influence of Academies" (1864) and "The Function of Criticism at the Present Time" (1864), *Complete Prose Works* (Ann Arbor: University of Michigan Press, 1962), 2:232–57; 3:258–85; Eça de Queirós, "O Francecismo," cited by Alexander Coleman, *Eça de Queirós and European Realism* (New York: New York University Press, 1980), p. 9.

15. André Gide, introduction to *Anthologie de la poésie française* (Paris: Gallimard-Pléiade, 1962), pp. 7–8. Lanson is cited by Curtius, *Essai sur la France*, p. 190; Valéry, "Images de la France," 2:999–1006.

16. "La langue française ayant la clarté par excellence . . . rien n'est comparable à la prose française" (Rivarol, *De l'universalité de la langue française*, pp. 33, 34–35); "un ouvrage dangereux écrit en France est une déclaration de guerre à toute l'Europe" (de Bonald, "Pensées diverses," p. 345).

17. "Les ouvrages bien écrits seront les seuls qui passeront à la postérité. La quantité des connaissances, la singularité des faits, la nouveauté même des découvertes, ne sont pas de sûrs garants de l'immortalité. . . . Toutes les beautés qui s'y trouvent [dans le style] . . . sont autant de vérités aussi utiles et peut-être plus précieuses pour l'esprit humain que celles qui peuvent faire le fond du sujet" (Buffon, "Sur le style," 1:13–14).

18. "Le Stile, independamment de ce qu'il exprime, est une affaire importante en France. . . . Ailleurs, les Pensées font naitre les Expressions . . . ; ici il arrive le contraire; souvent les Expressions font naitre les Pensées" (Béat-Louis de Muralt, *Lettres sur les Anglois et les François et sur les voiages* [1728] [Paris: Champion, 1933], p. 261).

19. "Sur tout, qu'en vos écrits la Langue reverée / Dans vos plus grands excez vous soit toûjours sacrée" (Boileau, *L'Art poétique*, chant 1, p. 160).

20. "La langue française . . . est une eau pure que les écrivains maniérés n'ont jamais pu et ne pourront jamais troubler. Chaque siècle a jeté dans ce courant limpide ses modes, ses archaïsmes prétentieux et ses préciosités, sans que rien ne surnage de ces tentatives inutiles, de ces efforts impuissants. La nature de cette langue est d'être claire, logique et nerveuse. Elle ne se laisse pas affaiblir, ob-

scurcir ou corrompre" (Guy de Maupassant, "Le Roman," introduction to *Pierre et Jean* [1887], *Oeuvres complètes,* 29 vol. [Paris: Conard, 1908–1910], 19:xxvi).

21. "Sans la langue en un mot, l'Auteur le plus divin / Est toujours, quoyqu'il fasse un méchant Ecrivain" (Boileau, *L'Art poétique,* chant 1, p. 161).

22. "Je la trouve [la langue française] si peu maniable après vingt ans d'étude, que je ne pense pas . . . que nous autres Français, nous sachions notre langue; si nous ne savions que cela, nous le saurions mieux" (Honoré de Balzac, letter published in *Le Constitutionnel,* 20 October 1846, cited in Charles de Louvenjoul [Spoelberch de Louvenjoul], *Histoire des oeuvres de Honoré de Balzac* [Paris: Calmann-Lévy, 1879], p. 122).

23. Jorge Luis Borges, *L'Express,* 9–15 May 1977, pp. 34–36; "Moi, né à Corfou, je me sens un bâtard aimant de la France, amoureux fou de la langue française, qui est une de mes patries, et mes livres sont un arbre de Judée dans la merveilleuse immense forêt française" (Albert Cohen, *Le Monde,* 6 January 1980, p. 17); "Je crois que mon rapport à la langue me tient lieu de géographie, justement. Je crois que la langue française est ma plus chère malade et ma seule patrie possible. L'asile et l'antre, par excellence. L'armure et l'arme par excellence. Un des lieux, en tous cas, où je me tienne en ce monde" (Bernard-Henri Lévy, *Le Monde,* 5 January 1978, p. 1).

24. Edmond Goblot, *La Barrière et le niveau* (1927) (Paris: Presses universitaires de France, 1967).

25. "Pour extirper tous les préjugés, développer toutes les vérités, tous les talents, toutes les vertus, fondre tous les citoyens dans la masse nationale, simplifier le méchanisme et faciliter le jeu de la machine politique, il faut identité de langage. . . . L'unité d'idiome est une partie intégrante de la Révolution" (L'Abbé Grégoire, "Rapport sur la nécessité et les moyens d'anéantir les patois et d'universaliser l'usage de la langue française," in Michel de Certeau, Dominique Julia, and Jacques Revel, *Une politique de la langue—La Révolution française et les patois: L'Enquête de Grégoire* [Paris: Gallimard, 1975], pp. 300–17 [citation pp. 308–9]).

26. As late as 1870, according to one estimate, French was still a foreign language for fully half the population of France (Eugen Weber, *From Peasants into Frenchmen* [Stanford: Stanford University Press, 1976], p. 70 and chap. 6, passim).

27. "Le but est d'arriver . . . à la vraie parole. . . . Pour cela, il faut rompre et greffer la parole primitive, naturelle, vulgaire, et lui donner par l'art, . . . par la vraie culture et la grande éducation, une sorte de nouvelle forme, plus noble et plus élevée" (Monseigneur Dupanloup, letter [1873], cited by Antoine Prost, *L'Enseignement en France, 1800–1967* [Paris: Colin, 1968], p. 66). See also Aleksander Wit Labuda, "La Langue de l'Empereur: La Culture littéraire dans

les lycées sous le Second Empire," *Littérature* no. 22 (1976): 75–91; Gérard Genette, "Enseignement et rhétorique du XIXe siècle," *Annales: Economies, sociétés, civilisations* 21, no. 2 (1966): 293–305, reprinted in *Figures II* (Paris: Seuil, 1969); and Theodore Zeldin, *France, 1848–1945* (Oxford: The Clarendon Press, 1977), vol. 2, chaps. 6 (on the lycée) and 7 (on the university).

28. For the dictée in full see René Dumesnil, *L'Epoque réaliste et naturaliste* (Paris: Tallandier, 1945), pp. 103–5.

29. See *Lire*, July and October 1985, for the quarterfinal, semifinal and final *dictées*. On the domination of writing, see Michel de Certeau, *L'Invention du quotidien* (1974), republished as *The Practice of Everyday Life*, trans. Steven Rendall (Berkeley and Los Angeles: University of California Press, 1984), p. 136.

30. Albert Guige, *La Faculté des Lettres de l'Université de Paris, 1808–1935* (Paris: F. Alcan, 1935), pp. 14 ff.; *Projet de loi: Budget de l'Exercice 1862* (Paris: Imprimerie impériale, 1861); *Projet de loi du Budget Général de l'Exercice 1881* (Paris: Imprimerie nationale, 1880).

31. See Stephen Potter, *The Muse in Chains* (London: Jonathan Cape, 1937), and, on Cambridge, E. M. W. Tillyard, *The Muse Unchained* (London: Bowes and Bowes, 1958).

32. "Notre conscience linguistique n'est rien de moins que notre conscience nationale" (André Thérive, *Le Français—langue morte?* [Paris: Plon, 1923], pp. i–iii).

33. Michel Ragon, *Histoire de la littérature prolétarienne en France* (Paris: Albin Michel, 1974), p. 24; Frances Trollope, *Paris and the Parisians in 1835* (London: R. Bentley, 1836), p. 59. During 1985, the centenary of the deaths of Victor Hugo and Jules Vallès, any number of official celebrations honored the archetypal republican (including a commissioned symphony); the Communard, exile, radical journalist, acerbic novelist was virtually ignored.

34. "Le tort du peuple quand il écrit, c'est toujours de sortir de son coeur, où est sa force, pour aller emprunter aux classes supérieures des abstractions, des généralités. Il a un grand avantage, mais qu'il n'apprécie nullement: celui de ne pas savoir la langue convenue, de n'être pas, comme nous le sommes, obsédés, poursuivis de phrases toutes faites, de formules qui viennent d'elles-mêmes, quand nous écrivons, se poser sur le papier. . . . Voilà justement ce que nous envient, ce que nous empruntent, autant qu'ils peuvent, les littérateurs ouvriers. Ils s'habillent, ils mettent des gants pour écrire, et perdent ainsi la supériorité que donnent au peuple . . . sa main forte et son bras puissant" (Jules Michelet, *Le Peuple* [Paris: Hachette, 1846], pt. 2, chap. 2, p. 149). On the French worker-poets to whom (among others) Michelet alludes, see Edgar Leon Newman, "The New World of the French Socialist Worker Poets," *Stanford French Review* 3, no. 3 (Winter 1979): 357–68, which includes

samples of the poetry. See also the special issue of *Revue des sciences humaines* no. 190 (April–June 1983): 31–47, "Des Poissardes au réalisme socialiste."

35. "Pour nous, *la Francophonie est culture*, c'est un mode de pensée et d'action . . . c'est une communauté spirituelle . . . c'est, pardelà la langue, la civilisation française" (Léopold Sédar Senghor, *Liberté III: Négritude et civilisation de l'universel* [Paris: Le Seuil, 1977], p. 80 [emphasis in original]); Albert Memmi, *La Statue de sel* (1966)(Paris: Gallimard, 1977), pt. 2, chap. 2, "Le Lycée."

36. The Senegalese actor Douta Seck remembers six hours of detention at school for speaking a single word in his native Wolof (*Libération*, 16 July 1985, p. 35).

37. "Cet enjambement audacieux, impertinent même, semblait un spadassin de profession . . . allant donner une pichenette sur le nez du classicisme pour le provoquer en duel" (Théophile Gautier, *Histoire du romantisme* [1874] [Paris: Charpentier, 1877], pp. 107–8).

38. Céline rails against "le 'français' de lycée, le 'français' décanté, français filtré, dépouillé, français figé, français frotté (moderniste naturaliste), le français mufle, le français montaigne, racine, français juif à bachots, français d'Anatole l'enjuivé, le français goncourt, français dégueulasse d'élégance, . . . l'épitaphe même de la race française" (Louis-Ferdinand Céline, *Bagatelles pour un massacre* [Paris: Denoël, 1937], p. 167). Céline's anti-Semitic diatribe reveals the dark side of this linguistic sensibility and what happens when the association of language, culture, and country becomes an absolute. See Albert Sonnenfeld, "The Poetics of Anti-Semitism," *Romanic Review* 76, no. 1 (January 1985): 76–93, esp. 80–81 on language.

39. "Le vrai français légitime et officiel de France n'aime pas qu'on lui rappelle la marge grouillante où son identité disparaît. La langue française oscille bizarrement entre une absence exsangue de corps et un trop d'organes, un excès physique. Aucun autre pays, sans doute, n'est obligé de se partager aussi visiblement entre deux cultures, en presque complète contradiction. C'est une vieille histoire, l'actualité même" (Philippe Sollers, *Le Monde*, 22 August 1980, p. 12). Jacques Cellard (language editor of *Le Monde*) and Alain Rey (coeditor of the "Robert" Dictionary) edited the *Dictionnaire du français non conventionnel* (Paris: Hachette, 1980): "Notre dictionnaire est une sorte d'asile pour ces bâtards, ces exclus" (Jacques Cellard interviewed in *L'Express*, 6 December 1980, p. 28). On contemporary French feminist controversies, see Elaine Marks and Isabelle de Courtivron, eds., *New French Feminisms* (New York: Schocken, 1980); on the coercion exercised by the legitimate language, see Pierre Bourdieu, *Ce que parler veut dire* (Paris: Fayard, 1982), pts. 1, 2.

40. "La vie qu'on passe en Compagnie leur paroit une vie bien

passée, une vie passée dans l'Ordre. L'Homme est fait, disent-ils, pour vivre en Société." Les Français sont "Courtisans d'inclination & pour ainsi dire, de naissance." "Ils sont tentez d'apeller *Hibou* ou *Philosophe* toute personne qui témoigne quelque penchant pour la solitude" (Muralt, *Lettres sur les Anglois et les François*, p. 171).

41. Trollope, *Paris and the Parisians*, p. 57; "Nulle part nous ne pensons mieux qu'en société: le jeu des physionomies nous excite; nos idées si promptes naissent en éclairs au choc des idées d'autrui." "L'honnêteté n'y [en Angleterre] est pas le fruit des instincts sociables, mais le produit de la réflexion personnelle" (Hippolyte Taine, *Histoire de la littérature anglaise* [1862] [Paris: Hachette, 1887], 3, bk. 3, chap. 1, 109, 108).

42. Henry Lytton Bulwer, *France* (London: Richard Bentley, 1834), 2:216–17; Jean-Paul Aron, *Qu'est-ce que la culture française?* (Paris: Denoël-Gonthier, 1975), p. 10.

43. Paul Van Tieghem, *Le Romantisme dans la littérature européenne* (Paris: Albin Michel, 1948), p. 182; Jules Clarétie's remark about the "électrisation du talent" is quoted in Dumesnil, *L'Epoque réaliste et naturaliste*, p. 90. See generally Dumesnil, chaps. 3 and 4 on "Cafés et brasseries littéraires," and chaps. 5, 6, 7 on salons and cénacles.

44. "La conversation provoquait la pensée . . . avec l'échange des nouvelles, elle provoquait le commerce des réflexions" (Taine, *Histoire de la littérature anglaise*, 5:462).

45. "La parole n'y [en France] est pas seulement comme ailleurs, un moyen de se communiquer ses idées . . . c'est un instrument dont on aime à jouir et qui ranime les esprits" (Germaine Necker de Staël, *De l'Allemagne* [1810] [Paris: H. Nicolle, 1813], 1:82). See the whole of chapter 12 on conversation. "Il faut se mesurer avec les idées en allemand, avec les personnes en français" (1:86); "Celui qui parle est un usurpateur qui se sent entouré de rivaux jaloux, et veut se maintenir à force de succès" (1:86); on the nature of Parisian literary conversations, see 1:58; "En France on ne lit guère un ouvrage que pour en parler" (2:3); Bulwer, *France*, 2:218.

46. "Si la société, même littéraire, eût été divisée sous Louis XIV comme elle l'a été depuis, les grands écrivains d'un parti auraient été méconnus ou méprisés de l'autre, et nous n'aurions pas une littérature nationale" (De Bonald, "Pensées diverses," p. 313); Hippolyte Taine, *Notes sur l'Angleterre* (Paris: Hachette, 1890), p. 343.

47. "La force est tout dans la bataille des lettres" (Emile Zola, "Un prix de Rome littéraire" [1877] in *Le Roman expérimental* [Paris: Garnier-Flammarion, 1971], p. 324).

48. James Fenimore Cooper, *Recollections of Europe* (Paris: Baudry, 1837), p. 181. "Nun aber denken Sie sich eine Stadt wie Paris, wo die vorzüglichsten Köpfe eines grossen Reichs auf einem einzigen

Fleck beisammen sind und in täglichen Verkehr, Kampf und Wettei-
fer sich gegenseitig belehren und steigern, wo das Beste aus allen
Reichen der Natur und Kunst des ganzen Erdbodens der täglichen
Anschauung offen steht; diese Weltstadt denken Sie sich, wo jeder
Gang über eine Brücke oder einen Platz an eine grosse Vergangen-
heit erinnert, und wo an jeder Strassenecke ein Stück Geschichte
sich entwickelt hat. Und zu diesem allen denken Sie sich nicht das
Paris einer dumpfen geistlosen Zeit, sondern das Paris des neun-
zehnten Jahrhunderts, in welchem seit drei Menschenaltern durch
Männer wie Molière, Voltaire, Diderot und ihresgleichen eine solche
Fülle von Geist in Kurs geseszt ist, wie sie sich auf der ganzen Erde
auf einem einzigen Fleck nicht zum zweitenmale findet" (Johann
Peter Eckermann, *Gespräche mit Goethe*, 4 May 1827 [Jena: E. Die-
drichs, 1908], 2:314–15).

49. "La personnalité intellectuelle chez nous ne peut guère se
produire à l'état isolé, comme phénomène sans relations avec l'opinion, la mode, le goût régnants. Elle doit ou leur appartenir, ou se
prononcer contre eux. Depuis quatre siècles, l'évolution de nos arts
procède par . . . actions et réactions, manifestes et pamphlets" (Paul
Valéry, "Pensée et art français" [1939], *Oeuvres*, 2:1053); "Presque
tous nos chefs-d'oeuvre ont un chef-d'oeuvre pour réponse" (Paul
Valéry, "Le Destin et les lettres," *Oeuvres*, 2:1115; cf. André Gide,
"Le Dialogue français," *The Cornhill Magazine* no. 969 [1946]:200–
201); Albert Thibaudet, "Pour la géographie littéraire," *Réflexions sur
la littérature-II* (Paris: NRF-Gallimard, 1940), p. 139.

50. "Les livres ne sont qu'une des formes sous lesquelles
l'oeuvre si vaste de la culture des esprits s'accomplit et se répand. . . . Une des forces de l'esprit français est le lien étroit qui a
toujours existé parmi nous entre ceux qui font les livres et ceux qui
les lisent et les apprécient" (Renan, *Essais de morale et de critique*,
p. 340).

51. Matthew Arnold, article on Sainte-Beuve in the *Encyclopaedia
Britannica* (1886), quoted in F. W. J. Harding, *Matthew Arnold the
Critic and France* (Geneva: Droz, 1964), p. 135.

CHAPTER 6

1. "'L'écrivain' en France est autre chose qu'un homme qui écrit
et qui publie" (Paul Valéry, "Pensée et art français" [1939], *Oeuvres*
[Paris: Gallimard-Pléiade, 1960], 2:1053).

2. "Jean-Jacques n'écrit que pour écrire et moy j'écris pour agir"
(Voltaire, *Correspondance*, ed. T. Besterman [Geneva: Institut Voltaire, 1961], 65:150 [#13221, 15 April 1767]).

3. "Il ne s'éleva guère de grands génies depuis les beaux jours de ces artistes illustres; et, à peu près vers le temps de la mort de Louis XIV, la nature sembla se reposer.

"La route était difficile au commencement du siècle, parce que personne n'y avait marché: elle l'est aujourd'hui, parce qu'elle a été battue. Les grands hommes du siècle passé ont enseigné à penser et à parler; ils ont dit ce qu'on ne savait pas. Ceux qui leur succèdent ne peuvent guère dire que ce qu'on sait. Enfin une espèce de dégoût est venue de la multitude des chefs-d'oeuvre" (Voltaire, *Le Siècle de Louis XIV* [chap. 32, "Des beaux-arts"], *Oeuvres complètes de Voltaire* [Paris: J. Esneaux, 1822], 7:126). The sense of creative exhaustion was not limited to Voltaire or to the French. It was an eighteenth-century phenomenon in Europe generally. See Walter Jackson Bate, *The Burden of the Past and the English Poet* (Cambridge: Harvard University Press, 1970), which examines the dilemma of English neoclassicism and the romantic solution.

4. See Peter V. Conroy, Jr., "A French Classical Translation of Shakespeare: Ducis' *Hamlet,*" *Comparative Literature Studies* 18, no. 1 (March 1981):2–14.

5. "Vous vous plaindrez sans doute que ceux qui jusqu'à présent, vous ont parlé du théâtre anglais, et surtout de ce fameux Shakespeare, ne vous aient encore fait voir que ses erreurs, et que personne n'ait traduit aucun de ces endroits frappants qui demandent grâce pour toutes ses fautes" (Voltaire, *Lettres philosophiques ou lettres anglaises* [Paris: Garnier, 1962], letter 18, pp. 105–6); "Le génie poétique des Anglais ressemble jusqu'à présent à un arbre touffu planté par la nature, jetant au hasard mille rameaux, et croissant inégalement et avec force; il meurt, si vous voulez forcer sa nature et le tailler en arbre des jardins de Marly" (letter 18, p. 109). Garden images were commonplace. See also Peter V. Conroy, Jr., "Dramatic Theory and Eighteenth-Century Gardens," *University of Toronto Quarterly* 49, no. 3 (Spring 1980):252–65.

6. Voltaire's conservatism is qualified somewhat by his conduct during the "revolution" of Geneva burghers. Instead of siding with the "aristocrats," who were his friends and allies, he supported the artisans in their demands for the rights of citizenship. See the discussion in Peter Gay, *Voltaire's Politics: The Poet as Realist* (1959) (New York: Vintage, 1965), pp. 185–238. Gay stresses the practical political understanding and activity of Voltaire against the stereotype, perpetuated by de Tocqueville among others, of the philosophes, and Voltaire in particular, as engaged in abstract "literary" politics. See esp. chaps. 5 and 6 as well as Peter Gay, editor's introduction to Voltaire, *Philosophical Dictionary,* trans. Peter Gay (New York: Basic Books, 1962), pp. 3–52.

7. Voltaire was exiled to the provinces in 1716, imprisoned in the

Bastille for eleven months in 1717, received his famous beating by the lackeys of the Chevalier de Rohan in 1726, was sent back to the Bastille and then to exile in England until 1729. Voltaire compares the situations of French and English writers in *Lettres philosophiques*, letter 23, "Sur la considération qu'on doit aux gens de lettres."

8. "Le sage Addison eut la molle complaisance de plier la sévérité de son caractère aux moeurs de son temps, et gâta un chef-d'oeuvre pour avoir voulu plaire" (Voltaire, *Lettres philosphiques*, letter 18, p. 109).

9. "Tout honnête homme doit chercher à être philosophe, sans se piquer de l'être" (Voltaire, préface to *Dictionnaire philosophique*, édition de 1765 [Paris: Garnier, 1961], p. xxxii). Language was a perennial concern. In the *Lettres philosophiques* (letter 24, pp. 139–40), Voltaire proposed that the Académie française undertake to purify the great works of the seventeenth century of the stylistic defects in which they abound. All of Europe would then learn correct, pure French. For all his admiration of his predecessors, Voltaire did not hesitate to mete out criticism where he felt it due. In the 1752 edition of the *Lettres philosophiques*, for example, he went so far as to call Corneille's style "very bad" (*Lettres philosophiques*, p. 265, n. 172). See also pp. 139 ff. for comments on the purity of the French language and the "Discours de M. de Voltaire à sa réception à l'Académie française" (1746), *Mélanges de Voltaire* (Paris: Gallimard-Pléiade, 1961), esp. pp. 243 ff., where Voltaire notes that Montaigne's style was "ni pur, ni correct, ni précis, ni noble"!

10. On *L'Ingénu* as a bildungsroman, see my article "L'Ingénu: The Uses and Limitations of Naïveté," *French Studies* 27, no. 3 (July 1973): 278–86. "Je dis toujours naïvement ce que je pense, comme je fais ce que je veux"; "une espèce de prison où l'on tenait les filles renfermées, chose horrible" (Voltaire, *Romans et contes* [Paris: Gallimard-Pléiade, 1954], pp. 240, 257).

11. "Ainsi, à chaque action honnête et généreuse qu'elle faisait, son déshonneur en était le prix. Elle regardait avec exécration cet usage de vendre le malheur et le bonheur des hommes" (Voltaire, *Romans et contes*, p. 289); "D'où vient donc . . . qu'un si grand roi . . . se prive ainsi de tant de coeurs qui l'auraient aimé, et de tant de bras qui l'auraient servi?" (p. 261); "En un mot, je veux être utile: qu'on m'emploie et qu'on m'avance" (p. 264).

12. "Le sentiment avait fait autant de progrès en elle que la raison en avait fait dans l'esprit de son amant infortuné" (Voltaire, *Romans et contes*, p. 287); "Son génie, étouffé depuis si longtemps, se déployait avec tant de rapidité et de force. . . . la nature se perfectionnait en lui" (p. 274); "Son entendement, n'ayant point été courbé par l'erreur, était demeuré dans toute sa rectitude. Il voyait les choses comme elles sont" (p. 279); "ce n'est plus le même

homme; son maintien, son ton, ses idées, son esprit, tout est changé; il est devenu aussi respectable qu'il était naïf et étranger à tout. . . . L'Ingénu n'était plus l'*ingénu*" (p. 290); "Je serais tenté de croire aux métamorphoses, car j'ai été changé de brute en homme" (p. 270); "l'Ingénu, qui a paru sous un autre nom à Paris et dans les armées, avec l'approbation de tous les honnêtes gens, et qui a été à la fois un guerrier et un philosophe intrépide" (p. 301).

13. See *Mélanges de Voltaire*: "L'Affaire Calas" (pp. 525–62), "Traité sur la Tolérance à l'occasion de la mort de Jean Calas" (pp. 563–650) and also "Relation de la Mort du Chevalier de la Barre" (accused of impiety and sacrilege, tortured, and executed) (pp. 773–86), and "Avis au public sur les parricides imputés aux Calas et aux Sirven" (pp. 828–78).

14. "Dans chacune de mes trois carrières je m'étais proposé un but important: voyageur, j'ai aspiré à la découverte du monde polaire; littérateur, j'ai essayé de rétablir le culte sur ses ruines; homme d'Etat, je me suis efforcé de donner aux peuples le système de la monarchie pondérée. . . .

"Les orateurs de la Grèce et de Rome furent mêlés à la chose publique. . . . En France, . . . à compter du règne de Louis XIV, nos écrivains ont trop souvent été des hommes isolés dont les talents pouvaient être l'expression de l'esprit, non des faits de leur époque" (François-René de Chateaubriand, *Mémoires d'outre-tombe* [Paris: Gallimard-Pléiade, 1958], 2:935 [pt. 4, bk. 44, chap. 8]).

15. See Paul Bénichou, *Le Temps des prophètes* (Paris: Gallimard, 1977); and Frank E. Manuel, *The Prophets of Paris* (Cambridge: Harvard University Press, 1962).

16: "Quatre hommes auront eu une vie immense: Napoléon, Cuvier, O'Connell, et je veux être le quatrième. Le premier a vécu la vie de l'Europe! . . . Le second a épousé le globe! Le troisième s'est incarné un peuple! Moi, j'aurai porté une société entière dans ma tête!" (Honoré de Balzac, *Lettres à l'étrangère* [Paris: Calmann-Lévy, 1906], 2:301–2 [6 February 1844]).

17. Friedrich Engels is often quoted on Balzac's *Comédie humaine*: "Around the central picture he groups a complete history of French Society from which, even in the economic details . . . , I have learned more than from all the professed historians, economists and statisticians of the period together" (letter to Miss Harkness, quoted by Peter Demetz, *Marx, Engels, and the Poets: Origins of Marxist Literary Criticism* [1959] [Chicago: University of Chicago Press, 1967], pp. 173–74). However, as Demetz points out, Engels was repeating what was even at the time a commonplace of Balzacian criticism.

18. "S'en tenant à cette reproduction rigoureuse, un écrivain pouvait devenir . . . l'archéologue du mobilier social, le nomenclateur des professions"; "Dans certains fragments de ce long ouvrage,

j'ai tenté de populariser les faits étonnants . . . les prodiges de l'électricité . . . [le] magnétisme animal, . . . les belles recherches de Gall." (Honoré de Balzac, avant-propos to *La Comédie humaine*, 12 vols. [Paris: Gallimard-Pléiade, 1976–1981], 1:11, 16–17).

19. On Balzac and the Académie française, see Marcel Bouteron, "Balzac et l'Institut de France," *Etudes balzaciennes* (Paris: Jouve, 1954), pp. 218–49. His aspirations for literary and social mobility can be gauged by the dedications of the novels of the *Comédie humaine*. Of the eighty works that carry dedications, over a third (twenty-nine) are to titled aristocrats: five baron(esse)s, eleven count(esse)s, five marquis, two duchesses, five prince(sse)s, one lord. Ten more carry the *particule*, thereby reinforcing the aristocratic "aura." Maurice Bardèche insists on Balzac as a bourgeois *gentilhomme* of sorts, a rather vulgar arriviste ever on the make (*Balzac* [Paris: Julliard, 1980], inter alia, pp. 56, 170, 316, 347).

20. "La loi de l'écrivain, ce qui le fait tel, . . . ce qui . . . le rend égal et peut-être supérieur à l'homme d'Etat, est une décision quelconque sur les choses humaines, un dévouement absolu à des principes. Machiavel, Hobbes, Bossuet, Leibnitz, Kant, Montesquieu sont la science que les hommes d'Etat appliquent." He continues with a quote from de Bonald: "Un écrivain doit avoir en morale et en politique des opinions arrêtées, il doit se regarder comme un instituteur des hommes" (Balzac, avant-propos to *La Comédie humaine*, 1:12).

21. "Le Catholicisme et la Royauté sont deux principes jumeaux. . . . J'écris à la lueur de deux Vérités éternelles: la Religion, la Monarchie, deux nécessités que les événements contemporains proclament, et vers lesquelles tout écrivain de bon sens doit essayer de ramener notre pays" (Balzac, avant-propos, 1:13). On Balzac's political ambitions and maneuvers, see Bernard Guyon, *La Pensée politique et sociale de Balzac* (1951) (Paris: Colin, 1967), chap. 2, "L'Entrée dans la vie politique," pp. 375–430, and chap. 4, "La Conversion légitimiste," pp. 489–532; And Pierre Barbéris, *Balzac et le mal du siècle* (Paris: Gallimard, 1970), 2:1807–1921 (on *Le Médecin de campagne*).

22. Victor Hugo—no Marxist—saw a revolutionary Balzac close to his own conception of the public writer: "A son insu, qu'il le veuille ou non, qu'il y consente ou non, l'auteur de cette oeuvre immense et étrange est de la forte race des écrivains révolutionnaires" ("Funérailles de Balzac" [21 August 1850] in *Oeuvres politiques complètes: Oeuvres diverses* [Paris: Pauvert, 1964], p. 106).

23. Not until the end of the century was Balzac's reputation solidly established. See David Bellos, *Balzac Criticism in France, 1850–1900* (Oxford: Clarendon Press, 1976).

24. "Mon ouvrage a sa géographie comme il a sa généalogie et ses familles, ses lieux et ses choses, ses personnes et ses faits;

comme il a son armorial, ses nobles et ses bourgeois, ses artisans et ses paysans, ses politiques et ses dandies, son armée, tout son monde enfin!" (Balzac, avant-propos, 1:19).

25. "Il serait étrange qu'à cette époque, la liberté, comme la lumière, pénétrât partout, excepté dans . . . les choses de la pensée. Mettons le marteau dans les théories, les poétiques et les systèmes. Jetons bas ce vieux plâtrage qui masque la façade de l'art! Il n'y a ni règles ni modèles" (Victor Hugo, préface to *Cromwell* [1827], *Théâtre complet* [Paris: Gallimard-Pléiade, 1963], 1:434); "L'art n'a que faire des lisières, des menottes, des bâillons; il vous dit: Va! et vous lâche dans ce grand jardin de poésie, où il n'y a pas de fruit défendu" (préface to *Les Orientales* [1829] [Paris: Hachette, 1879], pp. 3–4); "Nous voilà sortis de la vieille forme sociale; comment ne sortirions-nous pas de la vieille forme poétique? A peuple nouveau, art nouveau. . . . [E]lle saura bien avoir sa littérature propre et personnelle et nationale, cette France actuelle, cette France du XIXe siècle" (préface to *Hernani* [1830], *Théâtre complet*, 1:1148). Biographical material is from André Maurois, *Olympio ou la vie de Victor Hugo* (Paris: Hachette, 1954); and Herbert Juin, *Victor Hugo, 1802–1843* (Paris: Flammarion, 1981), which makes good use of recent works about Hugo.

26. "Le romantisme . . . n'est, à tout prendre, et c'est là sa définition réelle, si l'on ne l'envisage que sous son côté militant, que le libéralisme en littérature. . . . La liberté dans l'art, la liberté dans la société, voilà le double but . . . voilà la double bannière qui rallie . . . toute la jeunesse et . . . tous ces sages vieillards qui . . . ont reconnu que . . . la liberté littéraire est fille de la liberté politique. Ce principe est celui du siècle, et prévaudra" (Hugo, préface to *Hernani* [1830], *Théâtre complet*, 1:1147–48); "Il serait facile de démontrer que cette grande secousse d'affranchissement et d'émancipation n'a pas été nuisible à l'art, mais qu'elle lui a été utile . . . nécessaire. . . . Un jour, juillet 1830 ne sera pas moins une date littéraire qu'une date politique" (Hugo, préface to *Marion de Lorme* [1831], *Théâtre complet*, 1:957, 958).

27. La langue était l'état avant quatre-vingt-neuf;

. . . .

Alors, brigand, je vins . . .
Et sur l'Académie, aïeule et douairière,
Cachant sous ses jupons les tropes effarés,
Et sur les bataillons d'alexandrins carrés,
Je fis souffler un vent révolutionnaire.
Je mis un bonnet rouge au vieux dictionnaire.
Plus de mot sénateur! plus de mot roturier!
Je fis une tempête au fond de l'encrier.

. . . .

Sur le sommet du Pinde on dansait Ça ira:
Les neuf muses, seins nus, chantaient la Carmagnole;
Aux armes, prose et vers! formez vos bataillons!
. . . et je criai dans la foudre et le vent:
Guerre à la rhétorique et paix à la syntaxe!
Et tout quatre-vingt-treize éclata.
. . . .
Oui, c'est vrai, ce sont là quelques uns de mes crimes.
J'ai pris et démoli la bastille des rimes.
. . . .
Tous les mots à présent planent dans la clarté,
Les écrivains ont mis la langue en liberté.
. . . .
Le mouvement complète ainsi son action.
Grâce à toi, progrès saint, La Révolution
Vibre aujourd'hui dans l'air, dans la voix, dans le livre
Dans le mot palpitant le lecteur la sent vivre.
(Victor Hugo, "Réponse à un acte d'accusation" [1854],
            Les Contemplations [1856], *Oeuvres poétiques*
                complètes [Paris: Pauvert, 1961], p. 382)

28. Victor Hugo, letter to Baudelaire, October 1859, quoted in
J.-B. Barrère, *Hugo* (Paris: Hatier, 1967), p. 92. The narrative *Le Dernier Jour d'un condamné*, the first of Hugo's protests against capital
punishment, was published in the same year (1829) as *Les Orientales*,
the collection of poetry usually taken to illustrate Hugo's aestheticism.

29. "Les besoins de la société, auxquels doivent toujours correspondre les tentatives de l'art" (Victor Hugo, préface to *Angelo* [1835],
Théâtre complet, 2:556). Two years later Hugo amplified his conception of the poet's duty:

Je vous aime, ô sainte nature!
        Je voudrais m'absorber en vous;
        Mais, dans ce siècle d'aventure
        Chacun, hélas! se doit à tous.
(Victor Hugo, "Fonction du poëte" [1837]
            Les Rayons et les ombres [1840],
            Oeuvres poétiques complètes, p. 239)

30. Le poëte en des jours impies
    Vient préparer des jours meilleurs.
    Il est l'homme des utopies;
    Les pieds ici, les yeux ailleurs.
    C'est lui qui . . .
    Doit . . .
    Faire flamboyer l'avenir!
    . . . .

Il rayonne! Il jette sa flamme
Sur l'éternelle vérité!
Il la fait resplendir pour l'âme
D'une merveilleuse clarté!
(Hugo, "Fonction du poëte,"
Oeuvres poétiques complètes,
pp. 239, 241)

31. "L'auteur de ce drame . . . sait que le drame . . . a une mission nationale, une mission sociale, une mission humaine. . . . Le poëte aussi a charge d'âmes" (Victor Hugo, préface to *Lucrèce Borgia* [1833], *Théâtre complet,* 2:289–90).

32. "Le drame . . . doit donner à la foule une philosophie, aux idées une formule, à la poésie des muscles, du sang et de la vie, à ceux qui pensent une explication désintéressée, aux âmes altérées un breuvage, aux plaies secrètes un baume, à chacun un conseil, à tous une loi" (Hugo, préface to *Angelo* [1835], *Théâtre complet,* 2:556); "A ce drame, qui serait pour la foule un perpétuel enseignement. . . ." (Victor Hugo, préface to *Marie Tudor* [1833], 2:414); "Le théâtre maintenant peut ébranler les multitudes. . . . Autrefois le peuple, c'était une immense muraille sur laquelle l'art ne peignait qu'une fresque" (Hugo, préface to *Marion de Lorme* [1831], 1:958); "Au siècle où nous vivons, l'horizon de l'art est bien élargi. Autrefois le poëte disait: le public; aujourd'hui le poëte dit: le peuple" (Hugo, préface to *Angelo* [1835], *Théâtre complet,* 2:557).

33. "Le sujet philosophique de *Ruy Blas,* c'est le peuple aspirant aux régions élevées; . . . le sujet dramatique, c'est un laquais qui aime une reine." Earlier in the same preface is another rhapsody on *le peuple:* "En examinant . . . cette époque . . . on voit remuer dans l'ombre quelque chose de grand, de sombre et d'inconnu. C'est le peuple. Le peuple qui a l'avenir et qui n'a pas le présent; le peuple, orphelin, pauvre, intelligent et fort; placé très bas, et aspirant très haut; ayant sur le dos les marques de la servitude et dans le coeur les préméditations du génie" (Victor Hugo, préface to *Ruy Blas* [1838] *Théâtre complet,* 1:1493, 1494).

34. Car le mot, qu'on le sache, est un être vivant.
La main du songeur vibre et tremble en l'écrivant.

. . . .

Oui, vous tous, comprenez que les mots sont des choses.
Ils roulent pêle-mêle au gouffre obscur des proses,
Ou font gronder le vers, orageuse forêt.
Du sphinx Esprit Humain le mot sait le secret.

. . . .

Oui, tout puissant. Tel est le mot. . . .

. . . .

Il est vie, esprit, germe, ouragan, vertu, feu;
Car le mot, c'est le Verbe, et le Verbe, c'est Dieu.
(Hugo, "Suite" à la "Réponse
à un acte d'accusation"
[1854], *Les Contemplations* [1856],
Oeuvres poétiques complètes, p. 383)
No wonder J.-B. Barrère defines Hugo's style in terms of a "degré orgiaque dans la jouissance du mot" (*Hugo,* p. 144) or that Hugo should think himself "l'homme de nos jours qui sait le mieux le français" and could allow himself to criticize Racine for writing quite bad French on occasion (Maurois, *Olympio,* pp. 468, 466). Symptomatic of his intense interest in anything to do with language was his assiduous attendance at the sessions of the Dictionary Commission of the Académie française, prompted by a fascination with etymologies (Maurois, *Olympio,* p. 530).

35. For a sense of Hugo's tireless activity in his later years on behalf of the disinherited of the earth, see *Choses vues: Souvenirs, journaux, cahiers, 1870–1885* (Paris: Gallimard-Folio, 1972).

36. The Hugolian dynamic of antitheses in *Quatrevingt-Treize* is analyzed by Victor Brombert, "Sentiment et violence chez Victor Hugo: L'Exemple de *Quatrevingt-Treize,*" *Cahiers de l'A.I.E.F.* (l'Association Internationale des études françaises) no. 26 (1974): 251–67. References to *Quatrevingt-Treize* (Paris: Garnier-Flammarion, 1965) include part, book, and chapter as well as page. "La société, c'est la nature sublimée" 3,7,6, p. 372).

37. See Guy Rosa, "*Quatrevingt-Treize* ou la critique du roman historique," *RHLF* (Revue d'Histoire Littéraire de la France) 75, no. 3 (March-June 1975):329–43, on the ambiguous position of this novel as a historical novel.

38. "Derrière l'oeuvre visible il y a l'oeuvre invisible. . . . L'oeuvre visible est farouche, l'oeuvre invisible est sublime" (3,7,5, p. 367); "En même temps qu'elle dégageait de la révolution, cette assemblée produisait de la civilisation. Fournaise mais forge. Dans cette cuve où bouillonnait la terreur, le progrès fermentait" (2,3,9, p. 167); Gauvain absout "le moment présent. . . . Parce que c'est une tempête. . . . Pour un chêne foudroyé, que de forêts assainies! La civilisation avait une peste, ce grand vent l'en délivre. . . . Devant l'horreur du miasme, je comprends la fureur du souffle" (3,7,5, pp. 371–72); "Il semblait que cela était sorti de terre. . . . Et cela en était sorti en effet. . . . Dans la terre fatale avait germé l'arbre sinistre. De cette terre arrosée de tant de sueurs, de tant de larmes, de tant de sang" (3,7,6, p. 375).

39. "Chaque siècle fera son oeuvre, aujourd'hui civique, demain humaine" (3,7,5, p. 371); "Je préfère, dit Gauvain, la république de

l'idéal" (3,2,7, p. 368); "Mon maître, je ne suis pas un homme poli-tique" (3,2,7, p. 229); "Gauvain parlait avec le recueillement d'un prophète" (3,7,5, p. 371); "Non! plus de joug! l'homme est fait, non pour traîner des chaînes, mais pour ouvrir des ailes. Plus d'homme reptile. Je veux la transfiguration de la larve en lépidoptère; je veux que le ver de terre se change en une fleur vivante, et s'envole" (3,7,5, p. 372; cf. pp. 341–42, 368, 370, 380 on ascension).

40. "D'ailleurs, que m'importe la tempête, si j'ai la boussole, et que me font les événements, si j'ai ma conscience!" (3,7,5, p. 372); "Le marquis de Lantenac s'était transfiguré. . . . Gauvain avait été témoin de cette transfiguration. . . . Au dessus de l'absolu révolu-tionnaire, il y a l'absolu humain" (3,6,2, pp. 336–37); "Une méta-morphose avait eu lieu. . . . Un héros sortait du monstre; plus qu'un héros, un homme" (3,6,2, p. 341); "Rien n'était ineffable et sublime comme ce sourire continué. . . . Il ressemblait à une vision . . . à un archange. . . . Le soleil, l'enveloppant, le mettait comme dans une gloire" (3,7,6, pp. 378–79); "Et ces deux âmes, soeurs tragiques, s'envolèrent ensemble, l'ombre de l'une mêlée à la lumière de l'autre" (3,7,6, p. 380).

41. See Brombert, "Sentiment et violence," p. 262, on Hugo's "stratégie de réconciliation." This reading also owes much to Sandy Petrey, *History in the Text: "Quatrevingt-Treize" and the French Revolu-tion*, Purdue University Monographs in Romance Languages, no. 3 (Amsterdam: John Benjamins, 1980). See esp. chap. 1 on the two texts of the novel, political-historical and moral-ahistorical; chap. 3 on the opposition of pastoral and history; and chap. 7, pp. 107 ff., for a discussion of *Quatrevingt-Treize* in relation to Hugo's personal and ideological ambivalence in the early 1870s. "Aimer c'est agir," the last words written by Victor Hugo two days before his death, 22 May 1885 (holograph reproduced by Henri Guillemin, *Victor Hugo par lui-même* [Paris: Le Seuil, 1954], p. 175).

42. Romain Rolland, "Le Vieux Orphée," *Europe* (Paris: Rieder, 1935), p. 12.

43. In *Les Déracinés* (Paris: Fasquelle-Charpentier, 1897) Maurice Barrès left a memorable account of Hugo's funeral, a night of com-munion, fraternity, and orgy. See chap. 18, "La Vertu sociale d'un cadavre," pp. 436–65. Romain Rolland, more restrained, neverthe-less evoked the "kermesse de Jordaens" and a "cortège Dionys-iaque" ("Le Vieux Orphée," pp. 15, 16).

44. The quai Voltaire (seventh arrondissement) was named in 1791, the boulevard Voltaire (eleventh arrondissement) in 1870. The latter, originally the boulevard Prince-Eugène, required quick post-empire republican baptism. The place de la République was not named until 1879, the place de la Nation until 1880, but the connec-tion of the boulevard Voltaire nevertheless remains marvelously symbolic of Voltaire's significance for what Julien Benda called the

"mystique républicaine." After tracing the ideas of Voltaire that inspired revolutionary legislation, Benda concludes that "c'est par un symbolisme fort juste que le buste de l'auteur du *Dictionnaire* [*philosophique*] trône dans toutes les mairies de la Troisième République" (introduction to Voltaire, *Dictionnaire philosophique*, p. i). Half of the present avenue Victor-Hugo was named in 1881 (permitting letters to be addressed to M. Victor Hugo, en son avenue!), the other half and the place Victor-Hugo in 1885 within days of the poet's death. The many official celebrations of the centennial of this event suggest that some of the mystique lingers on.

CHAPTER 7

1. "Il a le fumier épique! C'est l'Homère de la vidange! Il n'a pas assez de majuscules pour écrire le mot de Cambronne" (Marcel Proust, *Le Côté de Guermantes, A la recherche du temps perdu* [Paris: Gallimard-Pléiade, 1954], 2:499). Mauriac's reminiscence is cited by Jean Lacouture, *François Mauriac* (Paris: Le Seuil, 1980), p. 52.

2. "On m'attaque, donc je suis encore" (Emile Zola, quoted by F. W. J. Hemmings, *Emile Zola* [Oxford: Clarendon Press, 1966], p. 159).

3. "Si ma lutte continue, . . . c'est que mon attitude a toujours été la même. Et montrer que ce que je viens de faire dans l'affaire Dreyfus n'est que la suite de ce que j'ai toujours fait." (Emile Zola, "Impressions d'audience" [Zola's notes for a narrative of his trial], *L'Affaire Dreyfus: La Vérité en marche*, ed. Colette Becker [Paris: Garnier-Flammarion, 1969], pp. 245–46). Colette Becker cites Jean Jaurès's assessment of "cet acte qui n'était que la suite logique de toute son oeuvre" ("Zola et l'affaire Dreyfus," *L'Affaire Dreyfus*, p. 49).

4. "Quel drame poignant, et quels personnages superbes! Devant ces documents, . . . mon coeur de romancier bondit d'une admiration passionnée" (Emile Zola, "M. Scheurer-Kestner" [*Le Figaro*, 25 November 1897], *L'Affaire Dreyfus*, p. 68). About this, his first article on the Dreyfus case, Zola later remarked that "le professionnel, le romancier, était surtout séduit, exalté, par un tel drame. Et la pitié, la foi, la passion de la vérité et de la justice, sont venues ensuite" (p. 67). The sense of drama never deserted him. Cf. "Lettre à Madame Alfred Dreyfus" (*L'Aurore*, 29 September 1899), *L'Affaire Dreyfus*, pp. 169–70, and "Impressions d'audience," p. 241, for Zola's idea of using in a novel the "affreuse scène" where Dreyfus was stripped of rank. In his own trial Zola noted "la façon esthétique dont se composaient les audiences comme autant d'actes d'un drame poignant, construit par un grand artiste" (p. 244). Bernard Lazare, who had gone to enlist Zola's support for Dreyfus, noted

that the affair "ne l'intéressa que quand le mélodrame fut complet et quand il vit les personnages!" (quoted by Becker, "Zola et l'affaire Dreyfus," p. 32).

5. "Et l'acte que j'accomplis ici n'est qu'un moyen révolutionnaire pour hâter l'explosion de la vérité et de la justice. . . . Je n'ai qu'une passion, celle de la lumière, au nom de l'humanité qui a tant souffert et qui a droit au bonheur" (Emile Zola, "Lettre à M. Félix Faure" ["J'accuse"], *L'Affaire Dreyfus*, p. 124). Zola proclaimed France "ce pays de libre examen, de fraternelle bonté et de claire raison" (*L'Affaire Dreyfus*, p. 85), and in his "Impressions d'audience" (p. 244) he wished fervently: "Il faut que notre peuple soit le plus libre et le plus raisonnable. Il faut qu'il réalise le plus tôt possible la société modèle, celle qui est en enfantement dans la décomposition de la vieille société qui s'écroule."

6. "Il n'y a plus d'affaire Dreyfus, il s'agit désormais de savoir si la France est encore la France des droits de l'homme, celle qui a donné la liberté au monde et qui devait lui donner la justice. Sommes-nous encore le peuple le plus noble, le plus fraternel, le plus généreux? Allons-nous garder en Europe notre renom d'équité et d'humanité?" (Emile Zola, "Déclaration au jury" [*L'Aurore*, 22 February 1898], *L'Affaire Dreyfus*, p. 132); "Aussi, ceux de tes fils qui t'aiment et t'honorent, France, n'ont-ils qu'un devoir ardent, à cette heure grave, celui d'agir puissamment sur l'opinion, de l'éclairer, de la ramener, de la sauver de l'erreur où d'aveugles passions la poussent" (Emile Zola, "Lettre à la France," brochure published 6 January 1898, *L'Affaire Dreyfus*, pp. 101, 102).

7. "L'innocent qui souffrait à l'île du Diable n'était que l'accident, tout le peuple souffrait avec lui. . . . [E]n le sauvant, nous sauvions tous les opprimés, tous les sacrifiés" (Emile Zola, "Lettre à M. Emile Loubet" [*L'Aurore*, 22 December 1900], *L'Affaire Dreyfus*, p. 204).

8. See Victor Brombert, *The Intellectual Hero: Studies in the French Novel, 1885–1960* (Philadelphia: Lippincott, 1961), pp. 20–24, 31–32. Although the substantive can be found earlier, the term "intellectual" became common currency during the high point of the Dreyfus affair in the winter of 1897–1898.

9. On Sartre's literary criticism, see Benjamin Suhl, *Jean-Paul Sartre: The Philosopher as Literary Critic* (New York: Columbia University Press, 1970), and Joseph Halpern, *Critical Fictions: The Literary Criticism of Jean-Paul Sartre* (New Haven: Yale University Press, 1976).

10. "Nous recourrons à tous les genres littéraires pour familiariser le lecteur avec nos conceptions: un poème, un roman d'imagination . . . pourront, plus qu'un écrit théorique, créer le climat favorable à leur développement" (Jean-Paul Sartre, présentation, *Les Temps modernes* 1, no. 1 [October 1945]:19). Cf. "Nous ne voulons rien manquer de notre temps" (p. 4). Simone de Beauvoir notes that

"Sartre vivait pour écrire; il avait mandat de témoigner de toutes choses et de les reprendre à son compte à la lumière de la nécessité" (*La Force de l'âge* [Paris: Gallimard, 1960], p. 18).

11. "[L'écrivain] est *dans son métier même* aux prises avec la contradiction de la particularité et de l'universel. . . . Il trouve dans sa tâche interne l'obligation de demeurer sur le plan du vécu tout en suggérant l'*universalisation* comme l'affirmation de la vie *à l'horizon.* En ce sens, il n'est pas intellectuel *par accident,* comme eux [les autres intellectuels], mais *par essence*" (Jean-Paul Sartre, "L'écrivain est-il un intellectuel?" in "Plaidoyer pour les intellectuels," *Situations, VIII* [Paris: Gallimard, 1972], pp. 454–55 [emphasis in text]).

12. "Autrefois, le poète se prenait pour un prophète . . . ; par la suite, il devint paria et maudit. . . . Mais aujourd'hui il est tombé au rang des spécialistes" (Sartre, présentation, *Les Temps modernes,* p. 2).

13. In the first of four letters published on *La Nouvelle Héloïse* (1761) Voltaire took the foreigner Rousseau to task for his language: "Cet homme se met si noblement au-dessus des règles de la langue et des bienséances, et daigne y marquer un profond mépris pour notre nation" ("Lettres à M. de Voltaire sur *la Nouvelle Héloïse* [ou *Aloïsia*] de Jean-Jacques Rousseau, Citoyen de Genève" [Voltaire wrote the letters under a pseudonym and addressed them to himself], *Mélanges de Voltaire,* [Paris: Gallimard-Pléiade, 1961], p. 398); Ernst Robert Curtius, *Essai sur la France* (Paris: Grasset, 1932), pp. 159–67, cites Henri Bergson on this bias against specialized philosophy, which he locates in the conception of the French language as a generalized medium rather than a specialized discourse.

14. "Son but est . . . de forger des notions qui s'alourdissent profondément, progressivement" (Jean-Paul Sartre, "L'écrivain et sa langue," *Situations, IX* [Paris: Gallimard, 1972], p. 67). See pp. 71–79 for Sartre's defense of his "germanization" of French philosophical language.

15. "Les hommes, il faut les voir d'en haut. . . . Au balcon d'un sixième: c'est là que j'aurais dû passer toute ma vie. Il faut étayer les supériorités morales par des symboles matériels" (Jean-Paul Sartre, "Erostrate," *Le Mur* [1939][Paris: Gallimard-Pléiade, 1981], p. 262).

16. "C'est dégoûtant, pourquoi faut-il que nous ayons des corps?" (Sartre, "Intimité," *Le Mur,* p. 286); "Mais l'antisémitisme de Lucien était d'une autre sorte: impitoyable et pure, il pointait hors de lui comme une lame d'acier, menaçant d'autres poitrines" (Sartre, "L'Enfance d'un chef," *Le Mur,* p. 385); "Il faudrait qu'elle [l'histoire qu'il écrirait] soit belle et dure comme de l'acier" (Sartre, *La Nausée* [Paris: Gallimard, 1938], p. 210). Sartre's sexual imagery, which will strike even the casual reader, translates a dichotomy be-

tween the masculine writer-hero and the feminine, soft, viscous world that threatens to engulf him. See Halpern, *Critical Fictions*, esp. pp. 2–14 and also passim, and the remarks on similar associations in de Beauvoir in Brombert, *The Intellectual Hero*, pp. 234–35.

17. "Cette espèce pourtant se plaint; donc elle existe" (Paul Valéry, "Propos sur l'intelligence" [1925], *Oeuvres* [Paris: Gallimard-Pléiade, 1962], 1:1051).

18. Voltaire, Zola, and Gide (for his exposé of the colonial administration in Chad) are cited in Sartre's présentation, *Les Temps modernes*, p. 5. Sartre's judgment of Hugo is more qualified ("Autoportrait à soixante-dix ans" [interview, 1975], *Situations*, X [Paris: Gallimard, 1975], p. 195). On the ambivalent relationship to Hugo, see Victor Brombert, "Sartre, Hugo, a Grandfather," in *Sartre after Sartre*, a special issue of *Yale French Studies* (no. 68 [1985]), pp. 73–81.

19. See de Beauvoir, *La Force de l'âge*, pt. 1, passim, and Sartre, "Autoportrait," p. 178, on the Popular Front. Sartre specifies (p. 177) that *La Nausée* was in some sense the culmination of his "man alone" period.

20. On Sartre's sense of superiority, see "Simone de Beauvoir interroge Jean-Paul Sartre" (*L'Arc*, 1975), *Situations*, X, pp. 117–19. The American writer Nelson Algren was impressed with Sartre's "tremendous egocentricity" ("Last Rounds in Small Cafés," *Chicago*, December 1980, p. 237). In *Les Mots* (Paris: Gallimard-Folio, 1964), p. 211, Sartre admitted to it: "Dogmatique, je doutais de tout sauf d'être l'élu du doute." Given the exceptionally numerous short quotations from *Les Mots*, further references will be given in the text only.

21. "Tous les écrivains d'origine bourgeoise ont connu la tentation de l'irresponsabilité: depuis un siècle, elle est de tradition dans la carrière des lettres. . . . Si . . . [l'écrivain] emploie son art à forger des bibelots d'inanité sonore . . . [the reference is to Mallarmé's poem "Ses purs ongles"] c'est qu'il y a une crise de lettres et, sans doute, de la Société. . . . Ces tentatives isolées ne purent empêcher les mots de se déprécier chaque jour davantage. Il y eut une crise de la rhétorique, puis une crise du langage. A la veille de cette guerre, la plupart des littérateurs s'étaient résignés à n'être que des rossignols" (Sartre, présentation, *Les Temps modernes*, pp. 1, 3).

22. "L'écrivain français, le seul qui soit demeuré un bourgeois, le seul qui s'accommode d'une langue que cent cinquante ans de domination bourgeoise ont cassée, vulgarisée, assouplie, truffée de bourgeoisismes" (Jean-Paul Sartre, *Qu'est-ce que la littérature?* [Paris: Gallimard, 1948], p. 203).

23. "L'Américain, avant de faire des livres, a souvent exercé des métiers manuels, il y revient; entre deux romans, sa vocation lui

apparaît au ranch, à l'atelier, dans les rues de la ville" (Sartre, *Qu'est-ce que la littérature?* p. 203).

24. The flavor of Sartre's language makes the passage worth quoting in full: "Mais nous, bien avant de commencer notre premier roman, nous avions l'usage de la littérature . . . ; Avant même de nous être trouvés aux prises avec un ouvrage en chantier, . . . nous nous étions nourris de littérature déjà faite et nous pensions naïvement que nos écrits sortiraient de notre esprit dans l'état d'achèvement où nous trouvions ceux des autres, avec le sceau de la reconnaissance collective et cette pompe qui vient d'une consécration séculaire, bref, comme des biens nationaux; pour nous l'ultime transformation d'un poème, sa toilette dernière pour l'éternité, c'était, après avoir paru dans des éditions magnifiques et illustrées, de finir imprimé en petits caractères dans un livre cartonné au dos de toile verte, dont l'odeur blanche de sciure et d'encre nous semblait le parfum même des Muses. . . . En un mot la destination dernière de nos oeuvres nous avons cru longtemps qu'elle était de fournir des textes littéraires à l'explication française de 1980" (*Qu'est-ce que la littérature?* pp. 206–7). Ironically, that is where Sartre ended up, in the Pléiade edition of his novels, underway before his death (the "livre cartonné au dos de toile verte") and published in 1981.

25. "Grâce à ces modèles, à ces recettes, la carrière d'écrivain nous est apparue, dès notre enfance, comme un métier magnifique mais sans surprises où l'on avance en partie grâce au mérite, en partie à l'ancienneté" (Sartre, *Qu'est-ce que la littérature?* p. 210); "Notre route est tracée. . . . tout est écrit dans les livres, il suffit d'en tenir un compte exact"(p. 209).

26. "Flaubert, qui a tant pesté contre les bourgeois et qui croyait s'être retiré à l'écart de la machine sociale, qu'est-il pour nous sinon un rentier de talent?" (Sartre, présentation, *Les Temps modernes,* p. 4).

27. "En fait, le poète s'est retiré d'un seul coup du langage-instrument; il a choisi une fois pour toutes l'attitude poétique qui considère les mots comme des choses et non comme des signes. . . . Le poète est hors du langage. . . . La prose est utilitaire par essence" (Sartre, *Qu'est-ce que la littérature?* pp. 18, 19, 26).

28. See "Sur *l'Idiot de la famille*" (*Le Monde,* 1971), *Situations, X,* pp. 91–115. An amused Nelson Algren recounted a 1949 visit to Paris when Sartre defended his attachment to a particular woman on the grounds that her frequent and prolonged crying jags left him free to pat her on the shoulder and think about Flaubert! ("Last Rounds in Small Cafés," p. 237). In 1972 Sartre noted that at sixty-seven he had been working on Flaubert since he was fifty and that before then he had dreamed about the book ("Justice et Etat," *Situations, X,* p. 61).

29. "Cette légende de l'irresponsabilité du poète, que nous dénoncions tout à l'heure, elle tire son origine de l'esprit d'analyse. . . . Proust s'est *choisi* bourgeois, il s'est fait le complice de la propagande bourgeoise, puisque son oeuvre contribue à répandre le mythe de la nature humaine" (Sartre, présentation, *Les Temps modernes*, pp. 11, 11–12).

30. "Un des principaux motifs de la création artistique est certainement le besoin de nous sentir essentiels par rapport au monde" (Sartre, *Qu'est-ce que la littérature?* p. 50). Geneviève Idt observes that almost all of Sartre's narrative work takes up the myth of the origin of writing and the writer ("Sartre 'mythologue,'" *Autour de Jean-Paul Sartre: Littérature et philosophie* [Paris: Gallimard, 1981], pp. 120–21).

31. Sartre's insistence on the primary importance of the original decision to write is found in "Sartre sur Sartre," *Situations, IX*, p. 133. George Bauer has pointed out that while Sartre mentioned a number of autobiographical projects over the years after publication of *Les Mots,* he used the many interviews he gave as a substitute for the autobiography he did not wish to write ("Interview as Autobiography," *L'Esprit créateur* 17, no. 1 (Spring 1977): 61–69). The point is explored in depth by Philippe Lejeune, *Je est un autre: L'Autobiographie de la littérature aux médias* (Paris: Seuil, 1980), pp. 161–202.

32. In a brilliant analysis of *Les Mots* Philippe Lejeune posits the dialectical structure of *Les Mots:* the initial situation of nonexistence is followed by the child's confrontation of that situation; and resolved, in the final synthesis, in the writer's neurosis (*Le Pacte autobiographique* [Paris: Seuil, 1975], pp. 209ff.). The point of the dialectic is that each synthesis carried the thesis of the next progression so that Sartre in effect ends *Les Mots* with an opening toward the next self/personage.

33. See the script for the film directed by Alexander Astruc and Michel Contat, *Sartre by Himself* (1977), trans. Richard Seaver (Urizen Books, 1978), p. 89. See also Jacques Lecarme, "*Les Mots* de Sartre: Un cas limite de l'autobiographie?" *RHLF* (*Revue d'Histoire Littéraire de la France*) 75, no. 6 (November–December 1975): 1047–61.

34. "C'est, en somme, toute la dialectique philosophique de Sartre qui est en cause [dans la biographie], celle en particulier de l'être et de l'existence" (Victor Brombert, "Sartre et la biographie impossible," *Cahiers de l'A.I.E.F.* (l'Association Internationale des études françaises) no. 19 [1967]: 155–66 [quotation on p. 155]).

35. "Sartre sur Sartre," *Situations, IX*, p. 123.

36. "Il n'aimait en lui que sa révolte: elle prouvait qu'il résistait encore" (Jean-Paul Sartre, avant-propos to Paul Nizan, *Aden-Arabie* [1960], in *Situations, IV* [Paris: Gallimard, 1964], p. 166). Nizan's commitment at an early age contrasts with Sartre's tardy realization of the necessity of responsibility: "Il aura fallu beaucoup d'années et

que je comprenne enfin ma route pour que je puisse aujourd'hui parler sans erreur de la sienne" (avant-propos to *Aden-Arabie*, p. 150). Lejeune sees *Les Mots* as a dialogue with Nizan, Sartre's attempt to explain his earlier "blindness" to an alter ego of sorts (inseparable companions when young, Sartre and Nizan were often taken for each other) (*Le Pacte autobiographique*, p. 205).

Epilogue

1. See Claudine Garcia, "Un écrivain à la une: Etude des articles de presse parus à la mort de Sartre," *Pratiques*, special issue on "L'Ecrivain aujourd'hui" no. 27 (July 1980): 41–60.

2. A poll of five hundred prominent figures in the French book and publishing world, published in *Lire* (April 1981), listed only four literary figures among the top ten "most influential writers in France" (cited by Roger Shattuck, "Letter from Paris—Where Writing Outranks Politics," *The New York Times Book Review*, 10 May 1981, p. 7; and Hervé Hamon and Patrick Rotman, *Les Intellocrates: Expédition en haute intelligentsia* [Paris: Ramsey, 1981], p. 52).

3. Albert Thibaudet, *La République des professeurs* (Paris: Grasset, 1937), p. 229, and generally chap. 13, "Ecrivains et professeurs," pp. 229–35.

4. On American publishing, see Lewis Coser, Charles Kadushin, and Walter Powell, *Books: The Commerce and Culture of Publishing* (New York: Basic Books, 1982).

5. See Julien Benda, *La Frar :e byzantine: Essai d'une psychologie originelle du littérateur* (Paris: Gallimard, 1945).

6. In 1970, 19.5 percent of nineteen-year-olds in France and 16.2 percent of twenty-year-olds were enrolled in institutions of higher education; the analogous figures for the United States are 40.9 percent and 35.4 percent respectively (*Educational Statistics Yearbook* [Paris: Organization for Economic Cooperation and Development, 1974], p. 30). Put another way, the number of students in institutions of higher education per 100,000 inhabitants was 1581 (1970) and 2090 (1981) for France and 4148 (1970) and 5492 (1981) for the United States. In *both* countries the numbers increased by a factor of 1.3 ("Education at the Third Level," *UNESCO Statistical Yearbook* [1984]).

7. See Pascal Ory, *L'entre-deux-mai: Histoire culturelle de la France, mai 1968–mai 1981* (Paris: Le Seuil, 1983), esp. pp. 63–78; Pierre Cabanne, *Le Pouvoir culturel sous la Ve République* (Paris: Olivier Orban, 1981); Pascal Ory, "La Politique du Ministère Jack Lang: Un Premier Bilan," *The French Review* 58, no. 1 (October 1984): 77–83; and, specifically relative to books and writers, Jean Gattegno, "Bilan d'une action: La Politique de la Direction du Livre," in *Problèmes de la lec-*

ture, ed. Roger Chartier (Marseille: Rivages, 1985), pp. 207–15. Some of the projects, notably the planned Opéra at the place de la Bastille and the redesigning of the entrance to the Louvre by I. M. Pei, have prompted criticism of a "louis-quatorzien" complex.

8. "Le Français est bavard," (interview, 28 May 1980).

9. "Aucune autorité fondée . . . sur une Parole plus ou moins sacrée, ne tient dans cet espace ethnique, historique et idéologique polyvalent. . . . Car la civilisation américaine . . . n'est pas une civilisation du discours; c'est une civilisation de sons, de gestes, de couleurs, de chiffres" (Julia Kristeva, "Des campus pleins d'étoiles," *Le Nouvel Observateur,* 1 January 1978).

10. *Paris Match,* 8 May 1981, p. 32. "Paradis privilégié" is quoted from an interview in *Les Nouvelles littéraires* by Bertrand Poirot-Delpeche ("Un écrivain-né," *Le Monde,* 12 May 1981, pp. 1, 6).

11. Nicolas Brasart, "Etamaton: Le Portrait officiel de Jean Le Bon à Mitterrand," *Feuilles* no. 4 (Spring 1983): 40–57.

12. "Les mythes modernes sont encore moins compris que les mythes anciens, quoique nous soyons dévorés par les mythes. Les mythes nous pressent de toutes parts, ils servent à tout, ils expliquent tout" (Honoré de Balzac, *La Vieille Fille, La Comédie humaine,* 12 vols. [Paris: Gallimard-Pléiade, 1976–1981], 4:935).

13. This discussion draws on my articles "Thoughts for Food I: French Cuisine in French Culture" and "Thoughts for Food II: Culinary Culture in Contemporary France," *The French Review* 49, nos. 1–2 (October-December 1975): 32–41, 198–205. See also Jean-Paul Aron, *Essai sur la sensibilité alimentaire à Paris au XIXe siècle* (Paris: A. Colin, 1967), and *Le Mangeur du XIXe siècle* (Paris: Laffont, 1973).

14. See the report by the person named director, Jean Ferniot, "Rapport aux ministres [de la Culture, de l'Agriculture] sur la promotion des arts culinaires," April 1985.

Index

Compositor:	Graphic Composition Inc.
Text:	$^{10}/_{12}$ Palatino
Display:	Palatino
Printer:	Braun-Brumfield
Binder:	Braun-Brumfield